Alexander Sanger

# BEYOND

REPRODUCTIVE FREEDOM IN THE 21ST CENTURY

# CHOICE

PublicAffairs · *New York*

To my wife, Jeannette,

And

My Three Boys,

Ralph, Andrew, and Matthew,

With All My Love

Copyright © 2004 by Alexander Sanger.
Published in the United States by PublicAffairs™, a member of the Perseus Books Group.
All rights reserved.
Printed in the United States of America.

No part of this book may be reproduced in any manner whatsoever without written permission except in the case of brief quotations embodied in critical articles and reviews. For information, address PublicAffairs, 250 West 57th Street, Suite 1321, New York, NY 10107. PublicAffairs books are available at special discounts for bulk purchases in the U.S. by corporations, institutions, and other organizations. For more information, please contact the Special Markets Department at the Perseus Books Group, 11 Cambridge Center, Cambridge, MA 02142, or call (617) 252-5298.

BOOK DESIGN AND COMPOSITION BY JENNY DOSSIN. TEXT SET IN ADOBE SABON.

LIBRARY OF CONGRESS CATALOGING-IN-PUBLICATION DATA
Sanger, Alexander.
    Beyond choice : reproductive freedom in the 21st century / Alexander Sanger.
        p. cm.
    Includes bibliographical references and index.
    ISBN 1-58648-346-3 (pbk)
    1. Abortion. 2. Abortion—Moral and ethical aspects. I. Title.
    HQ767.S26 2004
    363.46—dc22

                                                        2003063248

10 9 8 7 6 5 4 3 2 1

# Contents

# Beyond Choice

# Introduction

My wife, Jeannette, and I have raised three boys. When Jeannette was about four months pregnant with our middle son, Andrew, we went to her doctor for a checkup and a sonogram. We had difficulty reading the screen, but the doctor assured us everything appeared normal. The doctor asked if we had any history of genetic diseases. My wife volunteered, "I have congenital hip displaysia. At age 30 I had bone transplant surgery to try to correct the problem."

The doctor—this was in 1981—leaned forward and said, "In a few years there is going to be a genetic test to determine early in a pregnancy if the fetus carries that defective gene."

Jeannette looked at the doctor and said quite firmly, "I would never kill my baby because he had hip displaysia."

As we walked outside the hospital Jeannette and I reflected on the conversation. While acknowledging that abortion ought to be legal, Jeannette said she did not know if she could ever have an abortion for any reason. Having an abortion seemed somehow "wrong." "I don't think I could ever have one."

My wife's opinion puts her squarely in the middle of America's broad range of public opinion on abortion. She simultaneously thinks that abortion should be legal and that it is in many cases wrong. She is pro-choice, mostly.

The mostly pro-choice American public acquiesces in and supports an increasing number of restrictions on access to abortion. Most Americans favor government regulations that officially discourage abortion and that make abortion difficult to access and available only to women who can pay for it on their own in private clinics. In this view abortion should be legal but available only after the woman surmounts some significant obstacles to get one. In contrast to this "centrist" position the pro-choice camp advocates that abortion be accessible and available whenever and wherever a woman decides to have one, and the pro-life camp advocates that abortion be re-criminalized. These two opposing points of view represent the stark choice that America faces— abortion can either be legal or illegal. In fact, it has been both at different times throughout our history. At this moment in America it is a little bit of both—technically legal but difficult for many to access.

I will argue in this book that this current state of affairs is wrong and that it is better for women, and for men and children too, that abortion be fully legal and accessible. I will argue that having abortion legal and accessible is morally right, not morally wrong. I will provide a framework for analyzing whether some decisions about childbearing and abortion *are* morally wrong and therefore should be prohibited by law.

## The Pro-Choice Versus Pro-Life Debate

What does it mean to be pro-choice? Being pro-choice means being in favor of allowing women to make up their own mind about whether or not to have a child. It means that a woman should have this power both before and after she is pregnant. She should have the choice in the first instance to become pregnant or not, and, if she is pregnant, she should have the choice not to be, that is to say, to have an abortion and terminate the pregnancy. Being pro-choice means being in favor of contraception's and abortion's being legal, available, and accessible to those who want to use them, no matter what their personal circumstances might be and what decision they want to make. Being pro-choice means believing that the government has the obligation to ensure that all its citizens have access to the health care they need, including birth control and abortion, both of which should be covered by insurance or Medicaid as a matter of public health and fairness. Being pro-choice means that decisions about childbearing are for the woman to make, not for other people or the government.

Until the middle of the twentieth century in America it was a matter of great controversy whether or not the use of contraception was moral. It is now generally accepted by most people, except the hierarchy of the Roman Catholic Church and some others, that contraceptive use is moral. The moral objection to the pro-choice position is now mostly centered on abortion. Opponents of legal abortion consider abortion the equivalent of murder. Life begins at conception, they say, and the human embryo or fetus is an innocent human being and is entitled to be born. Abortion is an act of violence that kills a baby who cannot protect or defend itself. In this view, an absolute moral standard that respects and protects life, sometimes expressed in religious terms and sometimes not, should overcome both the right of individuals to make personal choices about childbearing and the personal hardship that may result from having an unwanted child.

Opponents of legal abortion, and even some supporters of legal abortion, have additional concerns—they do not like the use that some people make of legal abortion, they do not like the decisions that are being made, and they do not like the social consequences of having abortion being legal. Opponents of legal abortion believe that abortion is used, wrongly, as a form of birth control. As they describe it, abortion permits lifestyle choices of which they disapprove. In their view legal abortion, like birth control, makes it easier to have sexual intercourse outside of marriage and contributes to the weakening of the moral fabric of society. Abortion opponents argue that legal abortion makes the non-use of birth control more likely and indirectly contributes to the rise in sexually transmitted diseases, unintended pregnancy, and abortion itself. Life is unfair, they say, and an unwanted pregnancy is another of life's challenges and vicissitudes that should not be dealt with by killing an unborn child. They argue that life is cheapened by legal abortion and that civilized society is the worse for it. The opponents of legal abortion range from those who are discomfited by it to those who are outraged by it. Underlying the views of some abortion opponents is the traditional view of women as mothers and caregivers of children. In this view liberating women from these roles through legalizing abortion is not beneficial for society.

Those of us who favor abortion's being legal counter these arguments with four basic arguments.

First, we argue that a woman has the right to use birth control and have an abortion because the pregnancy affects her body and her body only. A woman has the right to control what she does with her body and what happens to it. No woman should be forced to have a child if she does not want to. Having a child is a fundamental life-altering decision, and it is for the woman to make this decision. It is irrelevant if she is pregnant or not at the time she chooses to make this decision.

Second, we argue that as a general rule American citizens are entitled to live their private lives without unnecessary government interference. Our right to privacy includes such decisions as where to live, what to do for a living, whom to marry, and whether to have children and how we raise them.

Third, we argue that it is better for women's health if birth control and abortion are legal, safe, and regulated, rather than illegal, unsafe, and unregulated. History has shown that women will use these services even if illegal and clandestine, and illegal medical services of any kind are a danger to women's health and lives.

Finally, we argue that families and society will benefit from parents having children that are planned, welcomed, and properly spaced. Every child should be a wanted child.

These arguments for and against abortion's being legal, moral, and acceptable have been made in one form or another for the past thirty years since *Roe v. Wade* was decided in 1973. Advocates on each side, and I was and am one for the pro-choice side, have attacked each other's positions in a debate more noted for absolutism and acrimony than civility and reason. Despite this vociferous public debate, by and large the position of the American people on abortion has not changed in the last thirty years. There are even some indications that the American public is slowly gravitating more to the anti-abortion side than the pro-choice side. This is personally depressing. What have I been doing wrong for the past decades? Why have my pro-choice arguments not been persuasive?

I think there are four reasons. First, the arguments based on women's rights and on a woman's right to control her body are addressed primarily to women. These arguments do not directly address the reproductive interests of men, except indirectly under the altruistic assumption that men should be concerned with the well-being of their wives, girlfriends, sisters, daughters, and fellow humans of the opposite sex. These arguments ignore the reality that men have their own reproductive interests and that men want to have children when they want to have them. These interests are not addressed by arguments based on women's rights.

In addition, any argument based on a right to bodily autonomy must recognize that there are exceptions to this rule and that it cannot be absolute. For over a century public health authorities have been able to require vaccinations against infectious diseases, even if the vaccination may have serious side effects, to quarantine sick people who are contagious, and to prohibit us from consuming certain drugs and foods. Public safety and national security concerns can force travelers to undergo body searches at airports. While these examples of bodily invasions may not rise to the same level as requiring a pregnancy to continue no matter what the health or emotional costs to the woman, they do indicate that there are legitimate societal interests that may override our right to bodily autonomy.

The privacy argument—that we are entitled to live our lives without unnecessary government interference into our private lives—runs up against the realities of the modern world where there is less and less privacy. As the world gets more crowded, more connected, and more complex, personal privacy is becoming increasingly elusive, and the public is becoming inured to it. We no longer have expectations of privacy for conversations on the Internet. Cameras to deter crime photograph us as we walk down the street in major cities. The public increasingly supports government regulation of private behavior that harms others. Recently, municipalities have been passing ordinances prohibiting smoking in public places because they believe that secondhand smoke harms passersby. The AIDS epidemic has led to government efforts to discourage or prohibit certain sexual private behavior, notably gay sex in bathhouses, which might result in disease transmission. In these contexts personal reproductive decisions that have public consequences may not seem worthy of privacy protection.

Neither is the public persuaded that the pro-choice arguments we have been making answer the basic moral question of how one can support reproductive choice when one believes that bad choices are being made or that having the choice in itself leads to bad results. It is generally agreed that it is an essential part of being human, and is therefore morally good, that individuals have the choice and the ability to make personal decisions, rightly or wrongly, about how they will lead their lives. The public therefore generally supports individuals having the most liberty and freedom possible to determine the course of their lives. But abortion is seen by many as a choice not worthy of human dignity and freedom because it results in the unnecessary death of an unborn child. In this view abortion could be eliminated if women would only make the unselfish decision to have the baby and either rear it themselves or give it up for adoption. How can one support abortion's being legal if you think it facilitates women making seriously bad or immoral choices?

Traditional pro-choice arguments have not provided much guidance either when individuals confront the difficult questions that new reproductive technologies present. Reproductive science has developed to the point where genetic engineering and even human cloning are possible.

These technologies not only will enable parents to guard against their children's inheriting certain genetic diseases, but also may in the future allow parents to select certain genetic qualities that they want in a child. Cloning will permit a child to be conceived by replicating the genes of one person, rather than by mixing the genes of a mother and father.

New technologies are enabling the human race to assert dominion over its evolutionary future. The technologies will allow us to choose the genetic makeup of our progeny. This in my view is so dangerous that I cannot reconcile it with the absolute right to reproductive choice. These new technologies present difficult moral questions, whether or not one wishes to use the technologies oneself. Their advent makes it clear that reproduction is a matter for all of society to be concerned about. Personal decisions about reproduction do have public consequences.

The lack of relevance of traditional pro-choice arguments to these issues says to me that the world has changed and pro-choice arguments haven't. We have less privacy in the beginning of the twenty-first century than we did when we began advocating for legal abortion in the 1960s. New technologies are presenting new choices and new dangers that we have not addressed. These new technologies make the role of men in reproduction even more uncertain if women can reproduce on their own. The danger that new reproductive technologies may facilitate bad choices has become a more acute moral question.

Traditional pro-choice arguments do not provide as much guidance as the public needs and deserves. I submit that traditional pro-life arguments don't either. Traditional pro-life arguments do not distinguish between various life forms or between egg and sperm combined in a petri dish or in a fallopian tube. Respecting life, however defined, does not provide a basis for analyzing whether genetic engineering is a good thing or whether human cloning should be permitted. A more sophisticated analysis of these issues is needed from both the pro-choice and pro-life camps.

# The Unchanging Nature
# of Public Opinion on Abortion

In one sense the pro-choice movement is a victim of its own success. It scored an enormous victory in 1973 when the U.S. Supreme Court in *Roe* v. *Wade* declared state criminal abortion laws unconstitutional. The political fights that were left—defending *Roe*, fighting the appointment of judges who would overturn it, and fending off state restrictions on abortion access—though clearly vital, appeared less compelling, and as a result over the years there was decreasing passion in the pro-choice movement, especially among young people. As of 2003 those younger than age forty-five have never lived as adults when abortion was illegal, and thus do not know firsthand the danger of abortion being illegal. These young people benefited from the reproductive health services, including abortion, that Planned Parenthood and others provided so competently. Young people don't appreciate the consequences of *Roe* v. *Wade* being overturned and abortion's being made criminal again. As Katha Pollit of the *Nation* said, the pro-choice movement concentrated on the larger political battles and the provision of needed services and "we've let the grassroots education and activism slide." As a result, many young people not only support increased restrictions on abortion access but even favor abortion's being totally illegal.

Compounding this apathy and ambivalence, few abortion supporters talk about abortion positively. Many supporters of choice carefully distinguish between being pro-choice and pro-abortion. Many say, "I would never have an abortion, but it should be legal." President Bill Clinton, when he talked about abortion, said it should be "safe, legal, and rare." If something is good, why should it be rare?

The result is that while public opinion has been relatively static on abortion for the last thirty years, some polls show that the support for the pro-choice position has recently been weakening. Support for a fully pro-choice position (abortion should always be legal)—as for the fully pro-life position (abortion should never be legal)—was never that strong to begin with. Approximately 20–25 percent of the American people support each position, with the remaining half of the American people having a mixed position. These figures have remained remarkably constant over the past quarter century.

Two years after the 1973 Supreme Court decision in *Roe v. Wade*, the Gallup Poll first asked the American people for their opinion of the legality of abortion. The Gallup Poll of April 1975 reported that 21 percent of the American people said that abortion should be legal under all circumstances, 54 percent said that it should be legal only under certain circumstances, and 22 percent said that it should be illegal in all circumstances. In a poll taken in May 2002, a quarter of a century later, Gallup reported "very similar" results: 25 percent said abortion should be legal under all circumstances, 51 percent under certain circumstances, and 22 percent illegal in all circumstances. The slight differences in the results fell within the margin of error for the polls.

In the twenty-five years between these two polls there has been an acrimonious national debate—political, legal, religious, moral, medical, and sociological—over abortion. And national opinion, at least as recorded in the Gallup polls, hasn't changed significantly. However, and more ominously, other polls have shown a declining support for abortion rights in recent years.

In a nationwide poll done in November 2002 Zogby International reported that 22 percent of those surveyed said they supported abortion always being permitted, while 25 percent said it should never be permitted. These results are similar to, and within the margin of error of, the Gallup polls. But the Zogby poll went further and asked if the respondents were currently more or less in favor of abortion than they were a decade ago. Twenty-two percent of respondents said they were less in favor, while only 11 percent said they were more in favor. Younger people tended to be more opposed to abortion than those in the baby boom generation. One-third of people ages eighteen to twenty-nine said that abortion should never be legal, while only 23 percent aged thirty to sixty-four said this, and 20 percent over age sixty-five. This bodes ill for the future of reproductive freedom.

On the twenty-fifth anniversary of the *Roe* decision in January 1998, the *New York Times* conducted a poll jointly with CBS News and reported, similar to Gallup, that the American public was "irreconcilably riven" over abortion and that "despite a quarter-century of lobbying, debating and protesting by the camps that call themselves 'pro-choice' and 'pro-life', that schism has remained virtually unaltered."

On some issues surrounding abortion, public opinion seems impervious to change. I was once on a call-in television talk show where I debated parental consent laws with two supporters of these laws. Before the show the audience in the studio and those at home calling in and sending in e-mails registered their views on the issue. They were 75 percent in favor of parental consent laws and 25 percent opposed (about the same as the national polls). After over an hour of vigorous debate where I, at least, thought I was extremely persuasive, the producers took another poll of the audience in the studio and at home. The result was identical—75 percent in favor of parental consent laws and 25 percent opposed. I hadn't changed a single mind. Maybe those watching were not persuadable, but I also had not yet developed the arguments in this book.

Not only, according to the 1998 *Times*/CBS poll, was the American public as a whole split on the abortion issue, but so were individual Americans. A majority supported the *Roe* decision and believed that abortion should be legal and a matter for a woman and her doctor to decide. Half of all Americans simultaneously believed that abortion was "the same as murdering a child," yet often "the best course in a bad situation." While saying that abortion was not the government's business, most Americans in the poll supported government restrictions on abortion access, including waiting periods, restrictions on funding, and a ban on certain abortion procedures. And while saying that the abortion decision was the woman's to make, an overwhelming majority disapproved of abortion after the first trimester, and increasing majorities opposed allowing abortion for economic reasons, or because the woman would not marry the father, or because having a child would interrupt a young woman's education. On the other hand, there was strong support for abortion being legal when the woman "had been raped, her health was endangered or there was a strong chance of a defect in the baby."

Many of us in the pro-choice movement summarized this state of affairs by saying that the average American supported abortion rights for "rape, incest, and me." About the only things that were clear from the polling were, first, that any polling results on abortion should be read skeptically; second, that polls fail to capture the realities of women's reproductive lives; and, third, that the American people appeared to hold totally contradictory ideas about abortion simultaneously. They approved of choice but not of abortion. They approved of women making the decision but not the decisions that were made. They did not want the government involved but approved of the steps that government did take to reduce abortions.

Reporter Carey Goldberg called the gradations in support or opposition to abortion, which varied by the particular circumstances, a "hierarchy of sin." Peter Steinfels, a *Times* religion reporter, said that the poll results reflected America's "bad conscience about abortion" and a "considerable moral confusion."

## The Moral Confusion and Political Weakness of the Pro-Choice Movement

In 1995 Naomi Wolf wrote an article for the *New Republic* arguing that the pro-choice movement was weakening because it had failed to address this moral confusion. The piece, entitled "Our Bodies, Our Souls," accused the pro-choice movement of relinquishing "the moral frame around abortion" and of ceding "the language of right and wrong to abortion foes." Wolf asserted that the abandonment of an ethical core had caused the pro-choice movement to lose political ground: "By refusing to look at abortion within a moral framework, we lose the millions of Americans who want to support abortion as a legal right but still need to condemn it as a moral iniquity." For Wolf, abortion was a "necessary evil" and a "sin."

Her prescription was:

> to contextualize the fight to defend abortion rights within a moral framework that admits that the death of the fetus is a real death; that there are degrees of culpability, judgment and responsibility involved in the decision to abort a pregnancy; that the best understanding of feminism involves holding women as well as men to the responsibilities that are inseparable from their rights; and that we need to be strong enough to acknowledge that this country's high rate of abortion—which ends more than a quarter of all pregnancies–can only be rightly understood as what Dr. Henry Foster was brave enough to call it: "a failure."

Putting aside the fact that Wolf ignored that there are traditions of theological support for birth control and abortion in virtually all the world's religions, she hit a nerve when she called abortion evil, a sin, and a failure. She should be credited with trying to frame the issue in a new way in order to advance it. However, I could not agree with either her diagnosis or her cure. I could not admit that I had worked to advance "evil" and "sin." I had always felt that my colleagues at Planned Parenthood and I worked within a moral and religious framework. We believed that there were responsibilities that went with the exercise of reproductive rights. But Wolf's diagnosis that we were losing political ground because we did not have an ethical core had to be addressed.

Because of the less-than-overwhelming public support for unfettered reproductive choice, the pro-choice movement has been losing ground in the political arena. Ever since the *Roe* decision a steady stream of federal and state legislation has been enacted designed to overturn *Roe*'s result. Legislation has restricted access to abortion services by denying Medicaid reimbursement for abortion, prohibiting abortions from being performed in public hospitals, requiring minors to notify or get the consent of a parent before an abortion, criminalizing certain abortion procedures, and requiring a husband's consent before his wife may have an abortion.

The pace of legislating appears to be accelerating. In the years between 1996 and 2001, Planned Parenthood reported that 264 pieces of anti-choice legislation had been enacted by state legislatures around the country. By July 2003 NARAL Pro-Choice America reported that the number had risen to 335. I used to think that this was a result of pro-life forces being better organized politically than pro-choice forces are. This may be true, but there is a lot more to the pro-choice political problem than our relative inability to get our supporters to the polls to vote our way. Our problem, I believe, is with our approach to the issue of choice.

## Why We Need to Fight a New Battle for Choice

The impetus for this book grew out of a very simple but heretical question. How many more pieces of anti-choice legislation will it take to get the pro-choice movement to rethink its approach to the issue?

The pro-choice movement isn't making major headway with the American public. We are losing ground politically. *Roe* hangs by a thread. A change of one or two members of the Supreme Court could lead to its overturn.

This state of affairs is not what we in the pro-choice movement want.

I believe that to win the judicial battles and political battles we first must win the battle for the hearts and minds of the American people. We have failed because we have not fought this battle with ideas and language that the American people would understand and agree with. If the American people have moral confusion about abortion, then the fault lies with we who argue on behalf of reproductive rights. We haven't presented abortion within a framework or a system of ideas that is coherent and makes moral sense.

It has been said that no social change is permanent unless it survives two generations. We have been through a generation since *Roe*. We don't want America's negative opinion of abortion, which seems to have solidified since *Roe*, to last another generation and become permanent. We don't want abortion allowed grudgingly and only for the well-to-do, for the adult who can afford it. We don't want women treated as incapable of making this decision. We don't want abortion considered immoral. We don't want, as Peter Steinfels said, "that a permanently uneasy conscience about abortion may be the best that the public can achieve, an appropriate response to tragic situations."

It is time for a new look at our issues, our most difficult issues. It is time for a new look at our opposition's take on our issues. It is time for rethinking. The pro-choice movement will make political progress when it demonstrates that it has an ethical core and a moral perspective that can guide men and women on their reproductive journey through life. The pro-choice movement will make progress when its ideas are shown to be of more benefit to both individuals and humanity than pro-life ideas.

The central challenge for the pro-choice movement in the twenty-first century is to show that it has the ideas and philosophy to help people cope with the ethical dilemmas that new reproductive technologies present. While there are ethical dilemmas for each individual who wants to use genetic engineering, there is a larger ethical dilemma for society as a whole. These technologies threaten to change the nature of the human race and that affects all of us. The pro-choice movement must answer the question whether this particular individual reproductive "choice" is defensible. We must provide the moral framework to distinguish between those reproductive technologies that benefit humanity and those that hurt it. We must provide the public a view of the kind of reproductive world we want to live in.

I believe that the pro-choice position generally benefits humanity and that the pro-life position does not. We must be able to say this clearly and unequivocally. To do so we must rethink what we stand for and what we believe and provide new ideas for the American people to grasp and rally around. The pro-choice idea that abortion should be legal and available to all women who want one no matter what their circumstances garners in polling the support of about one-quarter of the American people. We have to do better than that.

Let me be clear. I believe that the traditional pro-choice arguments are right and moral. I have made them for years. Unfortunately, they have proved insufficient to persuade a majority of the American people of the rightness of our position. We should continue to make our traditional arguments because they do persuade our core supporters. But a new framework is needed in order to bring along the 50 percent of the public that is nominally pro-choice but which may believe abortion immoral and accepts restrictions on abortion access.

I believe that American and worldwide views of abortion will become more pro-choice only when we put abortion in a reproductive and biological context. Women who make the decision to have sex or not, use contraception or not, or have an abortion or not are making biological decisions. In many cases the word "decision" may be too strong a word. Sex may happen without rational forethought. A pregnancy may or may not happen depending on a variety of circumstances. A pregnancy may miscarry, and a live child may or may not be born. This is the fundamental human biological condition. The human use of methods to prevent pregnancy and childbirth are essential components of human biology. In many ways it is a misnomer to say that to do so is a "reproductive right." It is simply profoundly human. To the extent that the pro-choice movement is trying to advance "reproductive rights," this book is designed to shift our focus from rights to reproduction. If we can do this, then I believe that we will be talking in terms that every person can relate to.

The pro-choice movement has been called at various points in its history the birth control movement, the family planning movement, and the reproductive rights movement. To me, the first words of each phrase—birth, family, and reproduction—are the key to the future success of the movement, rather than the last words—control, planning, and rights. I believe we should argue for reproductive freedom because it supports successful birth, family, and reproduction. We all are here because of the successful reproduction of our ancestors. We all, or most of us, want to repeat the process and have children and grandchildren. Reproductive freedom, including abortion, makes this possible. Reproductive freedom is just as important to those men and women who want to have children as it is to those who don't want to. We must be on the side of men and women, no matter what their choice.

# CHAPTER ONE

# The Origins of Choice

T he roots of the arguments for and against reproductive freedom extend back in time way before *Roe v. Wade*, the U.S. Supreme Court decision that legalized abortion in 1973. Reproductive freedom has been a contentious issue in many societies around the world for eons. Reproductive freedom has been an issue of both property law and religious doctrine. It has been both a racial issue and a medical issue. It has been a sexual issue and a women's rights issue. Finally, it has been a biological issue and a legal issue.

The status of contraception and abortion has changed over time. They have been alternately favored and disfavored and legal and illegal. In the United States the status of birth control and abortion in the twentieth century has been largely determined by the courts. While my grandmother, Margaret Sanger, pursued legislative changes to restrictive birth control laws, she succeeded mainly in the courts. As a result the political discourse about reproductive freedom before and after *Roe* has been largely a legal discourse. Those who support *Roe* have the political goal of keeping the membership of the Supreme Court as it is, while those who oppose *Roe* have the opposite goal of changing the court's membership and appointing justices who will overturn it. The political dialogue is frozen in place as legal dialogue. Advocates for and against reproductive freedom pitch their arguments so as to give one's side the advantage in the ultimate Supreme Court case that will reconsider *Roe*.

The problem with considering the issue of reproductive freedom primarily in the legal arena is that for the most part it should not be a legal issue at all. How can an issue that is simultaneously a medical, religious, racial, sexual, and woman's issue be resolved as a matter of constitutional law? The Supreme Court in *Griswold v. Connecticut*, the 1965 case that legalized birth control, solved this dilemma by articulating a new constitutional right, a right to privacy that protected citizens from government interference in marital childbearing decisions that took place in the bedroom. The court saw no other way to translate a biological imperative into a constitutional right and thus get the government out of the business of regulating childbearing decisions. In so doing the court limited the abortion debate, at least in the legal and political realm, to a debate over rights—should there be a right to privacy? What is the extent of the right to privacy? What other interests or rights can override the right to privacy?

The Supreme Court thus set the terms of the modern abortion debate and left the most important issue off the table—the biological reasons for reproductive freedom in the first place. I believe that biology provides the most important reason for reproductive freedom and that we are not going to win the legal battles until we educate the American people that reproductive freedom is a biological imperative. So, how did we lose sight of the biological imperative for reproductive freedom and how can we reclaim it?

## Pre–Nineteenth Century Reproductive Freedom

The concept of reproductive freedom has been recognized to some extent throughout human history. Greek and Roman secular law and Jewish and Christian theology all recognized that there were times and circumstances where birth control and abortion were acceptable. At the time when the United States was founded, under English law, birth control and abortion were mostly legal, acceptable, and used.

My grandmother, Margaret Sanger, did not invent birth control. Contraceptive information appears in the earliest human writings. An Egyptian papyrus from about the year 1850 BCE contains a recipe for a vaginal suppository (of uncertain effectiveness and questionable hygiene since its main ingredient appears to be crocodile dung) to prevent pregnancy. Greek and Roman medical literature is rife with instructions for herbal methods of contraception and abortion (the French so-called abortion pill, RU–486 or mifepristone, is not a new concept). Greek and Roman law did not mention contraception but did regulate abortion as a matter of property law, requiring a husband's consent before his wife could have an abortion, since the fetus was considered the husband's personal property. Reproduction was a matter not only for the secular authorities in the Roman Empire; it was a matter for the new Christian Church as well.

The Christian Church brought quite a different perspective to reproductive matters than the Roman Empire did. As a persecuted religious sect and eager for defensive and theological reasons to increase the number of Christians both by birth and conversion, the early Church was firmly pro-natalist. The main problem that early Christian theologians faced was that neither contraception nor abortion was specifically mentioned in the Bible, except for Exodus 21:22 which addressed the penalties to be imposed when a person causes an accidental miscarriage. The penalties were levied under the same theory manifested in Roman law. Penalties were merited because the father had been deprived of his property. Traditional Jewish teachings favored childbearing in order to have the Jewish race continue, but these teachings permitted, and in some cases even required, that birth control and abortion be used. Christian doctrine, which slowly emerged over the centuries after the New Testament was written, declared both contraception and abortion to be mostly, but not always, sinful. Christian theology took a more severe tone on reproductive issues after the Black Death decimated Christian Europe in the mid–fourteenth century. Many historians believe that the Church launched the witch hunts and the attendant Inquisition to prevent midwives, who were the leading purveyors of birth control and abortion methods to the women of Europe, from plying their trade.

The Church was not, however, entirely anti-abortion. For centuries, using the current state of scientific knowledge, the Church debated when a fetus became "human" and thus came under the protection of Church law against abortion. Plato and Aristotle had opined that the fetus wasn't "formed" or human until forty days after conception for the male and eighty days after conception for the female. Although easily dismissed as a sexist joke today, this theory was based on the biological knowledge of the time, in which every fetus was believed to have begun as male, and the female fetus was believed to be an in utero mutation from the male. At any rate, this belief was adopted by Christian theologians in later centuries and became the doctrine of delayed ensoulment, that is, the time when the soul entered the fetus and thus the fetus became "formed" or "human." The time of ensoulment was moved forward in time by Christian theologians from the Platonic fortieth or eightieth day to the time when the woman first felt the fetus move, usually during the fourth or fifth month of pregnancy. Thus, the humanness of an unborn child coincided with the time a woman could first confirm she was pregnant. Before this time, under early Christian doctrine, there was no "human being," and abortion during this period was not a sin. Under this doctrine, the moral status of an early fetus was less than that of a more developed fetus.

Secular law eventually adopted this theological concept of delaying the declaration of a pregnancy and thus of human life until the woman could confirm she was pregnant. In the Middle Ages English law, based on the notion of delayed ensoulment, defined pregnancy to begin at "quickening," the time when the pregnant woman first felt the fetus move. Before quickening, termination of the "pregnancy" was not prohibited because the woman was not deemed under the law to be pregnant. Legal historians today are divided on whether abortion even after quickening was considered a crime. Justice Harry Blackmun said in *Roe v. Wade*: "it now appears doubtful that abortion was ever firmly established as a common-law crime even with respect to the destruction of a quick fetus."

The use of quickening to determine the beginning of a pregnancy made sense in terms of two other biological facts that were probably unknown to theologians and lawmakers of the time. First, a substantial percentage of fertilized ova never implant in the uterus and hence a pregnancy never starts. One study showed that 58 percent of fertilized eggs did not survive until the twelfth day after conception. Second, there is a substantial risk of miscarriage in the early months of pregnancy even after implantation, a risk estimated to be between 10 or 20 percent of pregnancies, or perhaps more, since many early pregnancies are undetected and unreported. Taken together, this means, as biologist Lee M. Silver of Princeton University has stated, that 75 percent of fertilized eggs do not survive the nine months of pregnancy. The concept of declaring a pregnancy officially beginning at quickening, at the fourth or fifth months, recognized the biological uncertainties of early pregnancy. This concept has a lingering effect on American public opinion on abortion. Americans overwhelmingly approve of abortion being legal in the first trimester, that is, before quickening, and disapprove of abortion thereafter.

English law was carried over into American law in 1776 when we declared our independence and in 1789 when we formed our new nation. In both colonial and post-revolutionary America, abortion was legal at least up to the point of quickening, and perhaps thereafter. Contraception was not forbidden in either English or American law. Although much contraceptive knowledge was lost due to the witch hunts in Europe beginning in the fifteenth century, in late eighteenth century America there were herbal methods for both contraception and abortion that were handed down from midwife to midwife and from mother to daughter. This is not to say that abortion was not a contentious issue in the colonies. In 1729 Benjamin Franklin was starting his career as a newspaper publisher and used the abortion issue to attack a rival publisher, Samuel Keimer. Keimer's paper thought it was providing a public service, or at least filling up its newspages, with entries from the encyclopedia. He started with the letter "a" and soon published the entry on abortion. Franklin, using the pen names Martha Careful and Celia Shortface, penned letters to another rival paper "feigning shock and indignation at Keimer's offense," as his biographer, Walter Isaacson, put it. Isaacson continued:

> As Miss Careful threatened, "If he proceeds farther to expose the secrets of our sex in that audacious manner (women would) run the hazard of taking him by the beard in the next place we meet him." Thus Franklin manufactured the first recorded abortion debate in America, not because he had any strong feelings on the issue, but because he knew it would help sell newspapers.

Throughout most of Western history, therefore, reproductive freedom, despite being a contentious issue, was permitted to a greater or lesser extent. Reproductive policy and law were the products of 1) the contemporary and limited understanding of reproductive biology; 2) the Christian Church's institutional need to increase the number of Christians (especially after the Black Death); and 3) the intertwining of Church and State which resulted in theological ensoulment being transformed into legal quickening.

## The Demise of Reproductive Freedom in the Nineteenth Century

The birth control movement that Margaret Sanger started in the early twentieth century was a reaction to the nineteenth century pro-life movement that succeeded in reversing American and British law and criminalizing both birth control and abortion almost entirely. The campaign to restrict reproductive freedom was not solely based on a respect for unborn life at its earliest stages. Rather it was a campaign founded upon the institutional imperatives of organized medicine, the Protestant reaction to Irish Catholic immigration, and the feminist and fundamentalist drive for social purity in sexual matters.

During the nineteenth century physicians began to unravel the mysteries of reproductive biology and fetal development. The ovum was discovered, as was the process of fertilization. The nineteenth century was also the time when university-trained physicians sought to control the practice of medicine. In our overly regulated society it is hard to imagine a time when there were few if any restrictions on who could "practice medicine." In fact, until university-trained physicians appeared on the scene, midwives and other non-university trained doctors called "irregulars," as well as outright quacks, were the main practitioners of medicine. They not only diagnosed medical conditions but also distributed all kinds of homemade drugs to their patients. Medical potions and patent medicines were concocted and sold with virtually no regulation or oversight. While official records are skimpy, it seems that the first legislative restrictions on the practice of abortion were enacted as a result of efforts by "regular" physicians to protect the safety of women to whom dangerous abortifacient potions were being given by "irregulars." There is some evidence that America's first law that banned the giving of a "potion" to cause an abortion in a woman "quick" with child, in Connecticut in 1821, came out of an effort by physicians to ban all homemade herbal remedies, whether for abortion or not, as simply being too dangerous. When New York enacted its ban on abortion in 1828, it banned abortion before or after quickening unless two physicians determined the abortion was necessary to save the woman's life (a vastly broader category of cases than in current times since modern technology, obstetrical skills, and antibiotics were not available to deal with the many pregnancy complications that untreated would often kill the mother).

University-trained physicians also had a financial motive to put their competition, the irregulars, midwives, and quacks, out of business. These irregulars made a healthy part of their income by providing contraception and abortion, as well as childbirth services. As a result, regular physicians began to pressure legislatures to put the control of pregnancy prevention and termination in the hands of physicians only. Thus the early statutes, like in New York, permitted abortions only when two physicians agreed, and other later abortion statutes allowed physicians to exercise their medical judgment and perform abortions when they thought it necessary.

The formation of the American Medical Association in 1841 by the physician regulars accelerated the legislative process of putting medicine in general and reproduction in particular into physician hands. The AMA made it one of its first items of business as the trade association for physicians to put the irregulars out of business. Over the next century, as their medical expertise grew, physicians took control of childbirth and largely succeeded in removing it from the home under the supervision of a midwife to the hospital under the supervision of a physician. With contraception and abortion physicians took a more drastic route—they sought to criminalize them both either entirely or if not done under a physician's supervision. They didn't bother to hide their financial motive. James C. Mohr, in his book *Abortion in America*, related that the Southern Michigan Medical Society in 1875 was reminded by one of its members: "Regular physicians are still losing patients, even long-time patients, to competitors willing 'to prevent an increase in their (patient's) families' by performing abortions."

On abortion this strategy dovetailed with new biological discoveries that pregnancy was a continuum from conception to birth and that quickening had no medical significance. Physicians began to agree with some religious leaders that pre-born life deserved their total respect and protection and that abortion should not be permitted except for therapeutic reasons. This belief was an historical part of their professional obligations, since the traditional Hippocratic Oath written by the Greek physician Hippocrates in about 400 BCE said: "I will not give to a woman a pessary to produce abortion."

The AMA alone was not able to bring about the criminalization of abortion. At the beginning of the doctors' campaign in the 1840s and 1850s they allied themselves with the Know-Nothings, a fledging political party of nativists, whose main platform consisted of opposing Irish-Catholic immigration into America, which had begun to increase exponentially. The Know-Nothings wanted to preserve their control over the then mostly Anglo-Saxon, Protestant society. The party's platform was a mixture of nativism, temperance, and religious bigotry. The platform called for limits on immigration, for restriction of political offices to native-born Americans, and for a twenty-one-year waiting period before an immigrant could vote. The Know-Nothings sought to limit the sale of liquor, to require that all public-school teachers be Protestants, and to have the Protestant version of the Bible read daily to all students in public school. Party members feared that they, the native-born Protestants, would soon be outnumbered and outvoted by the new Catholic immigrants. Their goal was to preserve the primacy of the Anglo-Saxon, Protestant religion, culture, and political power.

It did not escape Protestant notice that immigrant Catholic women had large numbers of children, while native Protestant women were having fewer. Since few new birth control methods had been introduced at this time—although there were the beginnings of condom and diaphragm manufacturing—the Know-Nothings suspected that Protestant women were using abortion as their method of birth control. Physicians studying who were having abortions confirmed this suspicion. Hence, the Know-Nothing men readily joined the AMA crusade to criminalize abortion. As contraceptive options increased in the course of the nineteenth century, those who favored the white Protestant hegemony also supported the criminalization of contraception.

Racial and ethnic fears were thus a major part of the impetus to control women's fertility. As one prominent physician said in 1874: "The annual destruction of fetuses has become so truly appalling among native American (Protestant) women that the Puritanic blood of '76 will be but sparingly represented in the approaching centenary."

Even though men took the lead in advancing the medical, political, and racial arguments for the criminalization of birth control and abortion, some women were also in favor of this legislation, as they were in favor of other "social purity" campaigns after the Civil War that sought to restrict various immoral pursuits such as gambling, drinking, and prostitution. In these campaigns the political odd bedfellows, the Know-Nothings and the regular physicians, were joined by some women's rights activists. As Ellen Chessler, my grandmother's biographer, described it: the native white Americans seeking to preserve their hegemony "were joined by religious fundamentalists, physicians looking to secure their status, and self-proclaimed feminists who believed they were promoting their own autonomy by regulating sexual behavior and by attacking pornography, alcohol and vice." Into the vice category fell any expression of human sexuality other than between married couples for purposes of reproduction.

Nineteenth century feminists, an admittedly small and relatively powerless group, supported what they called "voluntary motherhood." Voluntary motherhood was to be achieved not by promoting birth control and abortion but rather by controlling male sexuality. Some feminists believed that birth control and abortion did more than enable voluntary motherhood; they enabled husbands to consort more freely with "other women." Feminists believed that their own voluntary motherhood could be achieved by periodic abstinence and self-control, their own and their husbands'.

So, in the years after the Civil War, Anthony Comstock, an official of the YWCA who headed the New York Society for the Suppression of Vice, found ready allies in some feminist circles for his social purity campaign to prevent the dissemination through the U.S. mails of obscene materials. He defined these to include any information on human sexuality, reproduction, birth control, or abortion. Every publication or article "designed, adapted, or intended for preventing conception or producing abortion, or for any indecent or immoral purpose" was banned. After Congress enacted the Comstock Laws in 1873, which banned sexuality, birth control, and abortion information from the mails as contraband, individual states followed suit and criminalized the dissemination of contraceptive and abortion information and devices within their borders, though with some variations that permitted greater or lesser discretion to physicians. The result was that by the last quarter of the nineteenth century birth control and abortion had essentially been criminalized at both the state and federal levels.

The result was not that birth control and abortion were thereby eliminated from American society. Instead they largely went underground. Some forms of birth control methods remained available but were sold under euphemistic titles. Abortion potions were sold as a tonic for "female problems," diaphragms were "womb supports," and condoms were called "rubber goods." Andrea Tone in *Devices and Desires: A History of Contraceptives in America* stated: "legal leniency, entrepreneurial savvy, and cross class consumer support enabled the black market in birth control to thrive." It is difficult to estimate how widely contraception and abortion were used, whether the poor were able to afford them, or how safe and effective they were. We can surmise that many Americans had access to either birth control or abortion because the birth rate continued its century-long decline even after both were criminalized. My grandmother's personal experience told her, however, that all too many women lacked this access.

Reproductive freedom was a threat to the power structure in nineteenth century America. It threatened physicians, who wanted to monopolize the practice of medicine; it threatened Anglo-Saxon Protestants who wanted to maintain their control over American society, culture and politics; and it threatened those men and women who viewed any expression of sexuality outside the home as a threat to marriage and decency. The campaign to criminalize birth control and abortion found many allies, and it succeeded. Anthony Comstock became one of the most powerful men in America.

## Margaret Sanger and the Overturning of the Comstock Laws

It took my grandmother twenty years to dismantle the Comstock laws. In her campaign she brought to the American public her experience as a nurse that birth control was a human necessity and a public good. She broke the Comstock laws repeatedly and her court cases reinterpreted the Comstock laws in such a way that they became toothless. Physicians were granted the power to prescribe birth control for the well-being of their patients. In making these arguments, my grandmother soft-pedaled her often strident feminism and used the argument that the ability of a woman to control and limit her childbearing was good for the woman, her children, and the rest of her family, but was also good for the public health, society, and the economy. Birth control became family planning.

Margaret Sanger's opponents were powerful: physicians, Protestants, Catholics, feminists, purity crusaders, and politicians of all stripes. Anthony Comstock, the lead zealot enforcing his laws, was still alive and active. Comstock's crusade even reached to the rural areas of upstate New York to the Catholic community of Corning where Margaret Sanger's (nee Higgins) parents made their home. Both were Irish Catholic immigrants. Sanger's mother, Anna Purcell Higgins, was pregnant eighteen times, had eleven children, seven miscarriages and died in 1899 at age forty-nine. She died about fifty years after, and not far from, the site of the first woman's rights convention in Seneca Falls, New York. Anna Higgins was remembered by her daughter as always either pregnant or nursing and in poor health.

Margaret Sanger's father was a freethinker and rebel against conformity and had the unfortunate habit of confronting the local Catholic Church on various social issues of the day. This was suicidal from the family's economic point of view since Michael Higgins made his living carving tombstones in the local Catholic cemetery. Needless to say, as these commissions dwindled, the Higgins family fell into deeper and deeper poverty.

In the 1890's when Margaret was in her teens (she had been born in 1879), her older sisters pooled their meager resources and sent Margaret away to boarding school. She soon had to drop out due to the death of her mother to come home and take care of her father and the younger children. I am not sure she ever graduated from high school. After a period at home the sisters again financed her way out of Corning, and Margaret, after attempts at acting school and teaching kindergarten, enrolled in nursing school in White Plains, New York, about thirty miles north of New York City. Again I am not sure she ever graduated, but she received enough training to become a probationary nurse at the Manhattan Eye and Ear Hospital, where one day she met my grandfather, William Sanger. To say that this was an unusual match is an understatement since my grandfather was Jewish, the son of Orthodox immigrants from East Prussia. While Catholic-Jewish marriages are still fairly rare of today, they were almost unheard of in 1900.

Over the next few years the Sangers had three children and moved out of the city to the suburbs where Margaret became a full time mother. My grandmother kept many, many records of her life—letters, diaries and so forth. One of the few things we do not know about her was what method of birth control she used.

At any rate, in 1910 my grandmother described herself as restless in the suburbs and wanting to enter the bustling world of New York City and to nurse again. William was on the fringes of the radical community in the City and even ran for City alderman in the 1911 election on the Socialist Party ticket. Through her husband Margaret met many of the significant radical thinkers and doers of the day, including Big Bill Haywood, the leader of the Industrial Workers of the World (IWW), John Reed, who wrote *Ten Days That Shook the World* about the Russian Revolution, Mabel Dodge, who ran a radical salon, and Emma Goldman, the anarchist who had frequently challenged the Comstock laws. Margaret became an organizer for the Socialist Party and for the IWW, while simultaneously nursing for the Visiting Nurse Service.

In 1911 my grandmother had her first confrontation with Comstock when she, a nurse, was asked to write a column for the Socialist Party newspaper, the *New York Call*, on sex education. She thus became one of America's first, if not *the* first, sex columnist. The column was called "What Every Girl Should Know." Margaret started her series with columns on the birds and the bees, literally, and on plant reproduction. Her readers were understandably confused. Trying to recapture her reader's attention, Margaret wrote the next article on venereal disease. This got not only her readers' attention but also Anthony Comstock's. The Post Office, under Comstock's direction, seized that issue of the *Call* as being obscene and thus a violation of the federal Comstock law and refused to let it go through the mails. The *Call's* editor compromised with Comstock and reprinted the issue with the following in the place of Margaret's column: "What Every Girl Should Know—Nothing—By Order of the U.S. Post Office."

About this time Margaret Sanger began nursing on the Lower East Side of New York. Again and again she was called down to nurse women who had given themselves abortions or who had been to illegal, "back alley" abortionists. The Lower East Side in the 1910s was populated by Eastern European immigrants, mostly Jewish, who spoke little English. Living conditions were abysmal—the poverty and overcrowding were overwhelming. The birth control that escaped seizure by Anthony Comstock often didn't find its way to the women there. The preferred methods of self-induced abortion were, as my grandmother described them, "herb teas, turpentine, steaming, rolling downstairs, inserting slippery elm, knitting needles, and shoe-hooks." Some women used a household acid like Lysol. Usually the woman died before a doctor or nurse could get there. My grandmother often talked about of saving the life of one particular patient, Sadie Sachs. My grandmother told of spending several days and nights helping a doctor save Sadie Sachs's life after she had given herself an abortion. When Sadie Sachs was finally feeling better and it came time for the doctor to leave, Sadie asked what she could do to avoid getting pregnant again. "So," the doctor replied, "you want to have your cake and eat it too. The answer is 'Tell Jake to sleep on the roof.'" Eventually Sadie Sachs got pregnant again, gave herself another abortion, and died in my grandmother's arms.

It is not clear from my grandmother's version of events that this death needed to happen. After all, Sadie Sachs was under the care of a trained nurse, my grandmother, who surely knew, despite her public protestations to the contrary, how to prevent pregnancy. It isn't even clear whether Sadie Sachs existed or was a composite of several patients. Whatever the reality, my grandmother claimed that the death of Sadie Sachs was the central motivating incident of her life. I suspect that it triggered memories of her mother's early death, even though her mother's death resulted from multiple pregnancies, rather than the multiple abortions. But the root cause was the same—lack of birth control.

The only way to get birth control to women was to get rid of the federal and state Comstock laws.

My grandmother began her challenge to Comstock by publishing a newspaper called the *Woman Rebel*. The masthead read, "No Gods, No Masters," a slogan borrowed from the Industrial Workers of the World, a radical labor union of the day. The paper contained articles and editorials on a variety of topics: the labor movement, capitalism, the U.S. Government, militarism, and other fashionable leftist subjects of the day. But its central theme was "birth control," a term that my grandmother and her fellow conspirators coined for the third issue to replace the less felicitous Victorian terms "family limitation," "voluntary motherhood," and "prevention of conception."

In the June 1914 issue, in her statement of editorial purpose, Margaret Sanger wrote the following:

A woman's body is hers alone. It does not belong to the Church. It does not belong to the United States of America or any other government on the face of the earth. The first step towards getting life, liberty or the pursuit of happiness for any woman is her decision whether or not she shall become a mother.

While familiar now, this was the first time that these words or these thoughts had appeared in print in America—that a woman's body was hers, that every woman had the right to decide whether or not to become a mother, and that it was none of the government's (or any church's) business. This was the beginning of the pro-choice argument. The argument was especially radical at the time, since in 1914 women did not even have the right to vote. Additionally, my grandmother repeated at every opportunity the story of Sadie Sachs and made the point that it was better for women if birth control (and even abortion) were legal and done by doctors, rather than illegal and done by quacks. All of the now traditional arguments in favor of reproductive rights were created by my grandmother at the very beginning. Her goal was to use these arguments to change both the moral climate, which disapproved of birth control, and the law, which forbade it.

My grandmother followed her newspaper by opening America's first birth control clinic, on October 16, 1916. This was the founding of Planned Parenthood. She was promptly arrested and convicted of violating the New York Comstock law and served thirty days in the Queens County Penitentiary. She appealed her conviction even though she had clearly violated the law.

Up until my grandmother's case, the New York Comstock law prevented the distribution of contraceptives or contraceptive information with one exception—doctors could prescribe birth control "for the cure or prevention of disease." This language was understood to mean that a man could be given a condom when he went to a prostitute so that he could avoid contracting a venereal disease. Birth control could not be given by a physician to be used at home by a man with his wife to prevent pregnancy. The trial judge had in fact stated a woman had no right "to copulate without fear of pregnancy." My grandmother and her lawyer had argued that women had precisely that right, but that was not the issue before the court. The issues were women's health and the right of physicians to practice medicine.

My grandmother's lawyer pointed out the absurdity of the Comstock Law's double standard—that males were protected by the law's exception and that females were not—and used the testimony of the women who had flooded her clinic to show that pregnancy had serious health consequences for women and that there were often valid medical reasons for avoiding or postponing pregnancy. After considering the arguments, the all-male New York Court of Appeals affirmed Margaret's conviction on the grounds that she was a nurse not a doctor and had no doctor with her in the clinic. But at the same time the court expanded the authority of doctors under the exception to the Comstock law to practice medicine largely as they saw fit. The court specifically authorized doctors to prescribe contraceptives to a woman when there was a valid health reason for prescribing them.

The court said that the exception to the Comstock Law, which permitted physicians to prescribe contraceptives "for the cure or prevention of disease," was not intended to permit "promiscuous advice to patients irrespective of their condition" but was broad enough to "protect a physician who in good faith gives such help or advice to a married person to cure or prevent disease." The court then referred to Webster's Dictionary for a definition of "disease": "an alteration of the state of the body, or of some of its organs, interrupting or disturbing the performance of the vital functions, and causing or threatening pain and sickness; illness; sickness; disorder."

Without saying so explicitly, the court had defined pregnancy as a "disease," since in its broadest interpretation pregnancy was an "alteration of the state of the body." If the law was interpreted more narrowly, a woman needed to have some preexisting medical condition that a pregnancy could aggravate. Under the court's decision, promiscuous advice to single men and women was still illegal, but preventive contraceptive advice to married men and women was not.

The opinion in *Sanger v. New York* ("*Sanger*") was a subtle but stunning victory. It was the first crack in the Comstock laws. It breached the double standard of sexuality that permitted men but not women to enjoy sex without fear of pregnancy. It treated women as human beings with real health needs. It permitted doctors to practice medicine. It opened the door a crack to legitimizing and legalizing birth control. The price for this victory, however, was the medicalization of birth control. On this the court was firm. Birth control was not a matter for the layperson. It was not a matter for nurses (then mostly female), it was a matter for physicians (then mostly male), and physicians only, a distinction that profoundly irritated my grandmother. And it reiterated that sex and birth control were for married persons only.

The *Sanger* case enabled my grandmother to make a new series of arguments in favor of birth control: that having birth control legal and regulated and under physician control meant that it would be safer for women and that when children were planned and properly spaced women, children, and society would all benefit. Margaret Sanger reminded audiences of Sadie Sachs and even of her own mother, for whom unwanted childbearing was a death sentence. Women and children would not survive unless women could control whether and when they had children. It was to these biological arguments that my grandmother turned as she began the second phase of her campaign in the state legislatures and in Congress to overturn the Comstock laws. No longer would she emphasize the class or feminist arguments for birth control. She saw these as too limiting in their appeal, especially for men, who she knew had to become supporters of the movement in order for it to progress. These arguments were also offensive to physicians, who she also now knew she needed to convert to her side. Her arguments would henceforth be mostly biological, medical, and social, though her feminist arguments were never far below the surface in the birth control movement, and they resurfaced in the 1960s and 1970s as the primary arguments for the legalization of abortion.

Finally one day in the mid–1930s, after years of beating her head in seeming futility against the walls of Congress trying to get the federal Comstock law amended to permit the distribution of birth control information through the mails, Margaret was lamenting her lack of progress to Morris Ernst, a famed New York lawyer. Ernst reminded Margaret of her victory twenty years earlier in *Sanger v. New York*, where she had convinced the highest court in New York to "reinterpret" the New York Comstock law. Ernst believed they could use a similar strategy by brazenly violating the federal Comstock law in order to force a court to reinterpret it. My grandmother promptly asked a Japanese doctor to mail a box of diaphragms to the medical director of her New York clinic, Dr. Hannah Stone. Having been alerted ahead of time by Margaret to do their sworn duty, the U.S. Customs duly seized the package as contraband under the federal Comstock law, and Margaret and Hannah Stone filed suit to get their diaphragms back. The case, entitled the *United States v. One Package of Japanese Pessaries ("One Package")*, was heard by the Federal Second Circuit Court of Appeals in 1936. As Morris Ernst had predicted, the three-judge panel reinterpreted the federal Comstock law and declared it inapplicable to the importation, sale, or mailing of contraceptives on the ground that contraceptives had some legal uses under state laws such as New York's. Like the *Sanger* case before it, this was a stunning decision. The *One Package* court used two judicial sleights of hand to justify its ruling: first it reinterpreted the *Sanger* case and then it reinterpreted the Comstock law.

The federal Comstock law, unlike the New York Comstock law, had no exception for physicians that permitted them to use the mails to distribute contraceptive information or devices for the cure or prevention of disease. My grandmother and Stone had clearly violated the law, just as my grandmother had in *Sanger*. Nonetheless, Ernst introduced into evidence, through Dr. Stone, all the biological, medical, scientific, and social research that my grandmother had gathered over the years, proving the health and medical benefits of contraception for women and children. By so doing Ernst gave the court the opportunity to reinterpret the *Sanger* case. This the court was eager to do. It may have been because the judges were politically sympathetic to my grandmother's cause and detested what Comstock stood for, or perhaps because Learned Hand's daughter, and Augustus Hand's niece, Frances Ferguson, was a devoted and fervent supporter of birth control.

Stone testified that she prescribed pessaries "in cases where it would not be *desirable* for a patient to undertake a pregnancy" (emphasis added). Judge Augustus Hand, writing for the court, accepted Stone's testimony as the legal standard announced in and permitted under the *Sanger* case. Hand stated that "the use of contraceptives was in many cases necessary for the health of women." These statements, that birth control could be prescribed when a pregnancy was not desirable and that birth control was necessary for the health of women, go far beyond what the *Sanger* decision in fact permitted. Neither Dr. Stone nor Judge Hand required, prior to the prescription of birth control, as the *Sanger* case had, that there be a physician finding of a "disease" to "cure or prevent" or even that the patient be married. Thus, *Sanger* was reinterpreted by Hand to greatly expand the authority of physicians to prescribe birth control. Judge Hand then went on to rule that, even though the federal Comstock law specifically banned articles for preventing conception, the law did not "prevent the importation, sale or carriage by mail of things which might intelligently be employed by the conscientious and competent physicians for the purpose of saving life or *promoting the well-being* of the patients" (emphasis added) Hand was essentially saying that since physicians, under his reinterpretation of *Sanger*, had so much discretion about the circumstances where they could prescribe birth control, the old law shouldn't get in the way. The fact that Congress had intended the law to get in the way was disregarded.

The government declined to appeal the *One Package* decision to the United States Supreme Court. As a result, the *One Package* case by two clever legal sleights of hand essentially legalized birth control in America—at least at the federal level under physician control. The American Medical Association endorsed birth control within the year. The *Sanger* and *One Package* cases together took birth control in less than two decades from being illegal, prior to 1918, to being permitted for disease prevention, broadly defined, to finally being permitted when a pregnancy was not desirable or to promote the well-being of the patient.

The courts that made these rulings did so, not on the basis of feminist arguments or privacy arguments, but on the basis of the individual health and medical benefits of contraception. The courts based their rulings squarely upon the authority of doctors, indeed the obligation of doctors, to provide care for their patients. Underlying both legal victories were my grandmother's arguments that reproductive freedom was a biological and social necessity for women, men, and children. My grandmother had argued that birth control enabled women to better survive the rigors of childbearing and also gave children a better chance at life, health, and survival when they were properly spaced and planned. She argued that birth control was a moral imperative because it provided for a healthier, happier, and more prosperous human race. The initial legal battles for birth control were won because the courts came to realize that permitting the government to prohibit birth control made no sense from a medical and health point of view, and thus from a moral point of view. Birth control was necessary for the survival and health of humanity; government had to get out of the way.

The biological and moral underpinnings of the *Sanger* and *One Package* decisions would be obscured when the Supreme Court in 1965 finally addressed the constitutionality of the remaining state Comstock laws. Biological necessity could not be easily translated into a constitutional concept, and the route that the court took to overturn these laws by creating a right to privacy would change the terms of the debate on reproductive freedom forever. My grandmother had started with feminist arguments; then as she repeatedly broke the Comstock laws and went to court, she adopted more biological and public health and welfare arguments for birth control. Her victory over Comstock was sealed when she convinced physicians to switch sides from opposing birth control to supporting it under their control. The physician need to control the practice of medicine, which had led to the criminalization of birth control 100 years earlier, she strategically turned in her favor. The role of physicians cast a long shadow over the debate over reproductive freedom for the rest of the twentieth century.

## The Supreme Court Finds a Right to Privacy

The campaign to legalize birth control and to overturn the Comstock laws was on one level a campaign to define what America meant by the word "liberty" in its Constitution and to define to what extent the Supreme Court would defend that liberty from encroachment by the states. The *Griswold* case in 1965 found a right to privacy in the Constitution and set the terms of the debate over reproductive rights from then on. Lost amidst all the heated debate over the right to privacy was the constitutional principle that the American system of government was based on the notion that the government only has those powers granted to it by the people. It was not based on the notion that the people only have those rights granted to them by the government.

In the thirty years after *One Package* the states gradually eliminated or amended their Comstock laws so that they no longer applied to contraception. Connecticut and Massachusetts stubbornly refused to change their laws, and in the early 1960s Esther Griswold and Lee Buxton, the executive director and the medical director respectively of Planned Parenthood of Connecticut, were convicted of being accessories to the crime of using birth control under the state's Comstock law, which prohibited birth control *use* by married couples. In 1965 in the case of *Griswold v. Connecticut* the Supreme Court declared the Connecticut law unconstitutional because it violated the constitution's right to privacy.

The first thing to note about the case was that the Supreme Court didn't borrow the strategy of the *Sanger* and *One Package* cases and "reinterpret" the Connecticut law out of existence, or at least so that it did not apply to married couples. In fact, the Supreme Court did not cite *Sanger* and *One Package at all*. Why didn't the court go this route? The court clearly had other constitutional fish to fry. It wanted to set limits on what the government could and could not regulate in our private lives, and the *Griswold* case provided the opportunity. The *Sanger* court had affirmed that the New York Comstock law was constitutional and was a valid exercise of the state's police powers. So despite the rulings in *Sanger* and *One Package*, constitutional law, as it existed before *Griswold*, still permitted a state like Connecticut to criminalize birth control when it was used without any other health justification than for the prevention of conception.

In the aftermath of the approval by the federal government of the birth control pill in 1960, the Connecticut law was clearly an anachronism, but, to declare it unconstitutional, the court needed to find a provision in the Constitution that the law violated. This was easier said than done. The court could not simply base its decision on the almost universal opinion that the law was antiquated or out of step with reality. As one dissenting justice put it in *Griswold*: "I think this is an uncommonly silly law. As a practical matter, the law is obviously unenforceable. . . . But we are not asked in this case to say whether we think this law is unwise, or even asinine. We are asked to hold that it violates the United States Constitution." The court solved this problem by enunciating a constitutional right to privacy and then finding that the law violated it.

Justice William O. Douglas, who wrote the court's opinion, began by saying that the Connecticut Comstock law "operates directly on an intimate relation of husband and wife and their physician's role in one aspect of that relation." Neither the right to marriage nor the right to practice medicine are explicitly mentioned in the Constitution, and thus were not constitutional rights that Connecticut had violated. So Douglas analogized his way through the Bill of Rights to find a constitutional right of privacy. Douglas compared marriage to the freedom to associate, which he found in the First Amendment's "right of the people peaceably to assemble," and to other specific freedoms in the Bill of Rights that protect citizens from government intrusion into their personal lives. Douglas ruled that the point of the Bill of Rights was to create a zone of "privacy," which was to be protected from unwarranted governmental intrusion. His opinion contained the following impenetrable statement, which would be thrown back at future abortion rights advocates:

> The foregoing cases suggest that specific guarantees in the Bill of Rights have penumbras, formed by emanations from those guarantees that give them life and substance.

Douglas went on to say somewhat more clearly:

> The present case, then, concerns a relationship lying within the zone of privacy created by several fundamental constitutional guarantees . . . Would we allow the police to search the sacred precincts of marital bedrooms for telltale signs of the use of contraceptives? The very idea is repulsive to the notions of privacy surrounding the marriage relationship. . . .We deal with a right of privacy older than the Bill of Rights—older than our political parties, older than our school system. Marriage is a coming together for better or worse, hopefully enduring, and intimate to the degree of being sacred. It is an association that promotes a way of life, not causes; a harmony in living, not political faiths; a bilateral loyalty, not commercial or social projects. Yet it is an association for as noble a purpose as any involved in our prior decisions.

Three of the justices in the majority, Arthur Goldberg, Earl Warren, and William Brennan, even though they signed on to Douglas's opinion, were not entirely comfortable with it and sought to find a firmer basis in the Bill of Rights for the right to privacy. Goldberg wrote a concurring opinion, which stated that the Connecticut Comstock law also violated the Ninth Amendment to the Constitution, which read: "The enumeration in the Constitution of certain rights shall not be construed to deny or disparage others retained by the people."

Goldberg argued that the Ninth Amendment, which had been little used until then, stated a fundamental principle of the American system of limited government: that the government derives its powers from the people rather than the people deriving their rights from the government. There are fundamental rights, including the right to privacy, which citizens have and retain even though those rights are not expressly stated in the Bill of Rights. This right to privacy, in Goldberg's view, encompassed a couple's right to have children, or not. He argued that the Ninth Amendment would, for example, prohibit a state from enacting a law requiring sterilization of a married couple after they had had two children. Such a law, just like the ban on contraceptive use, was an unconstitutional invasion of the right to privacy.

Two justices, Hugo Black and Potter Stewart, dissented. While they found the Connecticut law "silly" and "offensive," they did not feel that the Supreme Court had the authority to declare it unconstitutional. Black said: "I like my privacy as well as the next one, but I am compelled to admit that the government has the right to invade it unless prohibited by some specific constitutional provision." Finding the law to be "arbitrary, capricious or unreasonable" is not enough, said Black, nor did finding that it "accomplishes no justifiable purpose, or is offensive to our notions of civilized standards of conduct." Black was reluctant to substitute his judgment for that of the legislature. He saw no specific provision in the Constitution that prohibited the Connecticut legislature from enacting the law. He found no right to privacy in the Bill of Rights.

The greatest legal victory of the birth control crusade was thus a somewhat muddled one—many different opinions and a majority agreeing on little except that the law was unconstitutional and that the Connecticut legislature had exceeded the powers granted to the states by the Constitution. But even though the legal rationale for the right to privacy was not agreed upon, the court set the terms of the reproductive rights debate for the next forty years by proclaiming that there was a right to privacy and that it was the constitutional basis for reproductive freedom. Under this right to privacy, citizens have a constitutional right to make decisions about intimate matters like childbearing and marriage, and the government cannot interfere in these decisions. While *Griswold* enunciated a new right of privacy, it in fact reiterated ancient constitutional principles about our system of limited government.

Although the *Griswold* decision was limited to married couples, within a few years in *Eisenstadt v. Baird* the Supreme Court overturned a Massachusetts law that prohibited unmarried persons from using contraception. The rationale for declaring the law unconstitutional could not be based on the institution of marriage and a couple's right to make childbearing decisions and instead was based on an individual's, a woman's, right to make that decision. The court finally agreed with what Margaret Sanger had argued in the *Woman Rebel* in 1914: that the foundation of a woman's liberty was her right to decide whether or not to become a mother.

In her birth control crusade my grandmother succeeded in redefining the word "liberty." In 1918 the New York Court of Appeals in *Sanger v. New York* most assuredly did not find the Comstock law to be an infringement of woman's liberty. A half century later the U.S. Supreme Court did. My grandmother's birth control crusade, based first on feminist arguments and then on medical and social arguments, led to a change in personal values and public perceptions about the importance, need, and morality of birth control. She made it inevitable that the Comstock law would be seen not only as asinine but also as unconstitutional. She elevated human sexuality from Comstock's gutter to a fundamental component of human liberty. She elevated the individual desire to control one's reproduction from being a crime to be a fundamental component of the constitutional right to privacy. It didn't matter to her that the word "privacy" did not appear in the Bill of Rights. The word "liberty" did. She brought common sense, fairness, and human dignity into constitutional law in a new way.

In *Griswold* and eight years later in *Roe v. Wade*, which legalized abortion, the Supreme Court established privacy and liberty as the basis for reproductive freedom. These cases set the terms of the debate.

The public debate tended to ignore the biological, medical, and social arguments that my grandmother had mustered over the previous fifty years. When the pro-life forces argued that killing an unborn child was impermissible and wrong and that any basis for it was a figment of Douglas's constitutional imagination, the pro-choice forces argued that the right to privacy had a basis in our constitutional scheme of limited government and that it was right for women to have the power to decide such an intimate matter that affected only them. Ironically, the opponents of a right to privacy, who argue that it is nowhere written in the text of the Constitution, argue that, even though abortion is not mentioned in the text of the Bible, that opposition to abortion should be one of the most important tenets of the Christian faith.

I believe our pro-choice arguments were and are right, but they are insufficient. They haven't won the day for us. The arguments on both sides were absolutist—either there was a right to privacy or not and either the unborn child was a life protected by our Constitution or not. The absolutism that the legal system engendered and the sidelining of the biological and medical arguments in favor of reproductive freedom inhibited the ability of the pro-choice side to make any headway in the moral discussion with the public. *Roe* froze the debate for the next forty years.

## The Supreme Court Expands
## The Right to Privacy to Include Abortion

When in 1972 the Supreme Court in *Eisenstadt* declared the Massachusetts Comstock law unconstitutional as applied to unmarried persons, it said:

> If under *Griswold* the distribution of contraceptives to married persons cannot be prohibited, a ban on distribution to unmarried persons would be equally impermissible. It is true that in *Griswold* the right of privacy in question inhered in the marital relationship. Yet the marital

couple is not an independent entity with a mind and heart of its own, but an association of two individuals each with a separate intellectual and emotional makeup. *If the right of privacy means anything, it is the right of the individual, married or single, to be free from unwarranted governmental intrusion into matters so fundamentally affecting a person as the decision whether to bear or beget a child.* (Emphasis added)

Thus the right to privacy became the right to choose. This sentence in the *Eisenstadt* opinion became the basis of the Supreme Court's opinion in *Roe v. Wade* in 1973 which declared the Texas abortion law unconstitutional.

The abortion legalization movement, in which the word "choice" was used prominently, was a product of many changes in society. Certainly, some of the original reasons for the criminalization of abortion in the nineteenth century remained constant. Developments in biology had increased the medical understanding of pregnancy as a continuum from conception to birth. The development of the ability to get photographic images of the embryo had given additional support to the argument that the embryo was "human" and thus a legal "person" entitled to the protection of the law. Abortion remained a major concern of some religious denominations on moral grounds.

But many factors had changed since abortion had been criminalized. Physicians were no longer united in their opposition to abortion, and many took the lead in urging legalization, not so much out of wanting to earn income from performing them, but from the personal agony of witnessing injuries and loss of women's lives as a result of illegal abortions. Every hospital had wards to care for women who had been damaged in self-induced or back alley abortions. A century of medical progress meant that abortion, if done by a physician, was no longer more dangerous than childbirth and in fact was in most cases safer. New prenatal diagnostic techniques were developed that increased the demand for therapeutic abortion. Abortion was a big business. It was a major money maker for organized crime. That in itself was not the impetus to legalize it, but estimates were that hundreds of thousands of illegal abortions took place annually in the 1960s and that the brunt of the medical damage fell on the young and the poor. The wives and daughters of the well-to-do could get relatively safe abortions from their family doctors or could travel to where abortion was legal. This discrepancy in health outcomes and the danger and shame of illegal abortion were major factors that led many in the nascent women's movement in the 1960s to demand that abortion be legalized. This demand fit in perfectly with the feminist call for fairness, dignity, and equal treatment for women.

The Texas statute at issue in *Roe* prohibited abortions unless necessary to save the life of the mother. Justice Harry Blackmun, writing for the majority and citing *Griswold* and *Eisenstadt*, declared that the right to privacy under the Constitution "is broad enough to encompass a woman's decision whether or not to terminate a pregnancy." But not entirely. Privacy had its limits. Blackmun declared that a woman did not have an unlimited right to do with her body as she chose and hence he did not declare that a woman had an unlimited right to abortion. *Roe* held that the government could restrict abortion access because of its interest in protecting maternal health and viable unborn life.

Blackmun balanced the interests of women and the government and came to three conclusions. First, that, although there was a government interest in preserving fetal life, a fetus is not a "person" under the Constitution and thus did not have an absolute right to life and liberty. Second, Blackmun concluded that it was the physician's decision in consultation with his patient whether to terminate a pregnancy or not (note that Blackmun did not say it was the woman's decision in consultation with the physician—Blackmun was in private practice the lawyer for the Mayo Clinic). Third, Blackmun concluded that states can protect fetal life after fetal viability and can ban abortion, so long as they make an exception for abortions necessary in the physician's judgment to preserve the life or health of the woman.

Blackmun's opinion in *Roe* confirmed the validity of my grandmother's strategy in *Sanger* and *One Package*, which put birth control under physician control. Blackmun noted the decline in maternal mortality and morbidity after New York had liberalized its abortion law in 1970. Abortions in New York started to be performed by physicians in clinics or hospitals in sterile conditions under state regulation. Thus central to Blackmun's opinion was the fact that it was the doctor, not the woman, who made the abortion decision:

> The decision vindicates the right of the physician to administer medical treatment according to his professional judgment up to the points where important state interests provide compelling justifications for intervention. Up to those points, the abortion decision in all its aspects is inherently, and primarily, a medical decision, and basic responsibility for it must rest with the physician.

Over the past two centuries, the fight for reproductive freedom has changed from a fight for physician supremacy and Protestant hegemony to a fight over the role of women and the meaning of our constitution. The fight to enact and then overturn the Comstock laws involved forces interested in larger issues—sex, race, ethnicity, religion, morality, the public health, the role of physicians, the status of women, the role of the judiciary, and the meaning of liberty. In many ways reproductive freedom is a pawn in these larger wars. What gets lost in the fray is what my grandmother tried to bring into the birth control debate a century ago—the reason why birth control is important in the first place. Why is it biologically vital that women control childbearing? The abortion debate in the last quarter of the twentieth century failed to address this issue. My grandmother talked about the importance of birth control for the well-being of women, children, and families. While this argument never entirely disappeared, it often got lost in the din. The pro-life movement in its counterattack on *Roe* was skillful in changing the subject.

# CHAPTER TWO

# The Reproductive Rights Debate That Ignored Reproduction

Reproductive freedom has been a contentious public issue for longer than any other issue in American politics, except race. We are approaching the two hundredth anniversary, in 2019, of the first law outlawing abortion in the United States. Powerful forces including feminists, civil libertarians, physicians, social reformers, and religious figures have been arrayed on either or both sides of the issue. Over the almost four decades since *Griswold* and *Roe* the arguments in favor of reproductive freedom have focused on women's rights, while the arguments against it have focused on moral values. In their own spheres both sides appear to have convinced the public of the rightness of their arguments. A majority of the public simultaneously supports choice, believes *Roe* should remain the law of the land, and believes abortion to be immoral.

Because *Griswold* and *Roe* were Supreme Court decisions and are, until overruled, the final constitutional word on the subject, the debate between supporters and opponents of abortion was largely confined to the realm of constitutional law—was there a constitutional right to privacy or not and, if so, how far did it extend? In the political world debates raged with both sides producing an array of medical, social, and moral arguments to support their cases. Technological developments that threatened to enlarge or restrict women's reproductive choices raised the stakes and added a new ferocity to the political combat. New contraceptives, such as the long-acting Norplant, which expanded the range of women's birth control options, became lightening rods for social engineering when some advocates and politicians proposed that women on welfare be required to use them as a condition of receiving welfare. New methods of abortion, including RU–486, a pill that could terminate an early pregnancy, and the dilation and extraction abortion, a procedure that could be used to terminate a pregnancy after its midpoint, became especially controversial. Abortion opponents argued that these methods made abortion too "easy" in the case of RU–486 and too "gruesome" in the case of what was called "partial birth abortion." Even emergency contraception, which consisted of a higher dose of birth control pills taken within five days of unprotected intercourse and which was extremely effective in preventing pregnancy, became controversial. Opponents argued that in their opinion it was the same as abortion and that it would make having unprotected sex easier.

What was missing in this often shrill and violent conflict was any discussion of why reproductive freedom was important to men and women in the first place. The debate focused on rights, on the effects, good and bad, on society of reproductive rights, on the medical and health aspects of contraception and abortion, and often on sex. What was not discussed was reproduction and human biology. This is especially curious given that deciding to get pregnant or not and to give birth to a child or not are biological decisions.

## The Pro-Life Attack on Roe

The pro-life movement took the offensive after *Roe* and attacked the decision as being a judicial usurpation of the rights of the states to enact moral legislation and based on a nonexistent constitutional right to privacy. Before *Roe* the pro-choice side had been the proponent of moral, social, and legal change; afterwards, the initiative switched to *Roe*'s opponents. Pro-lifers began to set the terms of the debate. They went on the offensive and attacked *Roe* from all sides arguing: that the fetus is a "person" under the Constitution and therefore cannot be deprived of its "life"; that there is no right to privacy at all, or at least not one that gives the right to women to have an abortion; and finally that there is never, or rarely, a valid health reason for abortion. The prochoice movement responded, defending Blackmun's opinion in *Roe* and the status quo. The strategy and rhetoric of both the pro-life movement, as well as the pro-choice movement, were set by the terms of the *Roe* decision. Both sides knew that *Roe* could only be overruled if future justices disagreed with its medical, social, and legal underpinnings. The fixed battle continued for decades, changing only when a new reproductive technology came on the scene.

One of the core holdings of *Roe* was the court's holding that a fetus is not a "person" and therefore was not protected by the Constitution's guarantee of a person's "life, liberty and property." This holding is absolutely correct from a constitutional law point of view—there is no authority whatsoever in constitutional law for saying that a fetus has the same rights as someone who has been born. In recent years *Roe*'s opponents have attempted to undermine this holding by passing laws that consider a fetus a separate person under the law with rights of its own. For example, the Bush Administration in 2002 issued regulations that made a fetus a separate "patient" when it expanded the federal prenatal care program. When a pregnant woman sought prenatal care under this program, she was not the patient, her unborn child was. Many states got into the act of establishing fetal personhood by passing versions of the "Unborn Victims of Violence Act," which made it a separate crime to injure or kill a fetus when a pregnant woman was assaulted in a crime. Abortion opponents argued that fetal personhood began when sperm and egg were joined no matter how that was done. Opponents of stem cell research argued that an embryo of just a few cells created in a petri dish was a separate person under the law and could not be destroyed in order to extract stem cells. All these laws and regulations—the prenatal care eligibility regulation, the unborn victims of violence laws, and the stem cell ban—were intended to legitimize fetal personhood in the public's mind, and in minds of the Supreme Court justices who would hear the next challenge to *Roe*.

In its campaign to discredit *Roe* the pro-life movement also attacked the idea that a woman has the intellectual or moral capability to make the abortion decision. In other words, *Roe*'s opponents argued that there should be no right to privacy because women don't deserve it. They alternately portrayed women as selfish when they made the abortion decision, or as not independent enough or morally capable enough to make it. They argued that women were powerless when it came to abortion and that men and doctors forced them into having the procedure. Pro-lifers are fond of saying that there are two victims of abortion—the baby and the mother. To pro-lifers women are not independent moral agents and are nothing more than a financial gold mine for "abortionists." Pro-lifers have been successful in many states in passing laws requiring doctors to read to any woman seeking an abortion a counseling script, which is designed to dissuade her from having an abortion. In addition, many states require that the woman must wait for twenty-four hours after hearing that script before having an abortion, as if she had not thought about her decision prior to coming to the doctor. Many states prohibit teenage girls from getting an abortion without telling one or both of their parents or getting their consent. Some states even passed laws requiring a married woman to get her husband's permission before having an abortion. While the Supreme Court has upheld parental consent laws for teens, it did declare husband consent laws unconstitutional.

The third prong of the pro-life strategy was to attack abortion as not being a part of the legitimate practice of medicine: Those who do abortions are "abortionists," not doctors. These abortionists are perpetrating a holocaust. Abortion is so evil that public hospitals and military hospitals should be closed to it, and Medicaid should certainly not pay for poor women's abortions. Abortion is so inherently unsafe, the pro-life movement says, that extra burdensome clinic regulations that only apply to facilities that do abortions, as opposed to other outpatient surgeries, are necessary. Abortion doctors are required in many states to file extensive reports on their practice and their patients with state regulatory authorities. All these laws and regulations are designed to undermine *Roe* and also serve to delay, inhibit, and block women and girls from having abortions.

William Saletan in his book, *Bearing Right: How Conservatives Won The Abortion War*, blamed the pro-choice movement for framing its arguments in a way that forgot the reproductive interests of the young and the poor. As Saletan put it:

(In 1986) they (pro-choice advocates) feared that abortion restrictions would roll back women's rights and condemn many women to the poverty of untimely motherhood. But they understood that most voters didn't share that concern. So instead of talking about women's rights, the activists portrayed abortion restrictions as an encroachment by big government on tradition, family and property. When the issue was framed that way, many voters with conservative sympathies turned against the anti-abortion movement. And the balance of power turned in favor of abortion rights.

From the beginning, the alliance was unstable. Only on the question of abortion's legality did voters who cared primarily about protecting traditional institutions from big government agree with activists who cared primarily about women's rights and poverty. As the debate moved to other questions—whether government should spend tax money on poor women's abortions, or whether teenage girls should have to get their parent's permission for abortions—the alliance fell apart. Voters who believed in tradition, family and property abandoned liberal advocates of poor women and teenage girls, leaving those advocates in the minority.

By framing the argument in terms of fending off government, the pro-choice movement, in Saletan's view, "saved *Roe*, but in the streets and in their souls they had lost the struggle to define it." The needs and interests of young and poor women were sacrificed to preserving legal abortion for the middle class adults who could afford it.

The pro-life movement was handed a major weapon in its war on reproductive choice when the dilation and extraction abortion procedure was invented in the early 1990s. This procedure made it safer to perform an abortion after the midpoint of a pregnancy. Abortion becomes increasingly difficult as the fetus grows in size, and there are greater risks of damage during the procedure to the woman's cervix and thus an increased risk that she will not be able to have children in the future. Doctors designed the dilation and extraction abortion procedure, which abortion opponents called "partial birth abortion," to minimize these risks. Pro-lifers portrayed the procedure as so inhumane that they succeeded in having many states outlaw it. The Supreme Court declared the first round of these laws unconstitutional in 2000 on the grounds that they unduly limited the discretion of doctors to select the abortion procedure that would best preserve a woman's health and her ability to have children in the future. In 2003 Congress passed revised "partial birth" legislation in an attempt to have it pass constitutional muster.

The pro-life attack on the capability of women and the authority of doctors bore fruit when the Pennsylvania law that required a mandatory lecture before an abortion and a waiting period reached the Supreme Court in 1992. The *Casey* case was the culmination of a nearly twenty-year campaign to discredit what *Roe* stood for. *Roe* just didn't stand for the right to privacy. It stood for the rights of those born over those unborn under the Constitution. It stood for the rights of women to make their own medical decisions, and it stood for the right of doctors to practice medicine and to use their professional judgment in the best interests of their patients. All these principles came under attack in the Pennsylvania law that the *Casey* court was asked to rule on. Because the pro-choice movement had not made persuasive arguments on behalf of the poor and the young, it left them vulnerable to a court that was willing to reinterpret *Roe*.

## The Supreme Court Responds to the Pro-Life Strategy in the Casey Decision

Abortion returned to the Supreme Court in over twenty cases during the 1970s and 1980s, and each time, though by diminishing majorities, the holdings of *Roe* were affirmed. Finally in 1992 the court announced a major modification of Roe in *Planned Parenthood of Southeast Pennsylvania v. Casey*. The *Casey* court announced that state-imposed restrictions on the right to decide whether or not to terminate a pregnancy would be permitted unless they constituted an "undue burden" on the woman. "Undue burden" was defined as any "substantial obstacle" in the path of a woman. Under this standard the *Casey* court upheld state requirements that, in this particular case, the woman receive mandatory scripted counseling that was biased in favor of childbirth and against abortion and face a twenty-four-hour waiting period thereafter before she could have an abortion. It also upheld a requirement that a teenager had to get the consent of one parent before an abortion.

The only provision of the Pennsylvania law that the court overturned was a provision that required a woman to get her husband's consent to an abortion. This, the court decided, was indeed a substantial obstacle in the path of the woman because it gave the husband an absolute veto over his wife's abortion. This result highlighted one major change that the *Casey* court—almost incidentally—made to Blackmun's decision in *Roe*. In *Casey* the abortion decision was explicitly assumed to be the woman's decision, not the physician's.

Justice Sandra Day O'Connor explained the transformation of abortion from a medical decision to a woman's right in her plurality opinion, which was joined by only two other justices:

> Though abortion is conduct, it does not follow that the State is entitled to proscribe it in all instances. That is because the liberty of the woman is at stake in a sense unique to the human condition and so unique to the law. The mother who carries a child to full term is subject to anxieties, to physical constraints, to pain that only she must bear. That these sacrifices

have from the beginning of the human race been endured by woman with a pride that ennobles her in the eyes of others and gives to the infant a bond of love cannot alone be grounds for the State to insist she make the sacrifice. Her suffering is too intimate and personal for the State to insist, without more, upon its own vision of the woman's role, however dominant that vision has been in the course of our history and our culture. The destiny of the woman must be shaped to a large extent on her own conception of her spiritual imperatives and her place in society.

This O'Connor opinion took abortion to some extent out of the medical realm and affirmed the right of the woman to determine her own future and to make her own moral judgments. It was a quasi-feminist position, quasi because O'Connor didn't believe a woman should be able to make up her own mind about abortion free of outside interference. O'Connor's ruling permitted the states to adopt an official view in favor of childbirth over abortion and "to enact rules and regulations designed to encourage her to know that there are philosophic and social arguments of great weight that can be brought to bear in favor of continuing the pregnancy to full term." Under the *Casey* ruling, states are permitted to discourage abortion and to favor childbirth over abortion. This is a change from *Roe*, and other decisions after it, which had said that the state must remain neutral in a woman's decision between childbirth and abortion. *Casey* thus took some of the constitutional absolutism out of *Roe* and permitted the pro-life forces more political leeway to enact more restrictions on abortion access. To that extent O'Connor's ruling was a profoundly political opinion designed to let political forces fight out abortion restrictions in the legislatures without judicial interference. It was a fight that to date the pro-life forces have won. Hundreds of pieces of legislation restricting abortion access have passed state legislatures and have been permitted to pass into law by the courts as not being "undue burdens" on women. While hundreds more restrictive legislative proposals have been defeated or declared unconstitutional, in many states it is extraordinarily difficult for the young, the poor, and women who cannot travel to access abortion services.

*Casey* was a political compromise and satisfied neither side. Pro-lifers attacked it because it upheld the core of *Roe*, and pro-choicers attacked it because it made it easier for states to put severe obstacles in the path of a woman trying to get an abortion. Immediately after the *Casey* decision was announced, I directed that my organization, Planned Parenthood of New York City, take out a full-page advertisement in the *New York Times* declaring that "Roe Is Dead." The ad set out in detail why *Casey* had overturned what *Roe* stood for. I got angry letters from lawyers saying that I was crying wolf and that *Roe* was still good law. They obviously had not waded through the over eighty-five single-spaced pages of the court's opinion as I had. There was some nice feminist language in O'Connor's opinion in *Casey*, but it still left *Roe* in tatters. *Casey* had reinterpreted *Roe*, just as *One Package* had reinterpreted *Sanger*.

*Roe* and *Casey* did not end the abortion debate in America. They just changed which side took the offense and what strategy the offense would adopt. Abortion opponents were back to where they were in the early nineteenth century—they were the ones seeking a change in the law. What was different was that the U.S. Supreme Court had laid down the law. This was not an insurmountable obstacle; the Supreme Court had been known to change its mind and overrule itself. It had done so with separate but equal public schools for whites and blacks in *Brown v. Board of Education* in 1954. In 2003 it did so in the matter of homosexual sodomy in *Lawrence v. Texas*.

Since 1973 *Roe*'s opponents have tried again and again to get the Supreme Court to overrule itself and have mostly failed. The pro-life legislative and judicial strategy followed the same pattern: A law would be passed restricting abortion access in violation of *Roe*, and the pro-choice movement would file a lawsuit to overturn it. The courts then would have the opportunity to reconsider *Roe* and either to affirm it, to overturn it, or to reinterpret it as they did in *Casey*. Many pro-life laws were upheld. Only a few—the "partial birth" law and law requiring a husband's consent to an abortion—were declared unconstitutional. In many states abortion became largely restricted to adults who had easy access to a clinic and who could pay for their own abortions. Given less-than-rigorous reporting of abortion procedures by physicians who were often operating under threats of violence, it is difficult to say whether abortion rates actually declined even though the reported rate did decline. It seemed that most women found ways to make the multiple trips required to the clinics, most young got judicial permission for their abortions without telling their parents, and most poor people found the money somehow. But some did not and the restrictions on abortion access promoted by the pro-life movement and allowed by the courts proved to be real, severe, and undue burdens. What was lost in the abortion debate, which proceeded loudly on legal, moral, religious, medical, political, and social grounds, was that what was being burdened was human reproduction.

## Eugenics and the Missing Scientific Arguments for Abortion

Missing from much of the debate over abortion was any discussion of the biological basis for giving humanity control over its reproduction. Legal abortion was defended as a better alternative for women's health than illegal abortion. This did not make the case why abortion was a good thing in the first place. Pro-choice advocates were understandably leery of making biological arguments for abortion because biology had been misused by the eugenicists in the early twentieth century in their campaign to forcibly sterilize those they thought unfit to reproduce. My grandmother had supported some eugenic goals and this support continues to haunt the pro-choice movement today.

By being boxed into defending *Roe* on its own terms and on the terms that the pro-life movement set for the debate, the pro-choice side lost the opportunity to make other compelling arguments in favor of reproductive freedom. In pro-life terms the debate was about abortion and not about reproductive freedom. The pro-life movement read the same polls that the pro-choice movement did—Americans did not favor abortion but they did strongly support freedom and choice. The abortion debate was like two ships passing in the night. One side talked about babies, life, and abortion. The other talked of women, freedom, and choice. Each side was right in its own way. But neither side addressed abortion as, among other things, a biological and scientific matter.

After the *Sanger* case my grandmother spent decades gathering the scientific evidence that demonstrated that birth control was beneficial, indeed a necessity, for human betterment because it enabled the survival of women and children. But in the aftermath of *Roe*, when the terms of the abortion debate were rigidly fixed by the terms of *Roe* itself and by the pro-life attack on it, there was little opportunity for the pro-choice movement to advance scientific arguments for abortion. There was in the 1970s and thereafter little evidence that legal abortion contributed to human betterment, except for the fact that it was safer for women than illegal abortion, since it saved women's lives and preserved their fertility. The pro-choice movement also argued that properly spaced children were healthier and more likely to survive and that women were healthier and happier when they could control whether and when to have children. These arguments pretty much constituted the central medical and scientific arguments in favor of legalized birth control and abortion.

These arguments were based upon the undeniable reality that every society has only two choices about abortion: Either it can be legal and safe or it can be illegal and unsafe. The American experience had shown this. When my grandmother was called to try to save the life of Sadie Sachs, she saw firsthand the desperate choices that women were forced into when abortion is illegal. Making abortion illegal does not make it go away. It just makes it more humiliating, expensive, and dangerous. In a sense the pro-life arguments against abortion are based on the fantasy that, if abortion is made illegal, it will simply disappear. It won't. Despite this, many pro-life politicians have said that their goal is to have abortion "disappear." In their view there should not be either legal or illegal abortion, just as there should not be heroin, slavery, or murder—abortion, either legal or illegal, is immoral and evil. I would argue that the difference between these evils and abortion, and why abortion will not disappear, is biological. The traditional pro-choice arguments about the dignity of women and the importance of choice as a moral value miss this point.

*What the pro-choice movement needs to do is provide a compelling argument not for legal abortion but for abortion.* The primary focus should not be abortion safety or the health of women or the social benefits of reproductive freedom or the importance of choice, as important as these are. The primary focus of the pro-choice movement should be on why reproductive freedom is vital to humanity and why abortion is good. In my view, the most compelling and honest way to do this is to justify abortion on a biological basis. Abortion is, after all, a biological act. We can justify it as such.

In the immediate aftermath of *Roe*, however, no comprehensive biological argument was made for giving women and men control of what was clearly a biological function—childbearing. The field of evolutionary biology, which could provide the evidence for this argument, was in its infancy. But there was another reason for why little attempt was made to harness biological evidence in support of reproductive freedom. I believe the pro-choice movement was scared away from making biological arguments because of the birth control movement's disastrous foray into eugenics a half century earlier. This foray by my grandmother and others after the *Sanger* case and before the *One Package* case was an attempt to try to gain respectability and scientific credibility for the birth control movement. It was a mistake. Eugenics was not based on any verifiable science, and its programs were examples of government coercion of human reproduction at its worst. The reproductive rights movement had been once burned; it wasn't going to make the same mistake twice.

The eugenics movement at the end of the nineteenth century and the beginning of the twentieth sought to use new discoveries about genetics to improve the health of the human race. Scientists had long known about the benefits of selective breeding of livestock to improve the health, size, and strength of animals. At the end of the nineteenth century farmers and scientists rediscovered the work of Gregor Mendel, who decades earlier had discovered through the selective breeding of pea plants how dominant and recessive "genes" determined the inheritance of certain traits, including flower and seed color, seed and pod shape, flower position, and plant height. Even though the gene had not yet been discovered, scientists demonstrated that they could manipulate these traits by the selective breeding of various pea plants. Eugenicists believed that Mendel's principles of selective breeding could be applied to humans to eliminate undesirable traits and to improve the fitness of the human race.

Manipulating heredity seemed to many to be an easy way to solve some of the most severe social problems of the day, including poverty, poor health, and crime. The eugenicists believed that many human traits were determined by genetic inheritance just like the traits of Mendel's peas. Eugenicists believed that traits like alcoholism, criminality, certain physical handicaps, low intelligence, and "feeblemindedness"—a catch-all term used when there was no other specific diagnosis to explain why an individual was a low achiever—were all inherited. If these traits were inherited and not the product of personal and social circumstances, then the eugenic solution was to prevent alcoholics, or the carriers of disease, or the feebleminded, from having children. There was at the time little scientific knowledge of how diseases, birth defects, or mental and physical handicaps, or conditions thought to be handicaps, were inherited. There was no proof that in fact they were inherited. The "scientific" evidence consisted mainly of anecdotal observations that some children seemed to "inherit" epilepsy, or alcoholism, or low intelligence from their parents. Eugenicists leapt from these unscientific observations to the promotion of programs and laws that would encourage the "fit" to reproduce more and the "unfit" to reproduce less, or better still, from their point of view, not at all.

Eugenics was a tragic mistake. Its bad science made for bad public policy. Eugenicists failed to understand that behavioral traits in humans are complex, are not subject to objective definition, and have many causes in addition to whatever the genetic component might be. They ignored the effects of environment, education, parental upbringing, and societal influences on human behavior. Eugenic research was hopelessly amateurish, eugenics testing was biased, and eugenic data collection was unscientific. For example, early IQ tests, which were designed to test the intelligence of American-born whites, were given in English to recent immigrants from Eastern Europe. In the minds of the eugenicists, genetic dispositions were intertwined with race: the white, Protestant, Northern European was considered superior, and virtually everyone else was inferior. From this racist and scientifically shaky platform, eugenicists proposed laws to tighten already existing miscegenation laws that prohibited marriage between the races, laws to restrict immigration from Eastern and Southern Europe, and laws to sterilize the "unfit."

Eugenicists believed that the citizenry in general, and women in particular, owed a duty to their country to produce strong, healthy, and intelligent children and that they had a corresponding duty not to produce "unfit" children. The quality of a nation's children, indeed its entire population, was a valid societal concern because society had to foot the bill for the health care, institutionalization, and rehabilitation of the unfit. To eugenicists birth control was a tool for getting certain citizens to do their duty and to limit their reproduction. Birth control would either be, depending on the target audience, withheld, urged, or mandated. Citizens of good stock, generally the wealthier, whiter, and Protestant members of society, would be urged to refrain from using birth control and to have more children, while those from lesser stock, generally the poorer, non-white, and non-Protestant members of society, would be encouraged to use birth control and have fewer children. For those who were not just from lesser stock but who were also deemed to be "unfit" the eugenicists had the harshest remedy: mandatory sterilization.

The eugenicists, who generally came from the Protestant elites of the country, had an inordinate influence on government policy, and, as a result of their efforts, beginning in the early 1900s thirty states had enacted laws requiring the compulsory sterilization of the "unfit." A test case, *Buck v. Bell*, challenging the Virginia compulsory sterilization law, reached the U.S. Supreme Court in 1927. The court upheld the law as constitutional by an 8–1 vote. The plaintiff, Carrie Buck, was an institutionalized minor who gave birth to an illegitimate child. Buck's mother was also institutionalized. The Commonwealth of Virginia presented evidence that all three—grandmother, mother, and child—were "feebleminded." Justice Holmes, writing for the majority, upheld Virginia's power to sterilize Carrie Buck in order to prevent the birth of more inevitably "feebleminded" children, who would in turn become wards of the state. He stated famously: "Three generations of imbeciles are enough."

In addition to being wrong as a matter of public policy and law, *Buck v. Bell* was wrong on the facts and was a travesty of justice. Evidence uncovered long after the case was decided showed that the state's lawyers and the lawyers for Carrie Buck conspired to withhold certain exculpatory evidence. Buck was institutionalized after she had been raped and impregnated by a member of her foster family. Her commitment was part of a concerted effort by her foster parents to cover up the crime and protect their family. Buck's daughter and Buck herself were far from "feebleminded"; their school records clearly showed that both were of normal intelligence. None of this evidence was presented to the court.

Eugenicists and the government may have had a worthy goal in trying to alleviate societal ills by creating a healthier human race and thus a healthier society. They had other less worthy, even racist, goals as well. And not only was their science faulty, so were their views of human dignity and the methods they adopted to better society. State governments were interested in finding any way to reduce the expenses of caring for the poor, the sick, and the criminal elements in their society. The interests of the eugenicists and state governments coincided on the quick fix of the sterilization of the "unfit." Carrie Buck became a pawn in the efforts of eugenicists and governments to control women's childbearing, to breed a better race, and to minimize welfare expenses. Carrie Buck was from the wrong class, in the wrong place, at the wrong time. She and her future children were dispensable. *Buck v. Bell* has never been overruled.

Despite my grandmother's efforts to enlist eugenicists and her support of some, but not all, of the eugenic platform, they did not support her birth control crusade. Eugenicists wanted less birth control use by the fit and wanted more use by the unfit. They opposed giving women a choice in the matter. My grandmother believed that each woman was the best judge of whether and when to bring a child into the world and that when she used birth control, both her health and the health of her children would improve. Her efforts to enlist eugenecists in her crusade in an attempt to give it scientific credibility not only failed, they backfired. By the 1930s new research began to expose the unscientific nature of eugenics. At the same time eugenic thinking was taken to its illogical conclusion by the German Nazi regime, which proclaimed that Jews and certain other groups were genetically inferior to the "Aryan" race and must therefore be sterilized or exterminated. One of the first books thrown on the fire by the Nazis in their book-burning craze was my grandmother's book *Woman and the New Race*. The ardent eugenicists and the Nazis both opposed my grandmother's belief that a woman alone had the right to decide whether or not to have a child. This, however, does not excuse her attempts to use them for her cause.

Eugenics, and its misuse of biology, continues to taint the reproductive rights movement. Because eugenics claimed a scientific, genetic, and biological basis for its racist program, the biological and genetic sciences themselves were tainted as the bases for arguments about reproductive rights. Even though there were clear scientific arguments in favor of legalizing birth control, other arguments would have to be employed.

## The Use of Birth Control in Social Engineering

Birth control remained controversial even when it did not use eugenic arguments to gain support. Throughout the twentieth century there was fierce opposition, especially from the Catholic Church and Protestant fundamentalists. When eugenics was dismissed as the pseudo-science it was, my grandmother and others were forced to find non-biological, non-racial, and non-eugenic arguments to support their cause. My grandmother did continue to make some biological arguments for birth control, including that maternal and child health necessitated that births be spaced; that pregnancy carried health risks for every woman and should be undertaken only after consulting a physician; and that birth control was the best solution for the woman who had to delay or avoid pregnancy. But the argument that birth control could improve the state of the human race was largely muted.

Instead, my grandmother advanced the argument that birth control could benefit society, as well as individuals, and that society could be made healthier, safer, and more prosperous if birth control were made more widely available to its citizens. Birth control was thus an indispensable part of creating a just society. Racial engineering through birth control was out; social engineering was in.

While social engineering through birth control was based on the best of intentions, it had racial implications that proved almost as dangerous as eugenics to the cause of reproductive rights. This soon became clear.

My grandmother long argued that birth control should be part of a nation's public health system. Poor people, she believed, should have the same access to the same basic health care, including birth control, as wealthy people do in order to enable them to live as healthy a life as possible and to be productive members of society. This argument met with some initial success during the Great Depression in the 1930s when my grandmother argued that government should fund birth control services in public health clinics as a way to reduce the number of persons on welfare. She argued that every additional child born to a poor family would go onto the relief rolls at an additional cost to the taxpayer. It would be less expensive for the government to prevent births instead of paying welfare costs for a child's life. The racial and class biases of this argument became clear when two states in the Deep South, North and South Carolina, became the first states to include birth control services in their public health programs. African-Americans came to believe that birth control and sterilization services were being targeted at them in order to reduce their numbers. During the 1970s as law professor Dorothy Roberts said, "It was a common belief among Blacks in the South that Black women were routinely sterilized without their informed consent and for no valid medical reason. Teaching hospitals performed unnecessary hysterectomies on poor Black women as practice for their medical residents. This sort of abuse was so widespread in the South that these operations came to be known as 'Mississippi appendectomies.'"

More recently, in the 1990s, the advent of long-lasting contraceptives like Norplant created a new opportunity for the government to try to limit reproduction by welfare recipients and generated new fears in the African-American community. Norplant was a five-year contraceptive contained in permeable plastic capsules that had to be inserted under a woman's skin by a physician. The main advertised benefit of Norplant was that the woman did not have to remember to take a daily pill, and therefore human error was taken out of the contraceptive equation. As the device was being developed, few noticed that once inserted by a medical professional, it could not be removed except by a medical professional either. The "choice" of the woman to use the device was circumscribed at both ends. She could not use Norplant except with a doctor's permission nor could she stop using it without it. In these regards its use seemed uncomfortably similar to sterilization.

This similarity became almost immediately apparent in the 1990s when, shortly after Norplant was approved, some women convicted of child abuse were sentenced to use the implant as a condition of gaining parole, just as earlier in the twentieth century, certain criminals were sentenced to sterilization. As with sterilization, the poor became targets. Norplant, because it was reversible, provided the opportunity for social engineers to prevent not just child abusers but also welfare recipients from having children. Because African-Americans were disproportionately poor and on welfare, they became the target of proposals by some politicians and opinion makers that Norplant use be a condition of receiving welfare.

Two days after the Food and Drug Administration approved Norplant in 1990, the *Philadelphia Inquirer* published an editorial entitled "Poverty and Norplant: Can Contraception Reduce the Underclass?" The editorial lamented the fact that half of black children lived in poverty and stated, "The main reason more black children are living in poverty is that people having the most children are the ones least capable of supporting them." The editorial went on to urge incentives to encourage welfare recipients to use Norplant.

Many in the black community exploded in anger, believing that the editorial was a call for "genocide." There was, however, not total unanimity on this issue within the black community. Marion Barry, the African-American mayor of Washington, D.C., not only approved of incentives for Norplant use, but also of *mandatory* Norplant use by women on welfare: "You can have as many babies as you want, but when you start asking the government to take care of them, the government now ought to have some control over you." Nonetheless, the *Inquirer* retracted it editorial and apologized.

The Norplant saga illustrates the conflicts that arise when women's fertility becomes a permissible target for government intervention. Women's rights, societal rights, economic and tax interests, race, and class all intersect and conflict when a society believes it should control the childbearing of its poorest members. In the case of Norplant the interests of poor African-American women won out, and their right to determine for themselves how many children to have was preserved. No proposal to mandate Norplant use for welfare recipients ever passed, or even came to a vote, in state legislatures or in Congress. Few politicians wanted to appear to use discredited eugenic arguments to target the reproductive freedom of one race, no matter what the alleged fiscal and societal benefits might be. But eugenics disguised as social engineering wasn't dead yet.

In 2001 a study purporting to establish a relationship between abortion and crime rates was published in the *Quarterly Journal of Economics* by John J. Donohue III, a professor of law at Stanford University, and Steven D. Levitt, a professor of economics at the University of Chicago. The authors argued that the legalization of abortion after *Roe* permitted more poor, young, and minority women to terminate unwanted pregnancies. The authors assumed that because of the women's disadvantaged status, their unwanted children would have been more likely to become criminals than their wanted children. Before *Roe* these unwanted children would have been more likely to have been born. After *Roe* they were more likely to be aborted. The authors concluded that legal abortion disproportionately prevented potential criminals from being born, with the result that the rate of violent crime would begin to decline eighteen or so years later. In fact, the violent crime rate did begin to decline about eighteen years after abortion was legalized in various states. But whether this was a coincidence or was caused by the legalization of abortion was another matter. Other researchers pointed out that there were many social, demographic, and economic factors behind the fall in violent crime rates in the early 1990s. Violent crime rates could have fallen because there was reduced drug use, especially of crack cocaine, because there were fewer guns available, because the economy improved, because the police were more effective at deterring crime, or because prison sentences increased and took more criminals off the streets. To a greater or lesser extent all these occurred in the early 1990s, and any role that the legalization of abortion twenty years earlier might have played became murkier. After looking at these and other factors, other research teams came to diametrically opposed conclusions—one group of researchers said that legal abortion reduced violent crime rates, while another team said that legal abortion increased them, mainly because it increased illegitimacy by allowing more sexual activity outside of marriage and thus delinquent behaviors and attitudes. A third research team found no causal link at all.

Despite the inconclusive state of the research, some pro-choice advocates touted the initial research as being a reason to keep abortion legal. The best that can be said is that the case for the alleged causal relationship between the legalization of abortion and a decrease in crime rates is unproven. At its worst, this argument is eugenics in new clothing. As with the *Philadelphia Inquirer* editorial, the abortion-crime link is an effort to target poor, young, black women and to tell them that if they used Norplant or had abortions, their problems would be over—they wouldn't be poor, or they wouldn't give birth to criminals. While there are clear demonstrable benefits for parents and children in having planned families and wanted children, we must be careful not to overstate the case. Birth control and abortion are not panaceas for all societal problems. We must be careful not to turn birth control and abortion, which should be empowering for all women, into, as law professor Dorothy Roberts once said, "a duty for the poor."

In an effort to make a more compelling case for reproductive freedom, its advocates have portrayed it as a necessary component of human and societal betterment. But it is a short journey from urging as a public health matter that family planning should be a governmental program to having the government attempt to dictate certain reproductive results. The eugenics disaster did not prevent the Norplant disaster nor prevent some from urging that abortion be kept legal as a crime preventative.

Advocates of reproductive freedom need to distinguish between the societal good that comes from family planning and attempts to employ family planning to achieve specific social results. Eugenics was not wrong as long as its goal was to enable women to have healthier children and its methods were voluntary. Eugenics went wrong when it said that only certain people could reproduce and that it was government's duty to enforce this. Private voluntary eugenics is not controversial. Women naturally seek to have healthy children. Public mandated eugenics that denies the freedom to some women and men to have children is a holocaust. The pro-choice movement must remain vigilant about the difference between these two things. We cannot give the government any excuse to restrict reproductive freedom, even with the best of intentions. We can promote reproductive freedom without claiming that it will solve all of society's ills. When we make exaggerated claims for the benefits of reproductive freedom, we open the door for the government, as it did with compulsory sterilization, to take us at our word. Governments have shown themselves capable of combining shaky or nonexistent science with racist attitudes to do grave injustice to those who are powerless in our society. The Norplant experience and the effort to link legal abortion with the decline in crime rates show that bad science, public eugenics, and racism are still alive and well as we enter the twenty-first century.

The early-twentieth-century eugenics tragedy colors any attempt to use science and biology to argue on behalf of legal birth control and abortion. But it doesn't prevent it. In the last quarter of the twentieth century the science of evolutionary biology has demonstrated that the sexual reproduction of humans and other animals, while immensely complex, is complex for a reason. Our reproductive and mating system is messy, volatile and fraught with danger, but it enables us to survive and has done so since the beginning of the human race. Humanity has been a reproductive success. A vital and indispensable part of our reproductive success has been our ability to control our childbearing by various means, including by using birth control and abortion. The reproductive freedom that *Griswold* and *Roe* recognized is an absolute necessity for human survival. All of humanity has benefited when individuals have control of their reproduction. This is a biological statement, not a eugenic one. Humans know what is best for them when they reproduce. Humans haven't needed any social engineering from government or reformers to make them reproduce better. Humanity has done this on its own, well before *Griswold* and *Roe*, and well before the invention of Norplant. Successful reproduction is one of humanity's unique triumphs. All we have to do is not mess it up.

# CHAPTER THREE

# Putting Reproduction Back into Reproductive Freedom

The debate over reproductive freedom during the past two centuries has been about many things—race, class, religion, the sanctity of life, human dignity, the role of women, civil rights, and the right to privacy—almost everything except reproduction.

Reproductive freedom is vital to humanity. It is even more vital than all the other freedoms that we cherish—freedom of religion, freedom of thought and speech, and the freedom to live our lives as we see fit. Humanity has these freedoms, or should have them, because they add to human happiness and make for a better world. So does reproductive freedom.

Successful reproduction is a biological necessity. After all, if our ancestors had not reproduced successfully, we wouldn't be here. It is also a complex biological process. Successful reproduction involves a man and a woman, both of whom are capable of reproducing, finding each other, bonding, having sex, getting pregnant, and giving birth to a living child. Successful reproduction also means nurturing and raising that child, and having that child repeat the same process. The goal of successful reproduction is having a healthy child who will in turn reproduce successfully. Life does not exist without successful reproduction.

Reproduction involves trade-offs, choices, and obligations. Men and women can choose to mate, have sex, get pregnant, have a child, and raise the child. Each step involves a trade-off. As Professor Bobbi S. Low of the University of Michigan says: "energy spent on reproduction can't be spent on getting a mate or raising kids." Reproductive freedom allows men and women within the context of these obligations to choose to take the next step in the reproductive process, or not. The primary obligation they have is survival—their own and that of their child. A woman's survival, as we saw with Sadie Sachs, depends directly on her ability to control pregnancy and childbearing. Children's survival depends on their condition at birth, their parent's survival, especially their mother's survival, and the nurturing they receive from their parents.

The reproductive process is long, complex, and fraught with danger, especially for women. Successful reproduction requires men and women using conscious and unconscious strategies to give them the greatest chance of success. Successful reproduction is not a random event. It is a carefully calibrated system that has evolved through trial and error over the eons to provide for the greatest chance of human survival, that is, life. Life does not exist without successful reproduction and I believe successful reproduction is furthered by reproductive freedom. While reproductive freedom includes birth control or abortion, the ability to prevent or terminate a pregnancy is just one step in the process of creating life.

There are costs and benefits in every step of the reproductive process. How we exercise our choices during the reproductive process is a profoundly moral question since it involves the decision to create or destroy life. Moral codes have evolved as humanity has and have enabled us to survive. A proper morality must encourage the survival of humanity. The survival of humanity means that we must grant men and women the reproductive freedom necessary to insure their own survival and that of their children. And it means that not just legal abortion is good; it means that abortion is good.

## The Biological Framework for Reproductive Freedom

Reproductive freedom is not only important, it is necessary for human existence. To create and nurture life, humanity must have the right to get pregnant or not and give birth or not, when people choose to do so. These choices are the essence of human reproduction. The right to reproduce as one thinks best is what reproductive freedom is supposed to protect. While the movement to establish this freedom has been a major component of the women's movement, it is not just a woman's issue. Reproductive freedom concerns the entire human race. It impacts human health and survival and the improvement of the human condition. By exerting control over our biological destiny, we are insuring that destiny. The future of the human race has not been and can not be left to chance. We have survived because we have taken control of our reproduction and our biological destiny. Reproductive rights are vital because they help insure the survival of humanity.

I am proposing a new biological framework within which to argue on behalf of reproductive freedom. It is a framework based on biological reality and science, not on ideology. The freedom to reproduce is more than an abstract right; it represents our biological purpose here on earth. Reproductive freedom can be insured when it is grounded on reproductive realities.

Reproduction involves each one of us, whether we are male or female, or young or old. We have reproductive obligations to our children and their children. Reproductive rights emerge from our biological obligations. We have a biological obligation to reproduce. The alternative is that we die out. We carry out this mandate by surviving to adulthood, finding a mate, having sex, having a child, and ensuring that our child is healthy and survives to do the same. We also carry out this mandate, even if we are childless, by helping our close relatives or kin in raising their children. Others carry it out by adopting and raising unrelated children.

The new framework I am proposing is based on evolutionary biology. It is from a basis in science that reproductive rights emerge. This framework is not exclusive of a feminist or human rights framework. On the contrary, I will argue that understanding evolutionary biology and the role of reproductive control within it can lead to a stronger basis for the necessity of women's and human rights. I will argue that reproductive rights are beneficial to women, men, and families as they pursue their reproductive strategies.

I will also argue that a perspective based on evolutionary biology can simultaneously support both reproductive freedom and a proper respect for the sanctity of human life. The biological goal of the human race is more than mere existence of life. Biology tells us that "life" is something more than existence. "Life" includes the creation of life, its survival, its health and viability, and the reproduction of its next generation. The distinction I am drawing between life as mere existence and life as something more comprehensive is fundamental. Divinity or nature, depending on one's beliefs, created a process for the continuance of life after its initial creation. This process, created either by divinity or by nature, is a product of evolutionary forces and is designed so that each life organism, including each human, can survive and reproduce successfully. Evolutionary biology describes the process whereby every organism converts the resources it finds in its environment into additional organisms. This is the fundamental definition of evolutionary biology–organisms using resources to make more organisms. For humans this means that the human race has evolved to find ways to grow food and build shelter and protect itself and thus have the health, strength, security, and stamina necessary to survive and in turn to reproduce. This is not an easy process. It has evolved over time by a process of trial and error in which nature has tested a variety of strategies for the survival and reproduction of many species. Some strategies have been successful and some not. Evolution has weeded out those species and organisms that pursued unsuccessful strategies.

*Reproductive Freedom Makes the Difference*
*Between Reproductive Success and Reproductive Failure*

We can define one basic element of an unsuccessful reproductive strategy quite easily—it is when a boy or girl, or a man or woman, dies before having children. At that point the bloodline stops. Although the reproductive process involves many stages where successful reproduction can falter, the most serious challenge to survival and reproduction for women and children to overcome occurs in childbirth. To the extent reproductive freedom can lessen the danger of death in pregnancy and childbirth, it can lead to more reproductive and biological success for humanity. If a woman has control over the timing and spacing of her children, then both she and her children are more likely to survive. If a woman does not have control over her childbearing, either whether she should have children at all, when she should have them, with whom or under what circumstances, then she and her children are less likely to survive childbirth and its aftermath. Early death before any organism can reproduce is reproductive failure. It is a failure for humanity.

In the African nation of Mali, one of the poorest nations on earth and where more than 5 percent of women die of pregnancy-related causes, there is an expression: "A woman who gives birth opens her own coffin." Pregnancy-related complications account for one-third of the deaths for Malian women aged fifteen to forty-nine. In neighboring Guinea one of every seven mothers dies in childbirth and over 10 percent of infants die before their first birthday. In the United States, the richest nation on earth, where relatively few women die of pregnancy-related causes, still more than 40 percent of women giving birth experience complications. Modern medical science has not made the risks of childbearing a relic of the past.

Humanity evolved in conditions even more precarious to women's health than in present day Mali and Guinea. Until the relatively recent advent of antibiotics and modern obstetrical care, primary causes of premature death for women throughout human history were pregnancy-related. Even today around the world in about 15 percent of pregnancies women develop not just complications, but potentially life-threatening complications during the pregnancy itself, in childbirth, or in the immediate postpartum period. In 2002 over half a million women died worldwide from childbirth-related causes, including about 70,000 who died from unsafe abortions. As many health activists have pointed out, this death toll is the equivalent of a jumbo jet full of women crashing every four hours! Complications arise and women die in childbirth for many reasons; it is difficult to predict in advance who will develop complications and who will or will not survive. Unexpected complications can arise in any pregnancy. But some risks can be predicted. There are increased risks, for instance, if a woman's births are spaced too closely together, if she is very young, or if she has already given birth to four children or more. There are increased risks if a woman is undernourished or anemic or has high blood pressure. Many of these risks can be reduced by proper prenatal care, by skilled childbirth services, and by the woman's giving birth at a facility that can immediately deal with her complications. Many of these risks can also be reduced by the use of family planning to space, delay, or prevent births.

The 1995 World Health Organization Report *Health Benefits of Family Planning* stated:

> Contraceptive use reduces maternal mortality and improves women's health by preventing unwanted and high-risk pregnancies and reducing the need for unsafe abortions. Some contraceptives also improve women's health by reducing the likelihood of disease transmission and protecting against certain cancers and health problems. . . . Each year over 500,000 women die from causes related to pregnancy and childbirth. A significant proportion of these deaths could be avoided through the effective use of family planning; it is estimated that 100,000 maternal deaths could be avoided each year if all women who said they wanted no more children were able to stop childbearing.
>
> . . .
>
> Termination of pregnancies can be risky to a woman's health. Unsafe abortions and their complications are a major cause of maternal death and illness; approximately 70,000 women die each year as a result of unsafe or incomplete abortion and many more suffer complications.

Infertility due to tubal infections resulting from unsafe abortion is common in some areas. Using contraception to prevent unwanted pregnancies helps to reduce the toll of unsafe abortion.

. . .

The risk of maternal death increases for each successive birth after the fourth; the risk is 1.5 to 3 times higher for women with five or more children than for women with two or three children. Pregnancy and childbirth is riskier for these women as they are more likely to suffer from anaemia, require blood transfusions during delivery, and die of haemorrhage than women with fewer children.

It is in a woman's biological interest to take control of her childbearing, to use contraception, and to limit the number of children she has. It is also in her children's interest. Just as there is a risk to the mother in a risky pregnancy, there is increased risk to the baby. Poorly managed pregnancies and deliveries are largely responsible for the deaths of over 4 million newborn babies each year. The World Health Organization report continued:

It has been estimated that expanding contraceptive services to meet the needs of couples who wish to avoid pregnancy but currently are not using contraception could prevent as many as 850,000 deaths per year among children under age five. Child deaths are prevented through adequate birth spacing, prevention of births among very young women, and prevention of births among women with four or more children.

When used to space births at least two years apart, contraceptives save children's lives. When births are spaced less than two years apart, particularly less than 18 months, infants are more likely to be premature and have a low birth weight, two factors that lead to increased mortality. The average chance of dying in infancy increases by about 60–70 percent for children born less than two years apart; the chance of dying before the age of five years increases by about 50 percent. Achieving adequate birth spacing could reduce child mortality by 20 percent or more in some countries in Central and South America and North Africa, and by up to a third in Brazil and Egypt.

Short birth intervals also decrease the survival chances of the preceding child. The arrival of a new baby means that breast-feeding stops suddenly and the mother has less time to devote to caring for the older child. A birth interval of less than 12 months raises the overall average risk of death for the preceding child between ages one and five by at least 70 to 80 percent; a birth within 18 months raises the risk by 50 percent or more.

A 2002 study by researchers at the Demographic and Health Surveys (DHS) of the U.S. Agency for International Development confirmed and updated the WHO findings and found that "children born 3 years or more after a previous birth are healthier at birth and more likely to survive at all stages of infancy and childhood through age five." Compared with children born less than two years after a previous birth, children born three to four years after a previous birth are 2.4 times more likely to survive to age five, and mothers with similar birth intervals are 2.5 times more likely to survive childbirth. A second study done in 2003 by Dr. Gordon C. S. Smith of Cambridge, England, found that a second pregnancy occurring within six months of the birth of a prior child increased the risk of the second child's death more than three and a half times.

The DHS report continued:

While the biological and behavioral mechanisms that make shorter birth intervals riskier for infants and mothers are little understood, researchers suggest such factors as maternal depletion syndrome, premature delivery, milk diminution, and sibling rivalry. For instance, studies suggest that shorter birth intervals may not allow mothers enough time to restore nutritional reserves that provide for adequate fetal nutrition and growth. Fetal growth retardation and premature delivery can result in low birth weight and greater risk of death.

Maternal health and child survival are totally intertwined. If the mother does not survive, it is likely that the baby will not either. This is a double biological disaster. A 1994 World Bank Report on women's health in the developing world, entitled *A New Agenda for Women's Health and Nutrition,* stated:

> In developing countries, a mother's death in childbirth means almost certain death for the newborn and severe consequences for her older children. . . . Children whose mothers die are three to ten times more likely to die within two years than those with living parents. . . .
>
> When mothers are malnourished, sickly or receive inadequate care in pregnancy, their children face a higher risk of disease and death. The effect on perinatal outcomes is particularly strong. Each year, 7 million infants die within a week of birth and more than 20 million low-birthweight babies are born.

The United States has among the lowest rates of infant and maternal mortality of any country on the globe. It also has an extraordinary health care system, but this system is not the total explanation for these low mortality rates. Americans have among the highest rates of contraceptive use of any country in the world. Most Americans who are sexually active use some combination of birth control and abortion to avoid becoming pregnant or having a child when they don't want to. There are about 40 million women ages fifteen to forty-four in the United States who are fertile and sexually active and who do not want to become pregnant. Nine out of ten of them—90 percent—are practicing contraception. These women generally use contraception skillfully since only about 1.5 million, or 3.75 percent of them, report becoming pregnant unintentionally each year. An equal number of unintended pregnancies—1.5 million—are reported annually by the 10 percent of women who are sexually active, fertile, and who are *not* using contraception. This means that 37.5 percent of these 4 million women get pregnant annually, or ten times the rate of the women who use contraceptives. Just under half of these 3 million unintended pregnancies will end in abortion. Abortion is an extraordinarily safe procedure in the United States, safer even than childbirth.

Worldwide, women demonstrate the same desire to control childbearing. Estimates are that over 60 percent of married women are using some form of birth control. Forty-six million women have abortions each year around the globe. American women, and for the most part women worldwide, have decided that it is better to plan, time, and limit their births and are able to do so. Women have thirty years of fertility from ages fifteen to forty-four, and unspaced and unlimited births would mean that, if she survived, a woman would give birth to over twenty children. If a woman does not use birth control and abortion to reduce the number of her pregnancies, she must rely on abstinence and prolonged breast-feeding. Few women today or in the past had twenty children, indicating that one method or another is being used.

The ability to control one's childbearing is one of the strategies available to help ensure survival. There are others, including controlling with whom one will have children and the amount and style of parenting of those children. These strategies have a direct influence on, in fact determine, the likelihood of a woman's survival and the survival of her and her partner's children. The control over childbearing also means control over pregnancy and control over sexual activity. The decision, if it is a decision and not coerced, to engage in sex with the risk of pregnancy is the first thing that a woman and man can control. Then if pregnant, the woman can control whether or not to give birth. After birth the woman and man can control whether and to what extent to nurture and parent. Reproductive freedom, or rights, describes the control that women and men have at each stage of this process. Birth control and abortion are one part of that freedom and are essential tools in the human mating and reproductive process. Reproductive freedom is not something granted by law, custom, or religion, though it can be taken away by these societal forces. It simply is part of our human nature and our humanity. It was part of our creation and is part of us as we strive to exist and to ensure the survival of our children. It is part of the human instinct. We strive to survive and to have our children survive. We do whatever we need to do to make this happen.

The evidence is clear that women who take control over childbearing are more likely to survive, and the children they do have are also more likely to survive and in turn reproduce. Pregnancy and childbearing are dangerous to women, children, and their families. Women and their babies have a better chance of surviving childbearing and infancy if births are spaced, planned, and timed for when it is best to give birth. Those who call themselves pro-life should support all measures to increase the chances of women and children surviving pregnancy and childbirth. But they don't.

## The Pro-Life Problem with Reproductive Freedom

The pro-life movement expresses objections to birth control and abortion on religious and other grounds. Each, they say, is unnatural and frustrates God's plan for humanity. In their view, every life, potential or actual, is sacred. To take a life before or after birth dishonors God. Abortion contributes to the breakdown of marriage and thus of society. It permits men to avoid their responsibilities and to force women to kill their children.

Whether or not one believes this position, we cannot shy away from examining the costs and benefits of reproductive freedom. The cause of reproductive freedom can be advanced only when we show it has more benefits than costs, and if some reproductive decisions are too harmful to humanity, then we must stand up and say that they should not be permitted in the name of choice.

Throughout history most human societies have to some extent restricted reproductive freedom by law or custom. In many cultures marriage is not a mutual decision but is customarily arranged by parents. Many societies encourage fertility, and the refusal to have sex and infertility are grounds for divorce. Some societies have banned birth control and abortion; most societies have banned infanticide and the abandonment of babies. A tribe or community may, depending on its circumstances, view reproductive freedom as an impediment to its goals of propagating itself, dominating its neighbors, or defending itself from outside aggression. Men may also view reproductive freedom as granting too much control of reproduction to women and will seek the power to attain their own reproductive goals. As happened in the United States in the nineteenth century, special racial and medical concerns can also lead to restrictions on reproductive freedom. The geopolitical, social, and gender goals that underlie the opposition to reproductive freedom are generally left unstated by the religions that oppose it, and by members of the pro-life movement, who express their opposition in terms of preserving and protecting unborn life.

Religious leaders who oppose birth control and abortion do not generally admit that requiring women to have large numbers of children is their goal or that it is an acceptable risk that women may die in childbirth as a result. Martin Luther was quite callous on the subject: "If a woman grows weary and at last dies from childbearing, it matters not. Let her only die from bearing; she is there to do it." The only approved way for Catholic women to minimize their chances of death in childbirth or having large numbers of children is to be abstinent in marriage or use the Church-endorsed rhythm method of birth control. Pope Paul VI in *Humanae Vitae* in 1968 condemned "every action which, either in anticipation of the conjugal act, or in its accomplishment, or in the development of its natural consequences, proposes, whether as an end or as a means, to render procreation impossible."

This condemnation of artificial birth control was a renewal of a prior condemnation in an earlier *Encyclical Casti Connubii* by Pius XI in 1930:

> No reason, however grave, can make what is intrinsically contrary to nature to be in conformity with nature and morally right. And since the conjugal act by its very nature is destined for the begetting of children, those who in exercising it deliberately frustrate its natural power and purpose are acting against nature, and are doing something that is base and intrinsically immoral.

Archbishop Patrick Hayes of New York in his pastoral letter for Christmas 1921 attacked my grandmother by arguing that birth control was a greater evil than abortion because birth control prevented souls from coming into existence:

To take life after its inception is a horrible crime; but to prevent human life that the Creator is about to bring into being is satanic. In the first instance, the body is killed, while the soul lives on; in the latter, by frustrating God's laws, not only a body but an immortal soul is denied existence in time and eternity.

The current Church hierarchy and the pro-life movement tend to overlook Archbishop Hayes' theology and focus their objections to reproductive freedom on abortion. It is abortion that is satanic. Pope John Paul II in his *Evangelium Vitae,* issued in 1995, quoted the Second Vatican Council that put abortion in the same class as other threats to human life and dignity:

Whatever is opposed to life itself, such as any type of murder, genocide, abortion, euthanasia, or wilful self-destruction, whatever violates the integrity of the human person, such as mutilation, torments inflicted on body or mind, attempts to coerce the will itself; whatever insults human dignity, such as subhuman living conditions, arbitrary imprisonment, deportation, slavery, prostitution, the selling of women and children; as well as disgraceful working conditions, where people are treated as mere instruments of gain rather than as free and responsible persons; all these things and others like them are infamies indeed. They poison human society, and they do more harm to those who practise them than to those who suffer from the injury. Moreover, they are a supreme dishonour to the Creator.

Many pro-lifers, at least in the western world, would want marriage to be consensual and mutual and would permit and even encourage use of birth control to control the timing of pregnancy. So, not all reproductive freedom is an anathema to the pro-life movement, just abortion, which they equate to infanticide. Since the fetus is a human being, pro-lifers believe, abortion is the same as murder. There can be few, if any, exceptions to this. Abortion may be justified in limited circumstances depending on one's view, including permitting it to save the life of the mother. But even in this case there is the moral dilemma of whether it is permissible to take one life to save another. Even in a country with high maternal mortality, like Guinea, the death of one out of every seven women during childbirth is no justification in the pro-life view for permitting abortion, which kills another human being.

In the pro-life view, reproductive freedom has consequences so detrimental to individuals and society that it should be banned, or allowed only in very unusual circumstances, such as to save the life of the mother. Marriage is the bedrock of society, and reproductive freedom permits increased sexual activity outside of marriage, thus weakening the marital bond between husband and wife. Birth control and abortion serve to reduce the cost of sexual activity outside of marriage by preventing pregnancy or a child from being born. Marriage is both a moral commitment and a necessity for a stable society and the upbringing of children. Anything that weakens marriage should be discouraged or forbidden. In the pro-life view, when one moral commitment is broken, people are more likely to break others, leading to a breakdown of all of society's rules and institutions. In this view permitting abortion on demand is the first step on the slippery slope to moral and societal ruin.

Pro-lifers fear that legalizing abortion results in abortion not becoming a choice, but rather a duty. Instead of giving a woman a "choice," legalized abortion creates circumstances where abortion becomes the inevitable alternative. Because abortion is legal, the woman and her partner now have an easy "out"—the solution to their unintended pregnancy. Legal abortion relieves a man of his obligations to the woman and the child. Her choice becomes her obligation.

I would argue that few, if any, of the pro-life fears of the dire consequences of legalizing abortion have been realized. Most people still marry. Sex outside of marriage was invented long before birth control and abortion, and society, despite the naysayers, is not in total moral ruin. Women are exercising their choice whether or not to have a child in an often difficult environment. Sometimes men do take the easy way out. Sometimes the women don't want them around. One-third of births are to women out of wedlock. These women don't feel obliged to have an abortion.

Even if all the elements of the pro-life argument do not survive close scrutiny, one can see that reproductive freedom has both benefits and costs and that these differ for men and women. Reproductive freedom is intertwined with how men and women approach sex, marriage, and the upbringing of children. It is the job of society to evaluate the risks and benefits of reproductive freedom and to decide whether and to what extent to impose restrictions on the exercise of this freedom. In addition to the traditional arguments for and against reproductive freedom, I am adding to those in favor a biological argument. I will argue that there are more biological reasons to favor reproductive freedom than to oppose it. There will be instances, however, where complete reproductive freedom cannot be justified because of its adverse impact on society, and I will support corresponding limited restrictions on its exercise. Sex selection abortion, as practiced in some Asian cultures, and reproductive cloning are two exercises of reproductive freedom that I do not support. In both these cases the costs to humanity outweigh the benefits by a substantial margin. But otherwise, reproductive freedom benefits men, women, and children. It benefits their health and survival and therefore should be allowed to be exercised as individual humans believe it best for themselves.

We are approaching being able to choose our evolutionary and biological future with new technologies. While choice is a core value of humanity, in the area of human reproduction choice is not the only value; it may not even be in some instances the supreme value. Our challenge is to reconcile human moral agency with the dangers posed by new reproductive choices. We have to ask ourselves the following question: choice for what? Asking this question deliberately puts choice into a moral context. I believe that, given new technologies and the new environment we are in, there is insufficient moral support for giving all women and men unfettered choice about their reproductive futures. Americans concur with this in their almost total absence of support for human reproduction through cloning.

How we exercise our reproductive choices determines the kind of society and world we will live in. The issue is no less important than this. The essential value, as the pro-life movement points out, must be the preservation of life. But I define life to include its propagation, in addition to its existence. Life is nothing without it being propagated. For this we need reproductive freedom. But can we be trusted to exercise our reproductive powers wisely? On the other hand can we trust our governments to restrict our choices wisely? Can we be pro-choice and admit that there should be limits to reproductive choice? These are the fundamental questions of this book. Our beliefs about when life or personhood begins do not determine our positions on these questions. These questions go beyond choice and life.

## What Does Biology Have To Do with Morality?

I believe that the sciences can inform, change, and justify moral and ethical thinking. While I believe that there is a biological basis to morality, the reader does not have to agree with this proposition in order to agree with my argument. I believe that morality is a product of human evolution, is a profoundly human creation, and is vital for human survival. Others believe that morality is something transcendent, independent of human experience and God-given. There are those who believe in a middle ground that the essentials of morality, like the Ten Commandments, are of divine origin or are a part of "natural law," and the task that God has given humans is to devise moral principles for situations left uncovered by the essential rules. No matter which position you adhere to, I believe that it is consistent with either position that science must inform moral beliefs, and that human experience and the realities of life must also. Moral beliefs as well as religious beliefs have changed over time. There is not necessarily a dichotomy between religion and science. If a moral rule helps community survival, the rule will last. If it does not, it will wither away. Such is the case with the moral rules against birth control and abortion. These practices help humanity survive and reproduce successfully and many humans use them. Moral rules forbidding them will not stand.

It is possible to believe that morality is transcendent and independent of human input or experience without necessarily believing that morality is of divine origin. A belief or disbelief in God is not necessary to believe that there is a universal pre-existing common morality, or a natural law, that contains the ethical principles necessary for how to live a moral life. One can be an atheist and believe that there is natural law that can be discovered by human reason. Thomas Jefferson said as much in the Declaration of Independence when he said that "we hold these truths to be self-evident." (Actually, Benjamin Franklin added the words "self-evident"; Jefferson, in his first draft, said "sacred and undeniable.") Alternatively, one can be a believer in God and believe that God is a creator or universal force but not necessarily the author of a transcendent moral code. One can believe in God and yet believe that moral values are created by humans for human betterment. Therefore, both believers and non-believers in God can believe that the Golden Rule, for instance, is either a part of natural law or is of human origin.

For both theologians and secular natural-law philosophers, like Jefferson, abortion in particular and reproduction in general have not historically been a major focus of their writings on natural law. In fact, reproductive issues are notable more for their absence than their presence in discourses on natural law in all major religious traditions. It has only been in relatively recent times that abortion has become a central theological concern. Neither abortion nor birth control is specifically mentioned in the Bible. The Book of Genesis contains the injunction to be fruitful and multiply, but there are no further directives set out for either a minimum or maximum number of children to have to satisfy this command. This is in marked contrast, for instance, to the Old Testament's very lengthy and specific dietary rules.

Into this void entered various Christian theologians who have debated the nature of life, and when it begins and ends, for centuries. These debates were conducted more on a theological than a scientific plane since ensoulment—when the soul was deemed to enter the body—was the determining factor as to when life began. The theological definition of life evolved as science discovered how life as a biological organism was created and constructed. Theology has given way to biology and genetics, and many Christians now believe that life begins at conception because of the unique DNA that emerges when sperm meets egg. Whether this reading of genetics is right or wrong (I believe it is woefully incomplete and inaccurate—DNA does not equal life), it indicates that natural law can evolve as science uncovers new knowledge. One can be a believer in natural law and a believer even that morality is created by God and yet believe that true morality is still in the process of being discovered by humanity through reason and science.

Part of the process of discovering morality is incorporating scientific discoveries into human knowledge in order to refine ethical principles. I hope the reader who is a believer in natural law will do this, just as theologians in the nineteenth century used scientific discoveries about how conception occurs and as theologians in the late twentieth century used discoveries about DNA to establish their views of when life begins. The pro-life movement is using biology to try to turn its view of a biological and genetic event into a legal one. Pro-life theologians who use arguments based on DNA to support their argument that life begins at conception, and must therefore be protected by law, are using biological arguments. It is time that the pro-choice movement did the same. The traditional pro-choice arguments based on choice and women's dignity and autonomy do not answer or counter the biological arguments of the pro-life movement. I believe that the new scientific discoveries about the biological process of human reproduction that I will present do. I believe that science can help us understand that the decision not to reproduce and to have an abortion can be not only a biologically sound decision but also a moral one.

The principles of evolutionary biology provide the basis for much that follows. Depending on one's beliefs, it can be entirely acceptable for a religious person to believe that humans evolved according to the theory of evolution. There is a wide range of opinion among religious people about the role of evolutionary forces in human development. The Catholic Church believes that God creates through evolution. Pope John Paul II stated in a catechism in 1986: "Indeed, the theory of natural evolution, understood in a sense that does not exclude divine causality, is not in principle opposed to the truth about the creation of the visible world as presented in the Book of Genesis. . . . It must, however, be added that this hypothesis proposes only a probability, not a scientific certainty." As Eugenie Scott has stated, the official Catholic position, and that of many Protestant denominations, is that "God created, evolution happened, humans may indeed be descended from more primitive life forms, but the hand of God was needed for the creation of the human soul." Some Protestants who believe in Intelligent Design Creationism also allow for evolution within species after God created the species. One does not need to accept all of Darwin's theory of evolution to accept the fact that humans have and are evolving.

For those who believe, as I do, in morality being a creation of humanity and a product of human evolution, the process of incorporating science into moral beliefs is somewhat easier. I believe humans create moral codes to define acceptable and unacceptable conduct. The line between the acceptable and the unacceptable varies between cultures that have evolved in their own unique environments throughout history. Conduct that is acceptable helps the group survive. Unacceptable conduct harms the group. I would argue that moral codes have a biological basis and have become social norms as the result of humans with an instinct towards certain behavior, which we would define as acceptable or moral, surviving and producing more offspring than those who lack these instincts. The survivors incorporated their own instincts into the society's moral code. This is a case of history being written by the winners.

If we can understand the process of how our instincts for moral behavior and survival emerge, then I believe we can develop a wiser and more effective ethical system that can guide society and individuals as they face moral dilemmas. Moral principles are rules that enable society to function. They constitute a code of behavior that members of society accept because they know it is in their collective best interests to do so. Some parts of the moral code are enforced by collective societal disapproval, such as that lying is wrong. Other parts of the moral code are enforced by law, such as lying under oath. While the Ten Commandments contain an injunction against false witness, it is easy to see that this moral rule could have been developed during pre-history as a means of having a tribe function better. The tribe would survive better if its members were truthful about such things as food availability or outside threats. They would expel those who did not conform. A public consensus and an individual instinct in favor of honesty would be preserved and handed down to each new generation. A member of the tribe has the choice of whether to conform or not and face the consequences if he does not. More will conform if the behavior is viewed as being to their benefit. A particular human behavior can thus evolve into a societal rule as the non-conformers are forced out or leave the society. Whether or not there is a moral gene, there is an instinct in humans for moral behavior, at least by others.

"It would be," as Professor Richard D. Alexander of the University of Michigan said, "to the advantage of each individual that other individuals in his society—especially those not closely related to him—actually achieve the ideal of completely moral behavior." In other words, we benefit when others act morally, and when society encourages this.

When a moral rule is widely flouted and the non-conformists do not leave the society, then that rule will wither away. Abortion is such a rule. It is estimated that in the United States about 35 percent of all women will have an abortion during their lifetimes. These women aren't leaving the country. Societal consensus against abortion should become more difficult, just as it did against birth control when its use became widespread. How can the proponents of abortion being made illegal call 35 percent of American women immoral? The biological necessity of abortion has overridden the moral stricture against abortion for a large percent of the population, just as the moral stricture against contraception was overridden. The pro-life movement has been skillful at using shame to prevent women from talking about their abortions, and so the morality for or against has been slow to change.

Worldwide the frequency of abortion is similar to that in the United States. The World Health Organization reported in 2002: "Each year, 210 million women throughout the world become pregnant and a significant (22%) percentage of them resort to abortion. It is estimated that 46 million abortions are performed each year. . . ." Are these 46 million women who have abortions every year evil or wrong? The pro-life movement says yes. I say this isn't possible. These women are trying to survive and to ensure the survival of their current and future children. This is moral and right. To the pro-lifer the goal of these women may be worthy, but their means is not. How can we redefine the problem to see how abortion can be viewed as moral?

No matter what your beliefs about the origin of society's moral code, human reason, experience, and the evidence of science must inform the extent that we will believe in and follow the code. Morality has helped humanity evolve as a species and our moral code has evolved along with us. Women were thought inferior to men in many societies and this is now changing because of human experience. The biology of human reproduction and evolution can inform us about the necessity and importance of reproductive freedom. I believe that biology can help us understand that reproductive freedom is a moral good.

## Reproduction Is Childbearing Plus

A new societal consensus on the morality of abortion can be achieved only when we understand the biological basis of abortion, as well as the other methods of reproductive control, and create a moral model based on that knowledge. Abortion and birth control are only two of the ways that humans control their reproduction. As such, they can only be understood as part of the evolutionary process that guides human reproduction. Birth control and abortion relate directly to the human ability to use and control sex for their reproductive ends. Sex is what enables humanity to reproduce successfully. It is not always in an individual's reproductive interest to get pregnant or have a child after engaging in sex. The ability to use birth control and abortion to reduce the risk of pregnancy and childbearing is an integral part of human sexual and reproductive strategy. While there are almost as many human sexual and reproductive strategies as there are humans, the common goal of every strategy is successful reproduction. Most humans (and animals) go through the process of meeting and mating, having sex, getting pregnant, having a child, and nurturing that child to adulthood so that the child can repeat the process. Humans are reproductive strategists in their own way, acting out their strategy in their own environment to pursue their own reproductive goals.

Men and women share the desire to reproduce successfully, but biology has given them different interests. Women have more invested in the pregnancy and its aftermath and assume more risk to their life and health. But men and women have an identical interest in seeing their child grow to adulthood and reproduce successfully. The difference in their approach to parenting and future mating comes from their differing abilities to get pregnant again quickly and from their different levels of confidence that the child they are raising is actually theirs. Women always know who their children are, men do not. This has led to major differences and conflicts over how each sex approaches mating and parenting. There is a battle of the sexes and for good reason. It has enabled humanity to survive.

Other reproductive conflicts occur because humans use contraceptive and abortion technologies to reduce pregnancy and childbearing. Each technology has unintended consequences for men and women and society as a whole. Technology can lead to an increase in disease and a numerical imbalance between the sexes. New reproductive technologies threaten to eliminate the need for sexual reproduction altogether. Individual reproductive decisions have cumulative public consequences. As a result, this most private of human endeavors, reproduction, becomes a public matter. Before we can delineate the role for society's government to constrain our reproductive freedom, we must first understand the role that human evolution has in human reproduction and why reproductive freedom is vital for humanity's well-being.

Safe childbearing is only one part of the process of successful reproduction. It is the part most fraught with danger for mother and child. This danger alone justifies women's taking control over their pregnancy and childbearing. But taking this control will not, by itself, ensure successful reproduction. Successful reproduction is a life-long process. All along this process there are steps that women and men must control and fight to control. The science of evolutionary biology can explain why reproductive control is vital for human survival. Human reproduction is not random and is not guaranteed. The pro-life objections to reproductive freedom do not take into account the benefits to humanity of controlling its reproduction. Reproductive freedom helps in the preservation of human life and to that extent, it is moral. Reproductive freedom can only be understood and justified in the context of human survival.

A word of caution about science: No science is perfect or irrefutable, and none should claim to be. Biology seeks to understand the complexities of the natural world so that humans can try to improve the human condition and to reduce the harm of certain biological processes, such as aging, disease, giving birth and so forth. Biology can better understand the human condition by comparing humans with other animals and by examining their similarities and differences. Biologists observe, perform experiments, compare and analyze data, and draw conclusions. And then they repeat, or try to repeat, the process to try to confirm what they found. Science purports to explain things as simply as possible and to be as nondogmatic and nonideological as possible, even though every scientist has opinions and beliefs on contentious topics, including reproductive freedom. Science has a way of refuting or confirming ideologies. Every hypothesis is subject to being confirmed or falsified by future experiments and observation. Controversy is the norm in science. Preconceptions have a way of being demolished—the sun looked as if it revolved around the Earth, to everyone except Copernicus and Galileo. Truth gets uncovered by trial and error. The biological studies cited in this book may be found in the future to be, if not false, then at least not the full story. That is the risk I assume. Every scientific study will have its critics, whether or not they have proof that the study is false. Not every study confirms some scientist's ideology, or mine. These are the risks of any book using science to make its case.

# CHAPTER FOUR

# Reproductive Freedom and Human Evolution

Among all the animals humanity is distinguished by its rapid evolution, by its extraordinary ability to tame its environment, and by its rapid population growth. These biological hallmarks of humanity are all interrelated. They are all based in part on the facts that humans reproduce using sex and that humans exercise control over their reproduction. Humanity did not evolve and populate the planet by having sex and children indiscriminately or randomly. It did so by having both sex and children strategically. Humans evolved with men and women competing to mate with each other and cooperating with each other in parenting their young. This resulted in a dynamic in which healthy children were born and survived. Human courtship, mating, and parenting are all full of conflict and choice. Men and women often have different interests at each step on the road to reproductive success. Women have inherently more choices in some stages of the reproductive process than men, and men have more in others. Many societies recognize female choice and give women the legal freedom to have sex and children at times and circumstances of their choosing. Other societies do not, and women either find it impossible or difficult to have sex and children at the times and with the partners of their choosing. Men and women strive to control sex and reproduction—to exercise reproductive freedom—because it is a necessary part of their quest for their survival and that of their children. That is why birth control and abortion are vital—because they help humanity survive and propagate.

## Why Reproduction Isn't Random

In order to have reproductive success an individual must survive and their children must survive in the particular natural environment in which they live. The environment presents for everyone both a challenge and an opportunity. We have to use it and survive in it. Nature is a two-way street: Just as humans have shaped the natural world, the natural world has shaped humans. Darwin's theory of natural selection says that animals with the traits most advantageous for survival in a particular environment will be more likely to survive and pass down these traits to their progeny. Those without these traits will be less likely to survive. Advantageous traits should thereby become more prevalent in the population, thereby leading to greater rates of survival and population growth. Species that don't have advantageous traits for their environment will die out.

So far, humanity has been a reproductive success and it appears that we in general possess whatever traits are vital to our survival and to our being able to control the environment. There are now over six billion humans on the planet. The population growth in humans has been exponential over the past few centuries as humans have conquered diseases and as a result lived longer. But human evolution took place in an era before humanity had the ability to conquer infectious diseases. Antibiotics did not become prevalent around the world until there were three or four billion of us. So, how did humanity survive, evolve, and grow to such a degree when other species of animals didn't? And why did some individual humans survive while others didn't? Much of the answer lies not in the stars but in our genes.

No two people have the same genes. The process of sexual reproduction ensures that each individual has unique genetic traits. The part of the genetic material from each parent that is passed on when sperm and egg meet is entirely random. This is the only part of the reproductive process, however, that is random. The genetic combination of a random selection of the mother's and father's genes, along with genetic mutations in the reproductive process, creates a unique individual who possesses a selection of the characteristics and traits of his or her ancestors. Among these traits is the ability to resist certain diseases. The genes that a man or woman possesses that can ward off certain pathogens are likely in turn to be passed on to their children and will enable them to ward off the same diseases and survive.

Men and women each have an interest in finding a mate with "good genes" that can be passed on to their children. Those with the best genes will be sought after, and both men and women will compete for the mates that they perceive will have the right genes to mix with their own, as well as for other important qualities including parenting. Much of the process of assessing a potential mate for their genetic fitness is unconscious. Even so, the process is not random, and in order to find the right mate, everyone becomes a reproductive strategist. Because only women get pregnant, give birth, and nurse the child, they are especially vulnerable during the reproductive process. They have to be especially selective in choosing their mates. Choosing a mate means finding someone with the right stuff—not only genetic, but also the willingness and ability to be a good spouse, to provide, protect, and parent—that will complement one's own resources and situation.

Reproductive freedom is an essential part of courtship, mating, and parenting. The process of seeking a mate, meeting one, bonding, deciding to marry, having sex, getting pregnant, having a child and raising a child is not a linear one. While there may be a culturally approved order to some of these things, there isn't a biologically approved order—pregnancy, for instance, can come before marriage or even bonding. Sex, both procreative and non-procreative, is a vital part of almost every part of the process both before and after pregnancy. For instance, non-procreative sexual activity allows a couple to explore their compatibility and willingness to bond. After childbirth it creates a bond between the couple that improves the chances that they will remain together to raise the children. In using sex for purposes other than procreation, there is the risk of pregnancy even when birth control is used. A pregnancy forces a decision about whether the pregnancy helps or hurts the reproductive strategies that the man and woman are pursuing.

Every woman must assess her reproductive options depending on her situation and environment. Society may have one view of what a proper reproductive strategy may be, but individual members of society often have their own quite different strategies. There is huge variation in the age when women have their children and whether they do it when married or not. In the United States poor, inner city women, especially African-American and Hispanic women, have shown a tendency to have their children earlier than white women and to have them out of wedlock. The teenage pregnancy "problem" and the single-parent "problem" have been the subject of much social and political commentary over the last quarter century. What has been less discussed is whether this pattern reflects a reproductive strategy by those teens and young women who have poor health and face shorter life expectancies than other women, whose parents also face shorter life expectancies, and who may face increased medical risks if they give birth later. The moral of the story is that, despite what various cultures say, there is no single formula or pathway for reproductive success in life. It all depends on the totality of one's situation and the environment. Reproductive success comes from taking control and doing the best one can under one's circumstances.

I believe that humanity has reproduced successfully by not leaving reproduction to chance or to nature and by exercising as much control over it as possible. Humans succeed reproductively when they keep one eye on the environment in which they find themselves and when they strategize at every turn to meet their biological goals. Birth control and abortion are nothing more than strategies that humans use to increase their chances of reproductive success, which I define as having children who will survive in the particular environment and who will in turn reproduce successfully. The battle of the sexes is all about the control of reproduction. Each sex strategizes and fights to attain its own reproductive goals. Humanity, indeed all animals, has evolved because of this battle. It is for humanity's benefit that there is this battle. Successful reproduction also requires a great degree of male/female cooperation, especially in parenting. Men and women insure the survival of the human race when they strategize, compete, cooperate, and try to control their reproduction.

This chapter will explore many of the aspects of the reproductive process and the role of sex in human evolution. We have and need reproductive strategies in order to run the gauntlet that evolution has created for us. Reproduction isn't easy, either biologically or culturally. There are many different cultural systems on our planet relating to male/female relationships, marriage, reproduction, and child-rearing. Despite the variety of these systems and their greater or lesser formal and informal restrictions on reproductive freedom, I believe that women and men have found the way in most cases to exercise the reproductive freedom they need in order to have their children survive and prosper.

Professors Russil Durrant and Bruce J. Ellis of the University of Canterbury, New Zealand, outlined the alternative strategies for reproductive success and the trade-offs involved:

> There are essentially three strategies that individuals can use to increase their reproductive success: (a) Increase the fitness of their offspring by mating with individuals of high genetic quality, (b) increase the fitness of their offspring by enhancing parental investment (by one or both parents), or (c) increase the number of offspring produced. No one strategy is inherently better than any other, and the pursuit of one strategy usually involves trade-offs with the others. . . . For example, individuals who produce a greater number of offspring (c) tend to have lower fitness of offspring.

Thus, reproductive success does not necessarily come from having as many children as possible. As Professor Bobbi S. Low of the University of Michigan has said: "Yet despite our complexity, this simple observation is true: those of us alive today are the descendants of those that successfully survived and reproduced in past environments. . . . Fertility is complex. Although a simplistic interpretation might imply that the best strategy is to produce as many offspring as possible as soon as possible, this is seldom, in fact, a winning strategy even for relatively nonsocial animals."

## Why Evolution Means Survival for Most But Not All

Humans are biological creatures. We are a species of animal, although a very special animal. We have the ability to exercise much control over our behaviors, reproductive and otherwise. We don't act solely on innate instincts. All animals, including humans, have the innate instinct to survive and reproduce and must do both within the confines of the particular environment where they live. The animals and humans that possess the traits that enable them to adapt better to their environment will survive and reproduce more than those who adapt less well. These innate traits that increase adaptability to a particular environment are passed down to the offspring of the individuals who have them and enable the offspring in turn to adapt and survive. Traits are passed on by genes. The genes of both parents are randomly mixed in sexual reproduction. Genes interact with the environment in complex ways. The passing down of traits is inexact and often inefficient. But it seems to work. It is part of the process of natural selection, resulting in what Darwin called the survival of the fittest in his theory of evolution that he formulated in the mid–nineteenth century. Evolution benefits the species but not necessarily each individual.

Darwin saw evolution in action when he saw that the traits of certain species of animals in particular environments changed from generation to generation due to the forces of natural selection. Darwin hypothesized that each individual animal within a species has a unique collection of traits, and that some traits will, depending on the environment, enable the individuals that possess them to survive and reproduce better than those who do not have them. These advantageous traits, having been passed down through sexual reproduction to the descendants of the individual who had them, became more prevalent as the generations progressed. As a result some animals evolved to have longer beaks, a different color, or a different shape. Later scientists have concluded that social systems and cultures within which species live have also evolved and adapted. For instance, some animals have evolved to live alone and others to live in groups, some above ground and some in water, all for reasons of survival.

Science has since discovered that the advantageous traits for survival are passed down from generation to generation by genes. Darwin didn't know about genes—they weren't discovered until much later—but he had the theory right. Genes can make an animal taller or smaller, faster or slower, with fur or a hide, or with better or worse eyesight or hearing. Besides transmitting anatomical characteristics, genes transmit behavioral characteristics as well, such as instinct and coordination. When the animals with whatever characteristics enable them to survive and reproduce actually do survive and reproduce, these genes are likely to go to their progeny and so on. Those animals with the characteristics that inhibit survival and reproduction won't be able to do either, and those animals will eventually die out. It cannot be known in advance which genes are which. It isn't always the fastest or strongest or the animal with the best eyesight that survives. Look at the turtle, with no such traits, which has survived, or the bonobo (our closest genetic relative), with almost all of them, which is nearing extinction.

Genes are not cloned or copied when we have children. The transmission of traits via our genes to our children is an inexact process. A random selection of a man and a woman's genes are commingled in the process of conception. In addition, genes are subject to mutation in the reproductive process and by exposure to toxic chemicals in the environment. The random mixing of genes in sexual reproduction and genetic mutations create the enormous genetic diversity in the human population. The result, as every parent knows, is that every child of theirs is different. Just because one or both parents have a characteristic does not mean that the child will.

Some traits, such as eye color and blood type, are transmitted to our children by a single gene. So are some diseases such as Tay-Sachs and sickle-cell anemia and thousands of others. The vast majority of traits, behaviors, and diseases are passed on by multiple genes, including traits such as height, speed, and an aggressive nature. These genes interact with and are affected by environmental factors such as climate, nutrition, and exposure to chemicals. Poor diet can stunt the normal growth that a gene might have otherwise indicated. Genes also co-evolve with other genes that they encounter in the body, society, and culture in which they exist.

The passing down of the genetic traits necessary for survival and successful reproduction is an inexact business. It is neither simple nor predictable nor efficient. The process of natural selection seems wasteful. Why does nature subject our "good" genes to the random process of sexual reproduction and to mutation? Why does nature allow for individuals carrying a gene for a fatal disease to survive and reproduce? It would seem that cloning the fittest individuals would be much more efficient. The genes that made the person adapt and survive would pass down intact to their progeny. Why do we take the risk of mixing our genes with someone else's?

## Through the Genetic Looking Glass: Sex and the Red Queen

Humanity is programmed to have a lot of sex. Sex accelerates human evolution by enabling beneficial traits to become more widespread in the population and by more efficiently reducing harmful traits. In a competitive environment with many parasites, this is essential for human survival. Humanity is in a co-evolutionary race with pathogens for survival. Sexual reproduction creates the enormous genetic variety in the human population and makes it more difficult for a pathogen to adapt to us and kill us. Sex is more than fun. It is how life survives and propagates itself. It is no accident that we use sex to reproduce ourselves. Most species, including all mammals, do. It is the rare animal that reproduces by cloning itself. The whiptail lizard species is one; it is an all-female species that reproduces by cloning eggs. Amoebas also reproduce by cloning. Like the amoeba, almost all asexual species are small in size, have short life spans, and may live in stable environments. For larger animals, including humans, sexual reproduction is the norm. The species that reproduce sexually evolved differently from those that reproduce asexually. These separate evolutionary paths must have been necessary for the survival of both kinds of species in their different environments.

The asexual species are missing out on one of life's great pleasures. Psychologist Steven Pinker of the Massachusetts Institute of Technology says that humans aren't programmed by evolution to reproduce but rather are programmed to like sex and little children. These two instincts combine to make for successful reproduction. Whether we are programmed to reproduce or to enjoy sex, we have evolved to have a lot of sex, and not always for the purpose of reproduction. Early in our history we may not have known that sex and reproduction were connected. At whatever time we learned that sex led to reproduction, we also learned they were separable. Besides having non-vaginal sex, humans, for instance, have sex while a woman is pregnant and after a woman reaches menopause and can't have children. We have sex throughout a woman's reproductive cycle when she is not ovulating. We have sex with members of the same sex. Other than being pleasurable, are there reasons why we have a lot of sex? Some other animals don't have any sex other than reproductive sex. They have sex with fertile partners of the opposite sex only at those times when the act is likely to result in pregnancy.

So why all the sex?

There are two basic arguments for the advantages of sex. Gabriela

Ochoa and Klaus Jaffe, professors at the Universidad Simon Bolivar, stated: "Sex is adaptive in variable environments because it enables the rapid spread and creation of advantageous traits. Second, there are the mutation-accumulation models, which suggest that sex is adaptive because it performs the efficient removal of deleterious genes." In other words, sex spreads good genes and wipes out bad genes efficiently.

Evolutionary theory suggests that we are here because our ancestors picked the right people with whom to have sex and have children, who survived to do the same. If you don't survive childhood to have sex, then you don't reproduce. Your genetic makeup has a lot to do whether you survive childhood or not. Some young people die in accidents, environmental calamity, or battle, some of starvation, but a lot die of infectious disease. Infectious diseases are caused by parasites like viruses or bacteria. There are a multitude of them, many of them deadly. Why haven't germs and diseases succeeded in killing us all? Why didn't the black plague in the 1400s or the flu epidemic in 1918 kill everyone on the planet? Why hasn't malaria or HIV/AIDS?

Many evolutionary biologists believe that it is humanity's immense genetic variety that saves it from extinction at the hands of viruses. Sexual reproduction has saved humanity by creating genetically diverse humans, each of whom has different abilities to resist different parasites. Sexual reproduction enables humanity over time to constantly recombine genetically. The process of evolution through natural selection means that those genetic traits that resist pathogens and promote survival will become more common in the human race. The genes that help the body to survive a parasite are passed on via sexual reproduction along with the body's other genes to each succeeding generation.

Parasites can survive and reproduce only when they overcome the defenses of their host. In the case of malaria or HIV, the host is a human being. For other parasites the host is another species of animal. Each species has its own parasites. The unique and infinite variety of genes in each person makes it harder for a single parasite to penetrate our immune system, to adapt to us, live off us, spread to another individual, and kill us. If we had no genetic variety, that is, reproduced asexually, then it would be easier for a single pathogen to evolve to do all this. Pathogens are subject to the same forces of natural selection as humans are. Those traits that enable the parasite to survive, such as the ability to penetrate an immune system, will be passed down as the pathogen reproduces.

Biologists developed the "Red Queen Theory," a term coined by writer Matt Ridley, to explain why parasites don't succeed in killing us all. In Lewis Carroll's *Through the Looking Glass*, the Red Queen takes Alice on a long run that ends up where they began. The Red Queen explains: "Now, here, you see, it takes all the running you can do, to keep in the same place. If you want to get somewhere else, you must run at least twice as fast as that."

As Ochoa and Jaffe described the theory, "The Red Queen hypothesis states that sex is an adaptation to escape from parasites." Humans and viruses are co-evolving. Humans evolve through sexual reproduction in response to the attacks of parasites; the germs and viruses themselves evolve to try to penetrate the human body's defenses. Pathogens reproduce asexually and quickly, and any variation comes from mutation, as we have seen most recently with mutations in HIV. Humans reproduce slowly and sexually, but have in their favor their size and genetic variety and thus their complex immune systems. Just as humans who survive will pass on their pathogen-fighting genes to their next generation, so too will the parasites that survive the human immune system pass on their adaptive abilities to their next generation. Human beings and parasites are each trying to adapt to and outwit the other and survive. In a process of co-evolution the host (us) and parasite (the flu, for example) evolve together with neither side ultimately winning, and in fact, both ending up where they began, like Alice and the Red Queen, in a form of equilibrium—both alive and both continuously evolving and fighting each other.

This state of affairs is not one of "peaceful coexistence," as some have described it. Rather, evolutionary biologist Paul Ewald of the University of Louisville, Kentucky, and others have called co-evolution a "sexual arms race" (also somewhat of a misnomer since pathogens don't reproduce by having sex), with each side trying to outwit and outgun the other. Sometimes one side or the other wins, as when a disease like polio is conquered or, alternatively, when a disease conquers us the way smallpox did with Native Americans. It is rare for one side or the other to win completely. Life in all its forms, human and otherwise, has evolved to survive. Sexual reproduction is nature's way of giving humanity resistance to pathogens and insuring that the pathogens don't win the arms race.

The arms race can be illustrated by the evolution of human hair. Our ape ancestors were covered in hair, we are not. While some anthropologists believe we gradually lost our hair when we moved out of the jungle into the hot sun of the African plains, others believe that we lost our hair "to reduce our vulnerability to fur-loving parasites." Professor Mark Pagel, a professor of evolutionary biology at the University of Redding, England, and Sir Walter Bodmer of Oxford University pointed out that only seven of the more than 5,000 mammals are virtually hairless—the elephant, the rhinoceros, the hippopotamus, the pig, the walrus, the whale, and the naked mole rat. Pagel and Bodmer believe that humans as they evolved developed the ability to build fires and make clothes to keep warm. Fur then became a harmful luxury; it was a place where parasites could live, breed, and infect us. "Hairlessness would have allowed humans to convincingly 'advertise' their reduced susceptibility to parasitic infection and this trait became desirable in a mate," said Pagel. In a process of co-evolution with culture and with fur-loving parasites, those humans who had less hair had fewer parasites and thus survived longer, were selected by the opposite sex more, and reproduced more.

While the Red Queen theory has a large following among biologists, there are those who do not feel it is the complete explanation. Ochoa and Jaffe, for instance, argued that mating strategies also contribute to the development of what they call "optimal genetic configurations." Mating is not random, nor thus is the mixing of genes. Females and males choose mates who have "good genes" and will avoid mating with those who carry "bad genes." Bad genes will thus be more likely to disappear from the population. This non-random mating through sex is a vital component of human evolution. Sex in fact acts to accelerate evolution. Sex can efficiently create favorable adaptations and delete unfavorable traits.

Michael E. N. Majerus, professor of genetics at Cambridge University, in his book *Sex Wars: Genes, Bacteria and Biased Sex Ratios*, argued that the method of reproduction a species uses, either sexual or asexual, depends on the environment. He calculated the difference in the mutation rate between sexually and asexually reproducing species:

> The chance of two advantageous mutations occurring in the same individual is approximately 250 times greater in the sexual population than if reproduction is asexual. Here, then, we have a situation in which, if a population is faced with a changing environment and needs to adapt if it is to survive, sexual reproduction is advantageous over asexual reproduction. This is simply because sex leads to more rapid generation of a wide array of variants, some of which may be able to cope with the new circumstances.

Others argue, as Majerus explained, that "the advantage of sex lies in the removal of deleterious mutations." This is harder when a species reproduces asexually—the mutation continues unless it itself mutates. Sexual reproduction permits two individuals, "each carrying a different harmful mutation . . . by breeding together, (to) produce some progeny that are free of both mutations. The optimal class is thus continuously reconstituted."

Majerus concluded:

> Both types of hypothesis outlined above involve the fitness of populations. In the first, sex increases the adaptability of the population in a changing environment. In the second, sex prevents a gradual reduction in the fitness of the population by providing a mechanism by which individuals free from harmful mutations can be produced and, due to their high fitness, then be selectively favored. The bottom line is that sexual populations are likely to be longer lived than asexual populations.
>
> . . .
>
> We have already seen that sex increases the rate of evolution. It then follows that for species in highly competitive situations, faced not only

with competition for resources but also with a range of predators and parasites, sexual lineages will do better than asexual ones.

Sex is part of not only mating and the evolutionary process, but also the social life of the species. Male and female sex roles are not necessarily fixed in stone by biology. As biologist Joan Roughgarten of Stanford University said, traditionally men were depicted "as promiscuous and females as coy and discerning." Biologists no longer see this as an entirely valid stereotype for either sex. Sexual activity is used for more than propagation, said Roughgarten. It is a part of social bonding where individuals gain allies in the fight for survival: "Much of the sexual behavior observed in animals is not designed to propagate genes, at least not directly, but to make the protagonist socially acceptable to a powerful clique, thus ensuring him or her access to potential mates and a safe environment." Roughgarten called this "social selection" for social inclusion, which in turn can lead to reproductive success.

Sex and sexual reproduction are strategies that nature has given humanity to enable it to survive and evolve. Sex protects us against pathogens and accelerates humanity's evolution by more quickly reducing bad genes and more quickly spreading good genes throughout the population. Sex is also used for social inclusion. But aside from these evolutionary benefits, at the human level sex creates children. How we create children is not a random process. Humans have to use sex strategically to get the children they want.

## Everyone Is a Reproductive Strategist

Sex is not just a method for reproduction; it is a method of quality reproduction. It is a vital component of human survival by enabling the transmission of pathogen-resistant genes through the generations and by accelerating evolution in difficult environments. In order for genes that carry traits for disease protection to be transferred via sex, two people need to meet, decide to mate, have sex, get pregnant, have a child, and parent that child until it reproduces and even thereafter. Males and females each have choices and trade-offs at every step of this process. These choices include the choices encompassed by what I call reproductive freedom—the choice whether or not to get pregnant and whether or not to have a child. Males and females, because of their different biologies, will tend to analyze their reproductive options differently and will use different strategies to attain their reproductive goals. The trade-offs occur because the time, energy and resources spent in one part of the reproductive process inevitably take away from those necessary for another part. Thus, for instance, time spent on raising a child takes away from the time available for finding a new mate.

A reproductive strategy is a compilation of behaviors, conscious and subconscious, instinctual and deliberate, that a male or female will engage in at every stage of the reproductive process so that they will have successful offspring who will in turn successfully reproduce. Everyone has a reproductive strategy. Men and women often pursue strategies that they don't even know are such. They cannot be verbalized. As anthropologist Lionel Tiger of Rutgers University has said:

> . . . there is firm evidence that people, like other mammals, take actions they may not understand, to achieve reproductive ends they may not foresee or even consciously desire.

We engage in a reproductive strategy when we choose a mate and when we compete to get a mate to choose us. We engage in a reproductive strategy when we decide about engaging in sexual activity, getting pregnant, having children and in how we parent them. How males and females view their options and tend to behave in these situations, just like other human activities and behaviors, are passed on by genes.

We do not have procreative sex haphazardly with just anyone of the opposite sex, just as we don't marry just anyone of the opposite sex. In general men and women mutually select each other as mates, even though in some cultures parents select their children's mates. Rape followed by childbearing remains a relatively rare, but nonetheless abhorrent, exception. What anthropologists call "pair bonding" is the rule for humans, but lifelong monogamy is most definitely not. As Rutgers University anthropologist Helen Fisher said:

> Human mating has some general rules: women and men from western Siberia to the southern tip of South America marry. Many leave each other. Many depart around the fourth year after wedding. Many leave when they are young. Many divorce with a single child. And many remarry once again.

Sexual selection theory says that the biological differences of males and females will lead them to use different criteria in making the decision to reproduce with someone. The members of each sex who are selected by the other sex to reproduce will pass on whatever characteristics they have that the other sex liked to their progeny. These characteristics could include such things as coloring, size, or speed. The animal kingdom, of which humans are a part, has an immense variety of mating systems.

Sex differences between males and females can lead to different mating strategies. Men and women will each pursue both long-term and short-term mating strategies, that is to say, marriages and affairs. This appears universal. One study done in 2003 of over 16,000 people in fifty-two nations on six continents and thirteen islands found that "sex differences in the desire for sexual variety are cross-culturally universal." The difference was that "when men pursue short-term mates they desire large numbers of partners and are generally quick to consent to sex, whereas when women pursue short-term mates they appear motivated more by partner quality than by partner quantity." David P. Schmitt of Bradley University, the author of the study, believed this difference was the result of the difference in parental investment that each sex makes in their children and that in humans women traditionally make more parental investment than men do.

Whether males or females are pursuing a long-term or short-term mating strategy, they can attain reproductive success only when they are selected by members of the opposite sex to reproduce. Success is not measured as a couple, it is measured individually for each male and female, when they pass their genes down to the next generation. Reproduction is competitive on many levels because success is so uncertain. There is no guarantee that a person will be in a position to chose a mate or will be chosen. There is no guarantee that, if they have a child, the child will survive. If there are limited resources, they must compete for resources so that they and their children will survive. At every level those with the most successful strategy will win, reproduce and survive. As Bobbi S. Low wrote, "Individuals that use efficient strategies produce more offspring for the next generation than their competitors." But since biological success can only be attained by combining one's genes with the genes of another person, this means that success will come by adopting strategies that take into account the strategies of potential mates as well as competitors. Each partner must select a mate, and in turn be selected by that mate, whose genes will mix well with one's own and who will produce viable offspring.

It cannot be emphasized enough that men and women have different reproductive interests along with their common ones, such as both wanting their children to survive in good health and to in turn have children. And the common interests may not coincide with an individual man or woman's interest in having a particular offspring or having the most offspring survive into the next generation. An individual man's best reproductive strategy at a particular point in time may not be the same as his current mate's and vice versa.

As *New York Times* reporter Natalie Angier said in her book *Woman*:

"Human mating systems are characterized by conflict from start to finish." . . . The thesis of sexual dialectics is that females and males vie for control over the means of reproduction. Those means are the female body, for there is as yet no such beast as the parthenogenic man. Women are under selective pressure to maintain control of their reproduction, to choose with whom they will mate and with whom they will not—to exercise female choice. If they make bad mating decisions, they will have less viable offspring than if they are clever in their choices. Men are under selective pressure to make sure they're chosen or, barring that, to subvert female choice and coerce the female to mate against her will. "That dynamism cannot possibly result in a unitary response. . . ." (p. 342)

What Angier is saying is that the forces of natural selection affect the mating behavior of both males and females. If you don't get selected to mate, then your genes die out. Our genes have evolved to survive and not die out, and males and females will fight among each other and compete with each other to be sure that this doesn't happen. The battle of the sexes is real. The battle occurs, and men and women will have different reproductive strategies, before, during, and after sex.

## The Battle of the Sexes – Choosing the Right Mate

Winning the battle of the sexes for control of reproduction is more important to women than to men because only women bear the health risks of pregnancy and childbearing. Reproductive freedom, the freedom to decide with whom to have a child and under what circumstances, is therefore more important to women than men. Females need more control over the reproductive process than males do in order to be biologically successful. The female need for control begins way before a woman has sex with her mate.

The importance for females to control the reproductive process comes from the risk to a woman's life and health from carrying a pregnancy, giving birth and nursing the child. Pregnancy, childbearing, and nursing take significant time and energy for the mother. Only women die in childbearing. When a woman dies, her children are more likely to die. Natural selection favored those women who minimized these risks, survived childbearing and successfully raised their children. The women who did not failed to pass on their genes.

There is always a trade-off for men and women between current and future reproduction. The time and energy that men and women put into pregnancy, nursing, and parenting take away from future reproduction and constitute their "parental investment" in the child.

Human children need a massive amount of parental investment to survive and mature. Initially this comes largely from the mother, even though males can make a significant contribution by providing for a pregnant and nursing mother. Males and females can parent equally after birth and after the child is weaned. Each can provide warmth, shelter, food, nurturing, education, and survival skills, that is to say, resources. While it may seem obvious to us why we need parental investment in our children, the extraordinary amount required for human children is the exception rather than the rule among animals. Human children are helpless at birth and for a long time thereafter. They can't walk for a year and haven't the stamina for extensive walking, as any parent knows, for years thereafter. They can't feed themselves for years. They have much to learn to become functioning adults, aside from the formal education required in the modern world. Social skills, survival skills, and work skills are all complex and take years to develop, as does the sexual maturity necessary for that child to reproduce.

For those individuals who want to have children, a mate is more than a life companion. Having the right mate is important in ensuring the health and viability of one's children. Everything else being equal, a man and a woman will choose a mate who can provide parental investment, along with the other things that come with mating, such as companionship, emotional bonding, and happiness. But things aren't equal because of the significant parental investment the female makes in pregnancy, childbirth, and nursing and because of the fact that she cannot get pregnant again immediately. Females can only have one reproductive success at a time. Men are able to have multiple reproductive successes going simultaneously. Both males and females, however, want biologically to maximize their healthy offspring. The chances of this are increased when both make the parental investment necessary to insure that the child survives and prospers.

Males have more options here. Males can reproduce more readily than females because they don't get pregnant or nurse, a process that can take years. Men can use the time that they would otherwise spend parenting searching for a new mate. This is the biological trade-off that males weigh in making their parental investment decision. Because males make less initial parental investment in their offspring, have more immediate opportunities to parent again, and have, historically, until recently never been able to ascertain that they are in fact the genetic father of their children, males are more likely to not parent their children. Females thus run a greater risk of being abandoned to bring up their children alone. Men have to balance their chances of finding another mate against the risks to their child if they abandon that child for the quest.

Because the mother makes significant parental investment before and after birth, it is harder for women to abandon a current pregnancy for an uncertain future one. This is why women rarely abandon their children to have other children. It is as if the mother and father decide to build a house, but the work of digging and building the foundation is left entirely to the mother. After years of labor it is unlikely that she will abandon the project and start on a new house with a new "partner." She will finish the job with whatever help the father brings.

It is thus usually, though not always, the decision of the father whether or not the child will be brought up by one parent or both. The mother, because of the heavy investment she has already made in the child, will rarely abandon that child. This biological reality leads females to be more strategic and choosier about their mating partners. They want someone who will not only remain with them but who will also help with the upbringing of the progeny. Therefore, women choose mates not only for their favorable genetic characteristics, but also for their favorable parenting characteristics.

Being choosy about their mates has downsides for females. While women benefit from choosing the fittest males possible, there is a cost in lost time and energy in the search. There is a risk of violence from the rejected males. The press carries stories of violence against women from jilted lovers on a daily basis. A woman also faces the risk of contracting a sexually transmitted disease if she has sex with potential mates. The species may benefit from women having multiple partners because of the increased genetic variety of the children produced, but the risks to individual women who employ this strategy are real and substantial. There are also risks to her current children if she takes a new mate into her life. There is a far greater risk of violence against children from stepfathers than from fathers. As anthropologist Sara Blaffer Hrdy, of the University of California at Davis, has stated, a woman's "reproductive success depends not on the number of fertilizations but on the contingencies of her life, the qualities of the mates she chooses, and, above all, how successful she is at keeping alive such infants as she does produce."

Females of different cultures use a variety of strategies for accomplishing these goals. In cultures where women have traditionally had fewer resources than men and may need resources other than their own to survive and raise a family, women, or their parents choosing on their behalf, have tended to select mates with superior material, financial, or social resources. In cultures where there is more community or more female wealth, male wealth is less of a factor. In the modern world, as in the ancient, men have more economic resources than women. This is changing slowly, but is still true. Men for a variety of reasons still earn more than women, and it is not irrational for women to look for an income even greater than their own to enable themselves and their children to survive and prosper. As Hrdy wrote, "When female status and access to resources do not depend on her mate's status, women will likely use a range of criteria, not primarily or even necessarily prestige and wealth, for mate selection."

Mate selection based on desirable sexual and social characteristics is vital to men and women but is more important to women. Each sex looks for a mate with resources, broadly defined. The willingness of the male to parent and a male's ability to protect and provide are important parts of a female's calculus, unless she is able to survive and parent alone. The resources part of the female reproductive strategy, and the corresponding male strategy to accumulate resources, is a reflection of unequal economic and social status and different biology. This can and has changed as the world has changed. What has not changed is that each sex has a different strategy because of their differing biology. This is not biological determinism. It is only to state that biology makes mate selection a more important issue for women than men. It does not say that women cannot be biologically successful if they make a less-than-optimal mate choice or if they choose to parent alone. Different cultures and environments can lead to vastly different reproductive patterns: while in Japan almost no births are to single women, in the United States one-third of births are, and in Iceland two-thirds are.

Mate selection is an essential part of an individual's reproductive strategy. Because women bear the health risks of pregnancy and invest more in a child, at least initially, women must choose their mates carefully. They need support from the man during pregnancy and after childbirth, and they need the man to parent the child. Women have fewer reproductive opportunities than men, and a man, if his only interest is biological success, may leave sooner rather than later to find another mate. This can be harmful to the woman and her children. A woman needs to strategize to prevent this from happening and to keep herself and her children alive. Each sex is battling for reproductive control and success. A large part of reproductive success comes from choosing someone with a compatible genetic makeup.

## How to Find the Right Genetic Mate — Diving into the Gene Pool with Our Eyes Closed

The genetic selection component of mate selection is largely unconscious, but no less important than the other components. Parents with dissimilar genetic immune codes are more likely to have children who will survive and be healthy. In this sense dissimilar genetic parents are more compatible than those with similar genetic codes. This is why close relatives who have similar genetic codes are discouraged from having children. Humans and other animals send off hidden signals that communicate their genetic immune code. While this is no guarantee that successful mating will result, all indicators are that humanity evolved to be able to detect these signals and therefore to increase its chance of reproductive success.

Choosing the right mate involves more than assessing the resources and parenting abilities of a potential partner. A successful reproductive strategy requires women and men to assess each other's health and genetic compatibility. To keep up in the race against the Red Queen a couple needs to produce genetically fit children. Genetically fit children come from genetically compatible parents. Finding a mate who is genetically compatible is no easy task. Resources and parenting abilities are easier to identify than good health and genes. The physical appearance of potential mates can reveal much about their strength or general state of health. Studies indicate both that facial symmetry is an accurate health indicator and that woman and men in fact specifically look for symmetry in a potential mate's facial features.

But how do we assess a potential partner's genetic fitness? How does a woman know a man will be a good genetic match for her? Evolution has equipped us with some tools to increase our chances of mating with people with compatible genes–not identical genes, compatible genes. Compatible genes are those that will mix well with one's mate at conception and that will create genetic strength in our offspring. The portion of the human genome that relates to disease resistance and sexual attraction is the major histocompatibility complex (MHC). Scientists have concluded that couples having dissimilar MHC's will produce the strongest offspring genetically.

Why is MHC important? Manfred Milinski and Claus Wedekind of the University of Bern, Switzerland, who have done extensive research on the subject, stated:

Why do mice and humans prefer to mate with MHC-dissimilar individuals? The preference will increase the MHC heterozygosity of an individual's progeny.... MHC heterozygotes could be resistant to infections of multiple parasites; they might provide a moving target to rapidly evolving pathogens; they might reduce inbreeding by increasing overall genetic heterozygosity, which is likely to increase disease resistance.

In other words, MHC heterozygosity keeps our children in the Red Queen's race. Since we don't know our own MHC status, much less that of a potential mate, how do we match ourselves with someone to get the maximum MHC benefits for our children? Our bodies silently telegraph the information. Our body odor routinely conveys information about our MHC to the outside world, including to any potential mates out there. Our senses, including our sense of smell, are telling us that someone is a good genetic catch when we feel attracted to them or are swept off our feet. Studies indicate that females in general are more attentive to scent in the first place, their own and others. So it would seem that if any sex were to be picking up genetic clues from smells it would be the female. This makes sense since females have to be choosier in mate selection.

In trying to measure what the effect body odor has on mate selection Professor Wedekind and other scientists at the University of Bern devised a series of experiments in 1994 involving a group of men and women whose MHC had been chemically analyzed before the experiment began. The men were asked to wear the same t-shirt for two days and nights in a row and to avoid activities that might alter their natural odor, like bathing, wearing deodorant, being around a pet, having sex, or eating spicy food. The t-shirts were collected, and the women were then asked to smell and evaluate the t-shirts for pleasantness and sexiness. The women generally preferred for both pleasantness and sexiness the t-shirts worn by men with dissimilar MHC than their own, thereby indicating that genetic opposites do indeed attract. Professor Wedekind concluded that MHC opposites attract for a reason—better disease resistance in one's offspring. There are also better pregnancy outcomes. Many studies have confirmed that couples with similar MHC suffer from more spontaneous abortions and have children with lower birth weight than couples with dissimilar MHC.

Many scientists have come to believe that genetic information is telegraphed to the outside world not only by our body odors but also by our pheromones. Pheromones are airborne chemicals that are undetectable by the human sense of smell but are unconsciously detected by certain sensors in our brains. Scientists have established what every dog owner knows: that many animals use pheromones to send information about territoriality and sex. Recent experiments have shown humans also send out pheromones conveying genetic and sexual information. A 2001 study in Sweden found that pheromones, unlike smells, are sensed equally by men and women, but that they convey different information to each sex. Scientists at Huddinge University used a PET scan to examine the brains of men and women while the subjects "smelled" synthetic odorless versions of estrogen and testosterone. The presence of estrogen caused the men to have increased blood flow in the part of the brain that other animals use for pheromone detection. The presence of testosterone caused the same reaction for women. Estrogen caused no measurable brain response in the women, and testosterone likewise did nothing for the men. Despite the work of these and other researchers, there is still no consensus in the scientific community how pheromones work or what exactly they communicate, if anything. All these mysteries are still to be uncovered.

All this is to say that mate selection is neither random nor entirely conscious or rational. But evolution has created a system with a purpose. And that purpose is human survival. Presumably for each of us there are lots of potential mates who give off the right smells or pheromones, thereby indicating that they have compatible, that is, dissimilar, MHC's genes to ours, and that it is likely that one would have healthy, genetically fit children with them. Naturally there is no certainty here. A woman cannot be sure even by using all her senses that her prospective mate will combine with her to produce children who are healthy with good resistance to pathogens. But our sense of smell and our ability to detect pheromones do convey something. They form the basis of attraction. Successful reproduction depends on both sexes assessing their potential mates for genetic compatibility, as well as for resources, parenting ability, and compatibility. Control of mate choice is vital then on many counts. It is an essential part of reproductive freedom. Reproductive success depends on it.

The reproductive process we have described until now all takes place before there is any sex. It is an uncertain and competitive process, and there are no guarantees that the strategies, mating rituals, and fights that humans engage in and the signals they exchange will result in reproductive success. The battle of the sexes for control of reproduction is rigged so that neither sex wins all the time. The selection of a mate is the first event of the Darwinian process. Each sex fights to choose and get chosen. If your strategy is successful, your genes get passed down. If you are not successful, your genes don't get passed down. A good result is not biologically guaranteed just because you picked a mate with the right resources, genes, MHC, and parenting abilities, and the one you picked consented to mate with you. The person might be the wrong mate. Your children may not inherit the right combination of your and your mate's genes—that part of the reproductive process remains random. The children might be susceptible to pathogens and lose the race to the Red Queen and die early. All we can do is trust our instincts, strategize, fight the battle, control the variables we can, and do the best we can under the circumstances.

These same rules apply after a couple has sex and gets pregnant. A pregnancy is no guarantee of reproductive success. It may be at the wrong time with what turns out to be the wrong person. A woman's control over her options becomes even more crucial at this point.

## Reproductive Strategies in Bed—Why We Have a Lot of Sex and Why We Use Don't Always Use Birth Control

Males and females have evolved to control whether or not sexual activity leads inexorably to pregnancy and reproduction. This evolution occurred for the most part even before the invention of artificial birth control and surgical abortion. Our species arose about 3 million years ago, and the first written mention of artificial birth control found to date was in about 1850 BCE. It seems likely that most of human evolution occurred before its discovery. It is also likely that humans discovered that they could control their fertility through other means long before then. Humans, women especially, survived and evolved because they took control of their fertility. Women had to time and space childbirth in order to survive. High mortality for women in childbirth and for children born too close together or poorly nourished insured that they would not be favored by the forces of natural selection. Eons ago, human females evolved to become the first, and maybe last, of the sexually reproducing species to be able to consistently refuse to have sex while she ovulated. This was the first exercise of women's reproductive freedom.

While extended nursing provided some protection against pregnancies occurring too close together, this method was not foolproof, and women had to devise other methods to insure proper spacing of children. Women in tribes that migrated with the seasons or in search of food especially had to time their deliveries for a time when they were not traveling. When I was in the Philippines in the early 1990s, local health workers reported that there were tribes that migrated each year on a set schedule from one hunting ground to another and that they needed to time their births accordingly. The tribal women used with some effectiveness contraceptives made from various teas brewed from rattan roots and other native plants. Women in poor health, which included probably everyone in pre-modern days, had to preserve their strength to provide for the children they already had. In all these cases pregnancy control was literally a matter of life and death for both mother and child.

The central reproductive tension between men and women is that the length of a pregnancy and the extensive parenting required for the human child after birth took away opportunities for women more than men to have additional children, at least immediately. This conflict is especially acute for women because they are less robust during pregnancy and nursing. It is therefore in their interest to select men as partners who not only had the right genetic stuff but who also would commit to protecting and providing for the women and children at least until they could survive on their own. A woman and man often see that it is generally in their reproductive joint interest to stay together to parent their children. Natural selection may have favored children that had two parents protecting them rather than one. One strategy to cement the parenting relationship was to maximize the parents' sexual activity together without the risk of another pregnancy too soon.

Non-procreative sexual activities flourished in evolutionary terms because they kept parents together to raise their children. The use of birth control became a reproductive strategy to both prevent and aid reproduction. Non-procreative sexual activity and the use of birth control became prevalent, as did other successful reproductive strategies, because they assisted the successful transmission of genes to the next generation. For humanity, the use of controls on fertility have worked to provide reproductive success.

Having sex before committing to a potential mate is not risk-free. Not only is there risk of violence if the woman rejects the man but the woman puts herself at risk of pregnancy and of contracting a sexually transmitted disease. In the United States over 80 percent, perhaps over 90 percent, of men and women have sex before marriage. This practice is almost universal. Given the risks, why do men and women do this? If the goal of the courtship is eventual marriage or reproduction, then engaging in sexual activity before committing to marriage or before desiring to become pregnant is one test of sexual and emotional compatibility for the couple. A good relationship on many levels is necessary for a couple to have the viable partnership necessary for the long-term effort required to bring up children successfully. Sexual compatibility is one vital component of a good relationship. Throughout the world to a greater or lesser extent, couples test for this before marriage. Birth control makes vaginal intercourse possible without significant risk of pregnancy.

Because of the availability of new methods of birth control, a man and a woman can engage in different reproductive strategies while in bed with each other. Some methods of birth control are known only to the woman, and others are known to her sexual partner. Generally, only the woman will know that she is taking an injectable contraceptive such as Depo-Provera, or using an IUD, or taking the pill. There is little telltale evidence. On the other hand the condom, the only male contraceptive method other than sterilization, is presumably known to both partners, as is the female condom. Thus in one sense the female holds the upper hand in reproductive power. The female by use of undetectable contraceptive methods can have intercourse without the possibility of pregnancy and without the male knowing that a method was used. Conversely, she can also say she is using one of these methods of contraception and not in fact be using it. Undetectable contraception allows women to pursue their reproductive strategies more effectively. Some women may prefer to use a method that allows them the flexibility to decide on their own whether or not to risk becoming pregnant at the time of intercourse.

Undetectability of the method and flexibility to strategize in bed are not the only bases on which women choose a method of contraception. For each woman there is a varying mix of personal, financial, and medical factors that can dictate which method of contraception she chooses or is available to her. There is no one method perfect for every woman at every time in her life. Women's choices and flexibility are circumscribed by many factors.

Beyond these difficulties, women encounter cultural messages about appropriate sex and gender roles that can affect their contraceptive decisions. There is a substantial body of opinion that sexual activity is wrong when it takes place outside of marriage. The Catholic Church goes further and says that within marriage sex is permitted only if it is open to procreation ("the conjugal act by its very nature is destined for the begetting of children"—*Casti Connubii*). While these messages are widely ignored by an overwhelming majority of Americans—after all, over 80 percent or 90 percent of Americans have sex before marriage— this condemnation still resonates as part of a long tradition of sexual conservatism in this country. As a result some women and men who engage in sexual activity before marriage, even though they are in the huge majority that do, nevertheless think they are doing something "wrong" or "immoral." As sociologist Kristen Luker of UCLA pointed out, this may result in the woman's failing to seek contraception ahead of time, since planning for sex involves a level of additional wrongdoing. By contrast, if a woman just lets sex happen or falls into it, she can be forgiven for letting her passions get the better of her. Culture, therefore, often gets in the way of women, especially, controlling their reproductive strategy.

Advanced contraceptive planning can also affect the courtship.

When a woman and man decide to have sex, if a "decision" is what it is, then one hopes that a discussion ensues about contraception. We know this does not always happen. A woman's advance preparation for sexual activity is a cultural signal for the man. He may read it positively or negatively depending on his personal views about women and the particular stage of the courtship. The woman may not want to take the risk that her partner would view her negatively if she prepared for sex. Men often put pressure on women, "for religious reasons," they say, not to use contraception. Women, often rightly, view this as an attempt by men to take back some control over pregnancy and to ensure the woman's fidelity. And rather than submit to an endless series of pregnancies, women will use contraception secretly. When Depo-Provera was introduced, it became immediately popular in the Hispanic community in New York where women, who were often pressured by their husbands not to use birth control, could use it without their husbands' knowledge.

The battle of the sexes for control over reproduction continues in bed. While man and women may use sexual activity to determine if their relationship is something that should continue, others use it as a pathway to pregnancy with or without the consent of their partner. Women often find that they are not in complete control over whether or not they get pregnant. Men may demand that their partner not use birth control. Some women will use undetectable contraception in response. Some women will want the flexibility in their method to discontinue it on the spot in order to try to get pregnant without their partner's knowledge. These considerations can lead to patterns of episodic contraception for some women and to a lack of total control over their reproductive options. For medical, cultural, and social reasons, not to mention the cost, time, and hassle in getting contraception, women may forego effective contraception, whether or not they are in a relationship. The conscious, effective pursuit of a reproductive strategy can be trumped by one's culture. An unconscious strategy may result. Just as the choice of mate has many unconscious elements, especially as they relate to genetic compatibility, so too the "choice" to use contraception or not has similar unconscious, or at least cultural, elements that can seriously impact the course the woman takes. The result is that the one point in a person's reproductive strategy where women should be asserting the most control—the time of having sex when they might get pregnant—is often a time when women lack control. Reproductive freedom after pregnancy becomes then even more essential.

## Love Gone Wrong—Reproductive Strategies after Sex

A woman's or man's decision to use or not use contraception is also affected by how each views the costs and benefits of a subsequent pregnancy and by the options they have if they are pregnant to continue the pregnancy or not. The most acute phase of a woman's reproductive strategy occurs after she becomes pregnant. As Professor Kristen Luker said: "It is important to realize that pregnancy is more than a biological occurrence; it is an event of immense social significance."

The biological value of becoming pregnant while courting is that it confirms the woman's fertility, that is to say her ability to become pregnant. It also confirms the man's. The confirmation of fertility is of major importance for both sexes. Pregnancy and childbearing after all are the biological goals of mating. While many couples wait until marriage to see if they can have children, many couples do this before. Historically about one-third of children in America were conceived before marriage, and now one-third are born to single women, some of whom will marry or cohabit with the father.

Pregnancy during courtship performs the function of forcing the couple to commit to the relationship or not. As Kristen Luker stated, a pregnancy "can force a man to think through his conflicting obligations and declare his intentions." It is in a woman's interest to seek this declaration before engaging in sex because of the increased risks she faces. Men have historically been a bit more reluctant at this stage to declare their intentions about their willingness to marry or at least be in a serious, committed relationship. The prospect of having a child brings a whole different level of seriousness to the relationship. It is indeed a time for the man and woman to make a decision. Before legal abortion, the shotgun marriage reigned supreme. In the cases where the man or the woman's parents did not want a marriage, the woman went away to have the child, which was then generally taken away from her and put in a home or put up for adoption.

The legalization of abortion ended this system. Not that there were not plenty of abortions done before legalization, but the health dangers, financial cost, and legal risks were considered too high for many to attempt the procedure. Evidence indicates that legal abortion, which reduced or eliminated these costs, reduced the pressure on the man to commit to marriage. As a result, women were left with the alternatives of having an abortion or having a child as a single mother. But legal abortion also gave the woman the freedom to decide on her commitment to the relationship without the burden of knowing that her only alternative was to be a single mother or to give up their child for adoption. The availability of abortion eliminates the female's risk of having a child before she is ready to commit to the relationship.

I was invited to sit with a nineteen-year-old woman one day in a clinic counseling session. The counselor asked her in a noncommittal way why she had come to the clinic. The woman responded that she wanted a termination, an abortion. When the counselor asked if she was sure about the decision, the woman responded that her boyfriend had "split" when she told him she was pregnant. No, they hadn't been using "protection." He didn't want to take any responsibility for a child, and she didn't want to raise a child alone. While she wanted to have the child, the young woman unfortunately did not have the resources and family support to raise the child alone. This story is repeated again and again in women's health clinics. Much of the counseling for pregnant women coming in alone involves discussion of whether the woman can, or would want to, raise the child by herself. While no widespread surveys have been done, my own counts and those of others show that far less than half of women are accompanied by their male partner when they come in for counseling and an abortion. There can be many reasons for the male's non-attendance, but chief among them is that they have split. The female's reproductive strategy, if that is what it was, had not worked and she is starting over.

The man may have the same view. One study in 1987 found that a quarter of abortion patients were having an abortion because their boyfriend or husband wanted it. Counselors in clinics report that physical abuse is often a major factor in the relationship where the woman seeks to end a pregnancy. But even in cases where there is no abuse, women are often subject to family, social, and economic pressures from their partners. Parents frequently, in about 30 percent of cases, pressure their teenage daughters to have abortions. Aside from the question of whether a pregnant woman is exercising free choice in situations like this, these cases illustrate that a woman's reproductive strategy does not play out in a vacuum. A woman has to thread her way around many obstacles—her family, her economic and social status, the feelings of her community, and those of her boyfriend or husband. Everyone has a view about her reproductive strategy. These community views and those of one's kin cannot be underestimated. They are a part of the reproductive environment.

One day a woman from the Hasidic Jewish community in Brooklyn came into our Manhattan clinic. We had a Brooklyn clinic, and the Manhattan clinic was far from her home. That was why she came to Manhattan. She wanted to avoid seeing anyone she knew. Her father was one of the religious leaders of the Hasidic community. She lived with one foot in the Hasidic world and one in the outside world. She was unmarried, lived with her family, but worked outside the community in the fashion industry. She was dressed modestly in contemporary clothes, but her mother, who accompanied her to the clinic, was dressed in traditional Hasidic garb. The young woman was having an affair with a widower of the same age in her community who already had two children. She was pregnant with twins, and the man would not marry her, since he had children and did not want any more. During the course of many counseling sessions, the woman revealed her fear that this was probably her last chance to have children. While twins were particularly auspicious in the Hasidic community, having children out of wedlock was unacceptable. If she did, she would have to leave her home and her community. She had to make a choice between having children on the one hand and her family and community on the other. She was trapped between her biology and her culture. The woman's mother was unable to help her, even though she clearly wanted both grandchildren and for her daughter to stay at home and in the community. Under the Orthodox interpretation practiced in her Hasidic community, her pregnancy had passed the point where she could have an abortion. She and her mother, in consultation with the doctor and social worker at the clinic, decided that her abortion would be entirely permissible under her circumstances. She had the abortion and went home to her family and community.

The termination of a pregnancy is biologically counter-intuitive since it ends whatever reproductive success the pregnancy represents. But as we have seen, reproductive success consists of much more than giving birth to a child. The child needs extensive nurturing and care and investment over a long period of time. All throughout the courtship, mating, pregnancy, and childrearing, men and women evaluate their prospects for reproductive success. Their view may change as time passes. Especially during pregnancy, there may be changes in the environment, in behavior, in family dynamics, in income, or in any other circumstance that could affect a parent's view of the future, of his or her mate, and of the desirability of having a child. Men and women may have different views of the future and their future prospects and thus will have different reproductive strategies. Reproductive success, as Professor Bobbi Low reminded us, does not mean having a child every time you are pregnant.

Modern medicine has changed the dynamic for women in one major respect. A woman can now get unprecedented information during pregnancy on the health of her fetus and on its prospects for survival and a healthy life. More and more genetic diseases can be discovered during prenatal testing, usually after the midpoint of the pregnancy. The woman is thereby put in a biologically difficult situation because she has already invested four, five, or more months in the pregnancy, and it becomes more emotionally difficult, costlier, and medically riskier (even though still safer than childbirth) to terminate the pregnancy. Advances in intra-uterine surgery make correction of some fetal medical conditions possible but not guaranteed. Even so, abortions after the midpoint of a pregnancy are in fact rare. Opponents of legal abortion have used the unappealing nature of an abortion in the latter stages of a pregnancy as a weapon to try to criminalize many abortion procedures. There is no aesthetically pleasing method of abortion at any stage. No matter what the woman's reasons for terminating a pregnancy in its later stages, the abortion is a stark reproductive failure. Either the fetus is severely damaged or the woman's health or personal circumstances have unraveled to such a severe degree that she cannot have the child, even though she may have invested months in the pregnancy. The woman may have denied being pregnant, or couldn't raise the money for an abortion, or simply delayed a decision or getting to the doctor. She may have been at fault or not. That does not mean that she should lose control of her reproductive destiny.

Every pregnancy brings into high relief for the woman not only the prospects for that pregnancy but also her own prospects of reproductive success in this and in future matings. A pregnancy puts a woman in reproductive control. Abortion lets her choose which path her reproductive strategy will follow. She must evaluate not only her own health and condition, economic and otherwise, but also her prospects for the future. She must evaluate whether the father of her prospective child will be a good parent. She may want more children by the same or a different mate. A woman must decide how having a child affects her chances of finding a future mate. If the woman is poor and if there are relatively few men available, she may not see any avenue to a healthier, more prosperous life with another mate and may see having the child alone as her chance for reproductive success. Poverty can cut both ways. In the clinics that I oversaw at Planned Parenthood of New York City, women cited lack of money and lack of support, financial and otherwise, from the father as the main reasons they were seeking abortions. Woman after woman in our clinics would say, "I wouldn't be doing this if he would help me with the child." Men have their own agendas for their lives that often do not coincide with their partner's.

Even if their partners bring them to the clinic, women are often left alone to make their decisions and to assess their reproductive future. As Bobbi S. Low has concluded, "Abortion . . . appears more common in circumstances in which the birth of a child is likely to reduce the mother's lifetime reproductive success." If the pregnancy represents in her view a rare chance at reproductive success, then a young woman often elects to have the child on her own. For other women, a pregnancy is not a once-in-a-lifetime event. Many women have more than one abortion during their lives. Whether the pregnancies were intentional or unintentional, terminating them means that the woman is exercising control over her reproductive strategy.

One woman scheduled eight different appointments for an abortion in our Margaret Sanger Clinic, came in each time, and decided eight times not to go through with it. She talked to the social worker repeatedly. She was in her thirties, single, well-educated, and working in a health food store. She was in a long-term relationship with the man by whom she was now pregnant and had had two previous abortions with him. The man did not want to be a father and did not want the responsibility of raising a child. She agonized about what to do. Like the woman from the Hasidic community, she felt that this might be her last chance at having a child. But she did not face the cultural and community pressures that the Hasidic woman did. Despite the fact that she would be raising the child on her own, didn't make much money, and had serious childcare issues, the woman decided to have the child and raise it on her own.

A pregnancy, planned or unplanned, done consciously or unconsciously, brings the future into the present. The man and the woman, each with their own reproductive strategies, have to decide what to do. Legal abortion has led to a situation where there is little community pressure for the man to marry the woman and he often disappears, leaving the woman to make the decision on her own. At this point community pressure can have a decisive influence on her decision. Unmarried childbearing may not be acceptable where she lives, and she is forced to have an abortion, even if it is her last chance to have children. Perspectives on the decision to have a child or an abortion change with age and are a product of a woman's environment. As Leslie Rottenberg, director of social services at the Margaret Sanger Clinic, said: "Women see their life differently in their thirties than at eighteen or twenty-four. At thirty many women say that they thought their life would be different by then and it isn't. They thought they would be married, or have children or have settled down. They aren't, and in an abortion counseling session these women are in mourning for their life and are depressed with the men they are seeing. They aren't in mourning about abortion."

## Why Teen Pregnancy Can Be a Successful Reproductive Strategy

Many teenage girls in the United States, who one would think have a multitude of opportunities to have children in the future, nonetheless have children at their young age. There is a growing shortage of eligible men as women in poorer communities age. Young women's health, the health of the families, and their environment are such that it is riskier for these young women to postpone childbearing than to start now. Teens in poor communities, and their mothers, age quicker, grow sicker, and die younger than those in wealthier communities. In a culture where the extended family helps bring up the children, it is vital for child survival that the children's mother and grandmother and other relatives are as healthy as possible. All these factors lead young women towards early childbearing. There is also evidence that teenage girls give birth to healthier babies than they would if they waited until their twenties to give birth. While there is a risk that their children may not fare as well in life than the children of older women, for some young teens this is a risk worth running.

The received wisdom on teen pregnancy is that early childbearing makes even more problematic the already difficult lives of poor young people and retards their advancement out of poverty. Teen childbearing contributes to a cycle of poverty where the children of the teen mothers themselves are more likely to become teen parents and remain in poverty. One scholar of teen pregnancy stated that "when a sixteen-year-old girl has a child . . . 90 percent of her life's script is written for her." He might have added that 90 percent of her child's script is also written. This depressing and fatalistic assessment attributes to teen pregnancy an impact that should instead be attributed to the life circumstances that a poor teen finds herself in. Many teens believe that a baby will love them and be a positive force in their otherwise bleak lives.

In recent years new research has suggested that the teen childbearing problem isn't as socially devastating as we had thought, or at least is not caused by the things we thought caused it. There are other factors—poverty, unstable family life, and poor education among others—that have a significant negative impact on the life course of a young woman whether or not she becomes pregnant and has a child. Poor inner-city teens start life with two strikes against them. However, bearing a child while a teenager is not necessarily a third strike. There are even some indications that having a child can enhance the life prospects of a young woman in certain circumstances. One African-American woman in the South Bronx, then age twenty-two with a five-year-old child, told me that having a baby as a seventeen-year-old was the best thing that ever happened to her. Her life was in a rut of skipping school, messing around with many young men, and taking drugs. Having a baby, she said, "made me grow up and fast." She realized that she was responsible for this child and, even though she had help from her family, she was the one ultimately responsible. She stopped taking drugs, stayed in school, even got a part time job after school, and, when I met her, was well on her way in adult life. This is by no means a unique story.

America's youth are reaching puberty and able to have children at earlier and earlier ages. They are in the reproductive game beginning at age twelve. They, like adults, pursue their reproductive goals consciously and unconsciously. For most teenagers their reproductive strategy is to start reproducing when they are older. This does not mean, however, that they don't have sex. Eighty percent of American teens are sexually active during their teenage years, and 10 percent of teens become pregnant each year, with about half of them giving birth each year and the rest of the pregnancies ending in miscarriage or abortion. That 10 percent of teens adds up to one million teenagers each year. Over 500,000 of them have a baby each year. The vast majority of them are from poor and low-income families. Why do they do this? Do they see a reproductive benefit that 90 percent of their peers don't see?

Reproductive strategies vary by the different reproductive environments that humans find themselves in. As Professor Arline T. Geronimus of the University of Michigan has stated: "Fertility-timing varies among populations because of the contingencies members of different populations face in their efforts to provide for the survival and well-being of families." In the United States this can be readily seen by the marked variation between the races. Hispanics have the highest teen birth rates, but there has been more study done comparing black and white rates. For blacks 43 percent of first births are to teen mothers, whereas for whites just 22 percent are. Poor, young, black women in inner cities confront a markedly different environment than middle-class, white girls do in the suburbs. Young minority women see not only a landscape of poverty but also a landscape with fewer eligible men and shorter lifespans for themselves and their family members. They also are part of an extended kin network; African-American and Hispanic children are more likely to live in multi-generational homes compared to white children.

Environments that might lead teens to early childbearing can be found in many parts of the country outside of our inner cities. I was in a clinic in Iowa several years ago where I met three fourteen-year-old white girls who came in for pregnancy tests. They lived on farms outside of town and were best friends. All the tests came back negative; none were pregnant. They collectively burst into tears at the news. They said that they wanted to be pregnant and bring up their babies together. Early childbearing is not the exclusive preserve of inner city, minority youth, though they have been the most studied.

First, many young minority men and women live in an environment of poverty, a substandard educational system, and a lack of jobs in the immediate neighborhood. Young black men in particular are affected by this dismal environment, and as a result many are lured into lives of violence, crime, and drug use. Too many young black men in inner city communities get a poor education, are less employable, are either in jail or on parole (in some communities one-quarter of the black men are in jail or on parole), are on drugs, and all too often die young. As a result, young black women do not regard many of their black peers as suitable mates. Females are less affected by the environment, and thus eligible females outnumber eligible males by a growing margin as they age. Under these circumstances it is not an irrational strategy for a female to choose an eligible mate earlier in life while she can, rather than later. It is also not irrational that she chooses a man to be only the biological father of her child and not necessarily a partner to help her raise the child. For this she can rely on her kin network. All these environmental factors push a young woman towards making childbearing decisions earlier in life rather than later. Young men feel the same pressures, and becoming a father early insures that they have reproduced even if their life may be short.

Second, because of unhealthy living conditions, a substandard health system, and violence, poor men and women, both minority and white, suffer from higher morbidity and mortality than those with higher incomes who are disproportionately white. Professor Geronimus called this the "weathering hypothesis." The weathering hypothesis says that certain groups statistically will "weather," growing sicker as they age and dying faster than other groups.

One study by Professor Geronimus in 1999 revealed that poor blacks who had reached the age of fifteen had a relatively low probability of survival until age sixty-five. In Harlem only 37 percent of black men and 65 percent of black women who reach age fifteen survive until age sixty-five. For black men this represents half the probability of survival to age sixty-five as for whites nationwide. Black girls in Harlem who reach age fifteen have the same chance of surviving only until age forty-five as the average white girl of fifteen has of surviving until age sixty-five. Poor blacks get sicker faster and die younger.

The leading causes of early death in poor communities include diseases of the circulatory system, AIDS, accidents, homicide, and cancer. Poverty and race alone do not explain the entire difference in mortality rates. Other factors include crowded living conditions, poor health care, being a victim of crime, living amidst environmental hazards, and, as a result of all these factors, experiencing enormous stress. The evidence is clear that many black people in America cannot reasonably expect to live through middle age. Living with this prospect may affect their behavior in a variety of ways, including in risk-taking behavior and in reproductive patterns.

Studies testing the weathering hypothesis have found evidence of a correlation between the average life expectancy in a community and the age at first birth in that community. Generally the lower the life expectancy, the lower the average age of first birth. In one study done in Chicago in 1997 Professors Margo Wilson and Martin Daly of Mc-Master University found that the median age of women giving birth was 22.6 years in neighborhoods with low life expectancy compared to 27.3 years old in neighborhoods with a longer life expectancy. The timing of a young poor woman's childbearing is, I believe, a decision actively motivated in part by knowledge that her life and the lives of her parents will be shorter and less robust than those of other people, and a decision that, to meet her reproductive goals, she might be wise to have children earlier in her life. With parenting by not only parents but also grandparents being necessary in poor communities, it is natural for a young woman to have children while her extended family is alive and healthy enough to help care for them and help them grow.

In addition to a shortage of men and the weathering of the population, yet another environmental factor in inner cities favors early childbearing. Most research indicates that the risk of neonatal death decreases for all races as they give birth at older ages. For instance, Professor Maureen Glennon Phipps found in a study published in 2002 that, as a general matter, healthy infants born to teen mothers who survive until they are one month old are at a greater risk of dying by their first birthday than those infants born to mothers in their twenties. But the authors were unable to analyze the effects of poverty on these results. Other studies, however, have shown that black and white women have quite different neonatal mortality rates for their children depending on the mother's age and poverty. Professor Geronimus found that the risk of neonatal death for a black infant *increases* as a poor, black woman gives birth at older ages, while the risk of neonatal death for a white infant *decreases* as the white mother gives birth at older ages. The weathering hypothesis says that the effects of social inequality, poverty, poor health and nutrition, stress, and other negative environmental circumstances compound with age and have increasingly deleterious effects on fetal and newborn health as a poor, black woman ages and gives birth.

Professor Geronimus found that black mothers between the ages of fifteen and nineteen had the *lowest* incidence of low birth weight babies as compared to older black women. For example, the infant mortality rate in Harlem for teens giving birth is eleven deaths per 1,000 births. The rate for black women in their twenties is twice that—twenty-two per 1,000. Among whites, mothers in their teens and thirties experience slightly higher rates of poor birth outcomes than white women in their twenties. In other words, whites in their twenties have the best birth outcomes, while the best birth outcomes for blacks is while they are in their late teens. Black women as they age were found to smoke more during pregnancy and have higher rates of hypertension than whites. Black women as they age continue to live more in poverty than white women. Through their young adult years, black women's health deteriorates more rapidly than white women's health does, thereby leading to a greater risk of low birth weight babies. Poor women also generally get less prenatal care than wealthier women. The Geronimus study concluded: "The populations in which early births are most common are those where early births are the lowest risk, raising questions about the social construction of teen childbearing as a universally deleterious behavior."

This and other studies suggest that women may consciously or unconsciously time childbirth strategically by taking into account factors that include the status of their own health and their infant's potential health, as well as the health of those in their kin network who will be helping raise the child. It is arguably a better reproductive strategy for a woman to give birth earlier rather than later in these circumstances. Women know that their premature death will have serious negative consequences for their children. In an environment where life is short it makes evolutionary sense for women to have their children as early as possible.

Many campaigns against teen pregnancy talk of the cycle of teen pregnancy or the cycle of poverty that it perpetuates. The argument is often made, and I have made it, that it is likely that the child of poor teen parents will themselves have a child as a teen and be poor, repeating the pattern through the generations. Rather than viewing early childbearing as a pathology to be cured, I would argue that it is an adaptive reproductive strategy that is succeeding. In fact, the child of the teen parents is doing reproductively what she should: having children at a time where by her own experience there is a good chance they will survive to have children of their own. The child of teen parents may have more reproductive success if she repeats her mother's pattern and if her children repeat hers. As Geronimus said, "to postpone such goals as childbearing is to risk foregoing them."

What is left unexamined is whether those teens that choose to delay childbearing until their twenties fared any "better" in the reproductive sweepstakes. Did they have children? Did their children survive to have children of their own? Were their children as healthy? Did they have learning problems or poor educational performance? Were they as successful economically? While in one study Geronimus has found that sisters in a poor community who delayed childbearing did not fare markedly better than their sisters who had their children earlier, these are questions for which there are no conclusive answers yet.

From an evolutionary point of view, early childbearing could give an advantage since it reduces the time between generations and possibly increases the number of offspring. This advantage will compound over the generations and lead to an even greater numbers of descendants in comparison to the results obtained by later childbearing with fewer children in each generation. Even though the evidence is conflicting, it does not appear to be a guarantee of a disaster for maternal or child health for a poor teen to have a baby at or after about age sixteen. Earlier than that is more problematic, but childbearing in the later teenage years is not biologically contra-indicated. It may be inadvisable for other reasons, but again the evidence is not conclusive that economically or educationally it is a disaster. From a psychological point of view, being an immature mother can be harmful to mother and child, but at least some young mothers are part of an extended kin network that helps them raise their children. All these factors are part of the environment in which young men and women make their reproductive choices. Society may not like the choices they make, but given their circumstances, the choices made by poor teens are a clear indication of reproductive strategies at work.

Teen reproductive behaviors reveal how our human nature to reproduce adapts to our environment. This is not to say that human behaviors aren't also caused by chance or by social learning or experience in our culture. We must also remember that a correlation does not imply causality. In other words, just because the children of teen mothers may have poor results in school does not mean that these results were caused by these children being born to teen mothers. It may be caused by other factors such as their underlying poverty, differing patterns of maternal care, or the poor schools themselves. But the fact that the children of teen mothers may face a more difficult road in life than they might have had if their mother had waited until she was older to give birth just shows the extent to which young woman will take risks in pursuing a reproductive strategy.

In some cases, teen births can show the extent to which a teen's parents will take risks to have a grandchild. At the Margaret Sanger Clinic of Planned Parenthood of New York City one day a Hispanic woman in her thirties brought in her eleven-year-old daughter who was at that point over twenty-four weeks pregnant. The boy next door, age fifteen, had raped her. The girl was petite but wore baggy sweatshirts to disguise the pregnancy. The girl's mother finally noticed something was wrong and took her to the emergency room, which referred her to us. The boy's mother was best friends with the girl's mother, and both mothers had already been to the police. Though the eleven-year-old understood enough about being pregnant to disguise it, she didn't really understand what it meant to give birth and be a mother. She was in fifth grade and a good student and loved her history and gym classes.

The girl and her mother talked with Leslie Rottenberg about having an abortion, though at this point in her pregnancy, a doctor would have to certify that the pregnancy was a threat to her life or health. The doctor would have done this given the girl's size and age. They talked about adoption, but the mother wouldn't even consider it, even though the mother was poor and had no husband and the boy's mother disclaimed any responsibility for the child. Nevertheless, the mother decided that her eleven-year-old daughter would give birth, which she did safely; the mother raised the child as her own; and the girl went back to fifth grade. The baby was the mother's first grandchild. The reproductive strategy here involved great risk to the girl but great reward to her mother. For the mother, it was worth it.

There is no one fixed path to reproductive success. Reproductive strategies depend on one's environment. The environment can encourage a woman to give birth at a certain time and under certain conditions or it may discourage her. Teenagers in poor communities may see a variety of reasons not to postpone childbirth until they are older. They may have fewer choices of men, their health may worsen, and the health of their kin may also. It is also likely that they will give birth to healthier infants if they do so sooner rather than later. The role of her kin network cannot be underestimated. Parents want to be grandparents. They know their time is running short and they want to be around to help raise the child. While there are risks for the teen mother and her child, the families often think these are worth running.

The reproductive patterns of some poor teens are in marked contrast to those of some professional women who delay childbearing. These women, according to Bobbi S. Low, "who forego fertility or who delay it past 30 are probably not optimizing their trade-offs. As family size fell with the demographic transition, obviously so did variance in family size. So, it made some sort of sense for women to shift from pure 'reproductive value' (as in traditional societies) to some mixture of 're-productive plus resource value'—so far so good—except that when they delay beyond early 20s their lineage never catches up." This is only to say that reproductive strategies are acted out, and trade-offs calculated, within specific economic and social environments.

## Can We Repeal the Laws of Human Nature?

It is natural for humans to try to plan for having their children. While today we call this exercising reproductive rights, this desire to plan has deep roots in human biological history. Planning for one's family is not a cultural fad. It is not just an option that opponents of reproductive rights refer to dismissively as part of our "contraceptive culture." It is a vital part of human survival. Abortion and birth control can only be judged in the context of human reproduction and biology.

Biology is neither destiny nor irrelevant. While biology and evolution have shaped human nature, humans still have free will to the extent that they can know the consequences of their actions and make decisions accordingly. There are, however, defined patterns to human reproductive behavior. Human reproductive behavior, like that of other animals, is shaped by the forces of natural selection. Those humans who have traits that best enable them to survive in their particular environment will do so and will be able to pass down those traits to their progeny. Men and women have reproductive strategies which are shaped by the sex differences between males and females. We reproduce using sex in order to mix our genes, accelerate evolution, thwart parasites and give the human race more genetic diversity. Reproductive strategies evolved that better enabled males and females to find the optimal partner for mating and parenting. Men and women also select each other, unconsciously, for genetic compatibility. Sex is used for more than reproduction. It is a part of human courtship. It tests the relationship and tests for fertility. It should not, and does not, always lead to a pregnancy or childbirth. Men and women, women especially, time and space their children to give them the best chance of surviving. The new (in evolutionary terms) ability of males and females to control reproduction with modern birth control and abortion adds new costs and benefits into the pursuit of reproductive strategies. But it does not change the biological fact that women and men have been successfully controlling their reproduction for a long time.

Those who oppose the legalization of birth control and abortion show an abysmal ignorance of biology and human nature. Not all abortion opponents directly urge the criminalization of birth control as they do of abortion, but many call the birth control pill, the IUD, and virtually every other modern method of birth control "abortifacients," thereby indirectly calling for a ban on birth control. Even condoms come in for attack. Many abortion opponents call them ineffective and demand that the government stop promoting them. The official position of the Catholic Church that it is "intrinsically contrary to nature" to want to control one's fertility by use of artificial birth control and that abortion is evil, misguided and dangerous.

I believe that birth control and abortion are not contrary to nature. Rather, nature, through the forces of evolution, has given humanity the ability to control its own reproduction. Humanity has succeeded because it has not left reproduction to nature or chance. Humanity has thrived on Earth because each member of our species has innately sought reproductive success. We have thrived because we have used strategies to give our children the best chance of survival and in turn of reproducing. Some reproductive decisions work out and some do not. This is what evolution says. Humanity has demonstrated that it has thrived when members make their own reproductive decisions, not when they leave things to chance or nature or when the government, their religion, or their culture dictates certain results.

Those who favor more societal control over human sexual and reproductive behavior believe otherwise, or at least believe that society as a whole will be better off if certain human sexual and reproductive behaviors are circumscribed. Some societies do this by establishing cultural norms and others by laws. All societies have an incest taboo to a greater or lesser extent. Many societies ban homosexual activity. Many have ages of consent to sexual activity and to marriage. Some have banned birth control, and many now have restrictions on abortion. The issue is where to draw the lines. One can be an opponent of abortion and still agree with my argument that humans engage in reproductive strategies and that humanity benefits from reproductive freedom. Abortion opponents would just draw the line at abortion, or even at birth control, and would say that humanity does not benefit from these, that the societal and human cost is too high, or that the processes are immoral. I believe that defining the limits of permissible morality must be more than a matter of personal definition or a matter of following ancient rules blindly. To be legitimate, a moral code must comport with the requirements of human survival, including the requirements of human reproduction. Moral and cultural norms have effects on human reproductive behavior. How do religious figures and others who set social and moral norms and who make government policy know the impact of their norms on human reproduction? How do they know if they are helping or hurting? This is not an easy question to answer since the success and failure of reproductive strategies are not easily measured.

The banning of birth control and abortion may change some sexual practices of some people and thus some of their reproductive behavior. Human beings have, however, demonstrated a remarkable ability to circumvent legal restrictions to attain their reproductive goals. American women demonstrated this in the nineteenth century when, while both birth control and abortion were illegal, they made liberal use of both. Higher cost, increased danger to their health, and the risk of prosecution did not deter women from using birth control and abortion. I believe that the campaigns of Comstock and his successors to criminalize birth control and abortion are more cultural, religious, and political in nature, rather than campaigns with realistic behavioral or fertility goals. Banning reproductive choices will not have as much impact on sexual and reproductive behavior as its proponents say they hope for. No matter what the legal status of birth control and abortion, teen sex, premarital sex, and extramarital sex are biological fixtures in the human reproductive landscape. Despite this reality, proponents of bans on birth control and abortion pursue their sexual and gender goals. They have misgivings about the status of women, have especial misgivings about women as sexual beings, oppose all sex outside of marriage, and see both the "contraceptive culture" and "abortion on demand" as harmful to the family and thus to the stability of society. In their view, the sexual promiscuity that contraceptives permit leads to an increase in sexually transmitted diseases, ruins marriages, and harms children. They ignore the fact that promiscuity and infidelity appeared on the scene long before artificial contraceptives did and that promiscuity and infidelity may even have biological and evolutionary purposes.

Opponents of birth control and abortion are endeavoring to remove biology and evolution as factors in human behavior. They are trying to establish one set of ground rules for reproduction. They want a pregnancy to be the potential result of each sexual encounter and for each pregnancy to result in the birth of a child, nature permitting. They want all sexual activity and reproduction to occur within marriage. They want men to have more power than they currently do over human reproduction. Opponents of women's control over childbearing believe that they can impose societal and moral rules over biological realities. They believe that strict rules on sexual behavior and restricting reproductive freedom will not hurt, and in fact will help, human reproduction and survival.

I have argued that there is no one successful reproductive strategy. Successful reproduction depends on two different people competing and cooperating in their unique environment. Reproduction is more unconscious and more a matter of trial and error than a conscious, planned strategy. Trying to repeal the laws of evolutionary biology is a fool's errand. It is not just wrongheaded; it is dangerous. Abortion opponents cannot repeal the laws of natural selection. These laws favor women who take control over their reproduction. This means natural selection favors women who use birth control and abortion to plan, space, and limit their children so that those children have the best chance of reaching adulthood and in turn reproducing. Natural selection favors children with genetic variety. Natural selection works within a particular environment. Life and the environment can change after a woman is pregnant and it may not be in her reproductive interest to give birth at that time and under those circumstances. Humanity learned eons ago that it could separate sex from pregnancy. Sex, however, cannot be separated from reproduction. Humans make better choices about reproduction, including their sexual activity, pregnancy, childbearing, and child rearing than governments do. Laws restricting reproductive freedoms, because they hurt the cause of human life, are not just foolhardy, they are immoral.

Many pro-life advocates push for adoption as the cure for abortion. They ask why can't women who have an unintended pregnancy and for whom having a child is not what they can handle at this point in their lives have the child and give it up for adoption? Few women do. Less than 1 percent of parents in fact voluntarily give up their children for adoption. Why don't more women have a child, rather than abort it, and put the child up for adoption?

Adoption is counter-intuitive from an evolutionary vantage point of both the biological mother and the adoptive parents. Adoption requires a person to devote time and resources to raising a child that is not genetically related. Adoption also puts the future of a child in the control of a stranger. There are thus two obstacles to overcome: there will be resistance from the person giving up the child for adoption, usually the mother, as well as resistance from potential adoptive parents. Assuming that the potential adoptive parents are childless or do not have other close relatives that need their care and upbringing, adoption makes sense biologically in that it creates a culture that is caring of children. Generally speaking, this child-friendly culture would benefit all children in society and would thus be favored by natural selection. However, natural selection would also favor those genetic children who resisted their parents adopting other children, since they would get fewer resources and attention from their parents.

If however a woman finds that there is a potential adoptive family, why wouldn't she put the child into their care? It would appear that by so doing her genes would get a free ride into the next generation. Her genetic child would have a chance to grow to adulthood and in turn reproduce, without her expending any resources or energy. What could be the problem? One problem involves the difference between what we mean by a "genetic child" and a "biological child." Having a child means that you have a genetic child. But those genes get expressed in an environment. When the genetic parents raise the child, they are controlling, to the extent they can, the biological environment in which their genetic child's genes are expressed. When adoptive parent raise the child, they control the environment, and the child becomes their biological child. A child raised by adoptive parents may turn out very different in many ways. Even though the genes of the genetic parents get to the next generation, those genes may be expressed in very different ways than if they had raised the child. For instance, a child with a natural aptitude for the piano may grow up never playing in an adoptive home. Given the interplay between genes and the environment, a genetic parent has little assurance that their genetic child would grow up as someone they would recognize. These feelings run not only to the genetic parents, but also to the genetic grandparents and other close kin. They may foresee few or no other possibilities for a genetic descendant and will be loath to give one up.

Evolution and biology conspire to thwart adoption. Evolution has programmed women to be nurturers of the children they bear. This is how humanity has survived. During pregnancy the mother/child bond grows and grows. It is indeed a rare mother who can sever this bond. She is not programmed to on a biological level; it is "easier" in many ways for a woman to have an early abortion. She has had less time to bond biologically and emotionally with her child. She has invested less in the pregnancy. It is biologically counter intuitive to think that a society can implement a cultural change to make adoption the only answer for a woman carrying a child that she does not want. The risks of pregnancy and childbearing to a woman's are simply too great for a woman to go through them for a child that she will not raise. On an evolutionary basis her genes will be favored by her preserving her health to raise her current children or for a future pregnancy for a later child that she can raise.

Furthermore, the adoption system is not always friendly to parents who may want to give up a child for adoption. Adopted children frequently can find their genetic parents. The genetic mother could fear that the child would come back to her and demand an emotional attachment that she would not want to give. The genetic parents may fear future financial obligations that would hurt their ability to raise the children that they kept. The genetic mother's reasons for resisting adoption are therefore economic, social, emotional and biological. There may also be racial objections. Many states have a formal or informal preference to place children with families of a similar ethnic or racial background. Many adopting parents have the same preference. There is a resulting imbalance in the babies available for adoption and the families wanting to adopt. The "shortage" of babies available for adoption is not the fault of legal abortion, even though there are fewer unwanted children born. It is rather the result of these anti-adoption evolutionary pressures, plus the societal acceptance of single motherhood. More women give birth as single mothers than abort their children. What we have then as a result in the United States are childless couples going to foreign lands to adopt children. Making the adoption system friendlier in the United States, or adding economic incentives for adoption, will do little to change this picture. Proclaiming adoption as the "solution" to the abortion problem is a cruel hoax.

Men and women are engaged in an evolutionary battle for the control of reproduction. Women succeed when they control their reproduction. Men do, too. Each sex has developed strategies for control. Men have reproductive goals and strategies that are different from women's. Men have the same desire to reproduce, but, not being the ones to become pregnant, give birth, and nurse, can seek reproductive success differently. But the necessities of sexual reproduction and sexual selection mean that males and females must not only compete with and among each other, they must cooperate too. This chapter has mainly focused on the evolutionary strategies of women and the necessity for reproductive freedom for human survival. The male interest in women's reproductive freedom is more tangential, but is almost as vital as the woman's. There does not need to be a full-scale battle of the sexes over reproductive rights.

# CHAPTER FIVE

# Enlisting Men in Support of Reproductive Freedom

*Antoine stands on the sidewalk outside the Margaret Sanger Clinic of Planned Parenthood of New York City on a hot, humid July morning. He has dropped off his girlfriend for an abortion and is waiting to take her home. He wears a windbreaker that is zipped halfway up despite the heat. A social worker tells him that she works at the clinic and is talking to his girlfriend and asks him if he wants to come inside to discuss his girlfriend's decision. Antoine shakes his head a murmurs "No." The social worker and I wonder whether Antoine is armed and doesn't want to go through the metal detectors at the clinic entrance. The social worker gently persists and asks if he wants to talk about the abortion. Antoine declines again: "That's her business. It ain't mine." When we relay the conversation to his girlfriend inside, she says "Typical. He thinks he's being respectful. All I want is for him to talk to me and deal with our relationship."*

## Do Males Need Reproductive Freedom?

Just as my grandmother framed birth control as a woman's issue, reproductive rights advocates have framed abortion as a woman's issue. Men and women alike have long viewed birth control and abortion this way as well. But framing the issues of reproductive freedom as women's issues does not help garner male support because it doesn't provide satisfactory answers to a male's questions: When is abortion my business? Why should I support women's reproductive rights? What's in it for me? Don't I have reproductive rights too? Why should a woman's rights prevail over mine?

To get the support of males, reproductive rights advocates must address and support male reproductive interests. Just as women are more than wombs, men are more than inseminators. Men's reproductive interests and rights derive, as women's do, from their role in human evolution. Women's reproductive rights derive from the importance to women of controlling their own reproduction. Natural selection favored those women who did. The genes of women who controlled their reproduction had a better chance of being passed down than those of women who did not, because the women who controlled their reproduction had a better chance of surviving childbirth, as did their children. This chapter will argue that it is of equal importance for men to control their own reproduction and to have the right to do so. Men, like women, need reproductive freedom to achieve reproductive success.

Humanity needs both men and women to be reproductively successful. It is not in women's interest to make reproductive freedom their exclusive preserve.

Before we can try to define the extent of male reproductive freedom, we need to see what a man's reproductive interests might be. Even though males and females have different biological roles, the essential male reproductive interest is the same as a female's—successful procreation. Men will not achieve reproductive success unless mother and child survive childbirth and the child survives to adulthood to reproduce.

Therefore, men like women need to control the timing, spacing and number of children to maximize their offspring's chance of surviving and being healthy and prosperous. For men this involves more, however, than just using contraceptives so that births can be spaced and timed, although this is part of a successful strategy. Men, like women, need a complete reproductive strategy that involves finding and choosing the right mate, then their mate's having a successful pregnancy and a problem-free birth and then years of upbringing for the child.

*The biological differences between males and females mean that each sex will have divergent reproductive and sexual strategies to accomplish this biological goal. The battle of the sexes is over the control of reproduction.*

Each sex battles among itself and against the other sex for this control. But for men the process is fraught with special challenges. Because women generally do the choosing, men have to compete with each other to reproduce. Alas, not all men get chosen. Men therefore compete, often violently, among each other for dominance and high status. In an attempt to try to improve their chances of being selected, men will either try to control women directly by force or will indirectly try to attract women by controlling resources or by other means of demonstrating their reproductive fitness. Males have evolved to have sexual and other characteristics that demonstrate and communicate their health and genetic fitness in a myriad of ways. But since males get selected for not only their genetic fitness, but also their social standing, resources, kin network and parenting abilities, they need to demonstrate these also. Conspicuous displays of wealth or family ties are done for a biological purpose.

Next, men have to try to exercise influence over whether and when a particular partner conceives a child. But men have fewer options than women to prevent pregnancy and childbirth. Other than sterilization, the sole male methods of contraception are the condom and withdrawal. Both are evident to the woman. A woman has more power to control whether or not she gets pregnant and can do so without the male knowing or controlling what her decision is. Furthermore with abortion a woman can control whether or not she gives birth. The battle of the sexes so far looks like a rout for the females.

After childbirth the scales tip towards the males somewhat. Parenting presents a fundamental quandary for men. During and after pregnancy and childbearing men have more immediate opportunities than women to find another mate and parent another child. Parenting reduces a man's opportunities to take this path towards another reproductive success. A man has to make a choice between investing in parenting one child, or proceeding to reproduce with another person. Women because of their investment in the pregnancy have less of a choice.

The battle of the sexes for control of reproduction becomes even more of a rout for the females because of the male's basic biological problem that even if he succeeds in the competition and gets selected to mate, he has absolutely no assurance (until the advent of DNA testing) that he is the genetic father of the children that his "mate" produces. This is the problem of paternity uncertainty. Natural selection favors men who know who their children are. If a man devotes the time, resources, and energy to parent his children, it is more likely that his genes will get passed down. If he unknowingly parents some other man's children, he is helping some other man's genes, not his own, to get passed down. So how does a man improve his chances here?

Men have evolved to have a variety of strategies for ensuring their reproductive interests and achieving reproductive success. These include trying to prevent other men from having access to their mate or else trying to have sex with a variety of other female partners in the hopes of fathering a child. These are not mutually exclusive strategies and men often pursue a combination of these strategies. But so do women, hence the paternity problem for men. Men have responded by using the law as their weapon.

Laws restricting a woman's reproductive freedom by restricting access to birth control and abortion, or by increasing the penalties for a woman's adultery, are efforts by men to tilt the playing field so that they will be able to pursue their strategies while not allowing women the same leeway to pursue theirs. There are costs, however, to men when they restrict women's reproductive freedom: their own freedom is also restricted and their potential reproductive success is threatened. Therefore, men who have more status, and thus more reproductive chances, will be less likely to want to restrict women's reproductive freedom. A high status male, who has many prospects for mating, is less threatened by a female's ability to control her mating and reproduction than a low status male who has fewer prospects. The low-status male will get chosen less, if at all, for mating and must make the most of his few opportunities. He will want to invest in parenting and, if married, will want to preserve the marriage for the benefit of the children. Reproductive freedom is viewed by low-status men, and by their partners as well, as a threat to their marriage and to the well-being of their children.

The uneven biological playing field forces us to confront the issue of how we can get men of every status to support reproductive freedom for women when it may not be in their immediate interest. At the same time we must ask the extent to which certain male reproductive interests should be enshrined as male reproductive rights. In order to recognize male interests and freedoms, we must admit that male efforts to win the battle of the sexes are not necessarily inimical to women's interests. The solution to these knotty issues will come when we find a way for men and women to unite in some common reproductive strategies for their mutual benefit. If this is possible, then perhaps we can enlist men in support of women's reproductive freedom, and enlist women in support of men's.

How can we get men of every status to support reproductive freedom? I believe only by eliminating paternity uncertainty. Technology in the form of condoms and DNA testing now allows this. While condom use is not totally effective in preventing pregnancy, it will go a long way towards letting men control when they are going to father a child. DNA testing can give men certain proof, after the fact, that the child they are parenting is actually their genetic child (while the percentage of time this happens is relatively small, on the order of ten percent or less, the fear is substantially greater). Paternity certainty will have enormous implications. It should level the playing field, should lead to changes in men's and women's reproductive strategies and should lead to more cooperation and partnership between the sexes in childrearing. It could, if advocates of reproductive freedom position it properly, lead to increased male and female support for reproductive freedom, since men will have the same interest as their partners in controlling pregnancy and childbirth to obtain the optimal reproductive result for them.

Women's reproductive freedom will get increased political support when it is seen as being in a man's interest as well as a woman's. The same is true of men's reproductive freedom. It will gain in support when it is seen as being in women's interests. While since *Roe* we have seen increased restrictions in women's reproductive freedom imposed by legislatures and permitted by the courts, we have also seen increased restrictions on a man's reproductive freedom. Both men and women should view this with alarm.

## Male Reproductive Interests Do Not Automatically Translate into Male Reproductive Rights

The Supreme Court in its birth control and abortion cases ruled that both women and men had a fundamental right to decide whether or not to have a child. However, the courts have been more willing to restrict a man's rights than a woman's, even where there was no conflict between their wishes.

For example, some courts have ordered men behind on child support payments not to have any more children. In the summer of 2001 the Wisconsin Supreme Court approved a lower court ruling that David Oakley, a father of nine, who owed $25,000 in child support, could be ordered not to father any more children while on probation "unless he could prove to the court that he could support all of them." While the court took note of Oakley's past record of abusing his children, the court justified the sentence not on abuse grounds but on the sole ground of Oakley's "abysmal history" of non-payment of child support. The court asserted that the court order did not deprive Oakley permanently of his constitutional right to procreate since "he can satisfy the condition of his probation by making efforts to support his children as required by law." One judge in the majority stated that he supported the order because the defendant intentionally refused to pay child support. If the defendant had been indigent and unable to pay child support, the judge said, he would have joined the dissent and permitted the defendant to have more children.

The dissenting judges argued that the ruling "wrongly supports an economic test for would-be parents," adding, "The right to have a child has never been rationed on the basis of wealth. The majority has essentially authorized a judicially imposed 'credit check' on the right to bear and beget children." The dissent also noted that this ruling placed a terrible burden on a female that the defendant impregnated—either she gets an abortion or alternatively she has a child and the defendant goes to prison for contempt of court. All of the court's four male judges were in the majority, and all of the three female judges were in the minority.

In a similar ruling in Ohio in September 2002, a trial judge in Medina County initially ordered bachelor Sean Talty to avoid having children since he was $38,000 behind in child support for two of his six children. However, Judge James Kimbler, after hearing arguments from Talty's lawyer that everyone, even a deadbeat dad, had the right to have children, ordered the defendant to "take reasonable efforts to avoid conception." The judge allowed that Talty would not violate his probation if he could prove that he tried to use birth control but it failed (one wonders how the defendant would prove this).

The courts of Wisconsin and Ohio apparently have the view that being poor, or a deadbeat, disqualifies a man from having children. No court has said the same about women. So long as poor women do not abuse their children, they are entitled to have children and to go on welfare to get support for them. That in fact is what the welfare system is designed for. The Wisconsin and Ohio courts view poor men as having lesser "reproductive rights" than poor women, even when the right asserted by the men did not conflict with or affect a woman's right. In fact, Sean Talty's reproductive interests coincided with those of his current girlfriend, who was the mother of two of his children. She was not pleased with the verdict and complained: "It took me ten years to get two and I would like to have more."

In May 2002 a court in Louisville, Kentucky, took a more jaundiced view of the reproductive rights of a deadbeat dad and ordered him not only to stop having children but also not to have any more sex. The defendant, Luther Crawford, age forty-nine, had fathered twelve children by eleven different women and owed $74,000 in back child support for three of those children. It was not revealed how much child support he owed, if anything, for the others. Crawford was unemployed, blind in one eye, had heart disease and high blood pressure, and on the whole did not appear to be much of a reproductive "catch." Despite these handicaps he had been in some ways a reproductive success, even though there was no evidence presented on how well his children were doing. The no-sex sentence was part of a plea bargain that reduced Crawford's jail time for non-payment of child support. At a subsequent hearing Crawford's lawyer argued that even if Crawford had a vasectomy, he would still be in violation of the court order if he had sex. The court reconsidered, withdrew its order, and sentenced Crawford to one year in jail, thereby preventing him from having sex with women and impregnating them at least for that year. Judge Tom McDonald said: "I can't order you to be a loving father, but the law requires you to financially support them, and you have failed miserably."

Being in jail has proven to be an obstacle for non-sexual male reproduction, even with new artificial insemination techniques and overnight mail. William Gerber, an inmate serving a 100-year sentence in Mule Creek State Prison in California under that state's three strikes law, having been convicted of discharging a firearm, making terrorist threats, and using narcotics, wanted to impregnate his wife, age forty-four, by sending a sperm specimen to her by overnight mail that she could use for artificial insemination. Conjugal visits were not permitted for prisoners serving life sentences. Gerber unsuccessfully petitioned the prison authorities for permission to procreate by mail. The Ninth Circuit Court of Appeals, by a six to five decision, upheld the prison authorities, saying that Gerber's right to procreate was fundamentally inconsistent with his status as a prisoner. Even though Gerber and his wife both wanted children, the court ruled she had no right to have a child by mail with her male.

These decisions involving men's reproductive rights come perilously close to reinstating eugenics as a valid principle for government regulation of reproduction. The courts are willing to abridge a man's reproductive rights even when there is no apparent conflict between the man's reproductive interests and his partner's. Oakley's girlfriend and Gerber's wife both wanted to have children, and perhaps so did Luther Crawford's next girlfriend. Even though the courts paid lip service to a man's reproductive rights, they ruled that the compelling state interests of requiring men to support their children, of preventing child abuse, and of preserving the integrity and purposes of the penal system were sufficient to prevent these men from having more children.

These important state interests are applied differently, however, to men and women. The courts are much more likely to constrict the reproductive freedom of men than they are of women. A man can be ordered not to have children if he cannot or will not support them; a woman cannot be. A man in jail cannot father a child but a woman can bear a child (she may not be able to have an abortion, however, depending on where she is incarcerated). Courts appear to be stricter on men with a record of child abuse, than on women with one.

The case of Darlene Johnson is illustrative. A month after Norplant was approved in January 1991, a California judge, Howard Boardman, presided over Johnson's sentencing. She had been found guilty of three counts of child abuse. Johnson was twenty-seven, the mother of four and eight months pregnant with her fifth. She had a prior criminal record and faced up to seven years in jail. Judge Boardman gave her a choice—seven years in jail or, as an alternative, one year in jail with an additional three years of probation, plus having Norplant inserted in her arm. She elected the latter. The defendant's appeal of the sentence was never resolved because she violated other terms of her probation and was jailed.

Clearly at the time, Johnson was not a fit mother to her existing children and needed help. The children were going to be removed from her no matter what the sentence. And no matter which option the defendant took, she would lose her ability to have more children for the duration of the sentence—for seven years if jailed, assuming no conjugal visits, and four or five years if on probation. In fact, the Norplant/probation option would enable her to have a child sooner than the jail sentence, if she desired. What was galling to those of us who opposed the sentence was the blatant use of regulating and preventing fertility as a criminal deterrent, as well as threatening by implication a longer jail sentence unless she agreed to Norplant. Surely an alternative would be to say to the defendant that, unless she were deemed a fit mother, any children she did have would be removed from her care.

The fear that a person, male or female, may commit child abuse on an as-yet-unborn child is hardly a valid reason to forbid that person from having that child. The sentences imposed on the men above were harsher than that imposed on Darlene Johnson. She could have children at the end of her probation; the men's sentences were open ended. If they were never able to become financially solvent and meet their child support obligations, they would never be able to legally have more children. In each of these three cases, these men clearly had something to offer since their girlfriends wanted to become pregnant with them. Since it appears that the men were supporting some of their children or had deliberately refused to even though they had the means, these cases represent an elitist, eugenic view that reproduction is only for men of means.

Male and female reproductive interests can conflict. This can occur when a woman wants a child and the man does not, and vice versa, the woman does not want a child and the man does. When these conflicts occur before pregnancy and cannot be resolved, either party can take steps  to find a new partner. When these conflicts occur after the woman is pregnant, then the couple must try to resolve it privately. Often the disagreement boils over in the clinic. Leslie Rottenberg, the director of social services in the Margaret Sanger Clinic of Planned Parenthood of New York City, reported that, when a couple comes in together, in half the cases the woman wants the child and the man doesn't and in the other half it is the opposite. When it is the woman who wants to have the child, the most common response from the man is: "It isn't fair. I should have a say if I am going to be a father." Rottenberg explains as tactfully as possible that he had a choice before he had sex. In her experience men separate sex from potentially becoming a parent whereas women do not. As a result of this perceived unfairness, men can get violent not only towards their partners but also the staff at the clinic. In the summer of 2003 a man burst into the clinic despite the extensive security and demanded to see his wife, who he thought was there for an abortion. He wanted to stop the abortion and to have the child. He put the clinic supervisor in a choke hold and, after not getting any information out of her, said, "I'm not done with you yet." He left the clinic peacefully. We don't know which patient he was there to see, or even if she was there.

Other men want to be sure they are not going to be a father. One day in 2003 at the Margaret Sanger Clinic, a woman originally from Bangladesh, who had had an abortion a week earlier, came in with her boyfriend. She was nineteen, he was twenty-eight. She clearly adored him. His feelings for her were somewhat less ardent. They both came from the same province in Bangladesh, but his family was the most prominent in the province while hers was of a significantly lesser status. A marriage between them was unthinkable in their society, as was having a child out of wedlock. The purpose of the visit was for the man to examine the girl's medical chart to be sure that she had had the abortion. With her permission, he looked at the chart and they left the clinic together. There would be no child to interfere with his and his family's plans for his future.

Occasionally disagreements over childbearing end up in court. When a disagreement goes into court, the legal system will examine each party's reproductive interests to see if they rise to the level of reproductive rights. In most, if not all, cases, this will mean the interests of the female will become reproductive rights and will prevail since she alone bears the health risks of a pregnancy. Because of this the courts have ruled, correctly, in my view, that a woman has a right to make her own childbearing decisions, as well as the right to preserve her health and life. This is the current state of the law in the United States and in most other countries where abortion is legal. A husband's permission for a wife's abortion is required in several countries, mostly in the Middle East and Asia, including Egypt, Saudi Arabia, and Syria, thus giving a husband veto power over his wife's abortion.

Despite the clear holding to the contrary of the U.S. Supreme Court in *Planned Parenthood v. Casey* in 1992, American men persist in going to court to try to stop their wife's or girlfriend's abortions. In 2002 John Stachokus asked a court in Pennsylvania for, and got, a temporary injunction to prevent his former girlfriend, Tanya Meyers, from having an abortion. The two had broken up when she was eight weeks pregnant, and Meyers decided to end the pregnancy. Before the judge could read the *Casey* decision, find that Stachokus had no legal leg to stand on, and reverse himself, Meyers miscarried, thereby ending the proceedings.

If the polls are any guide, the American public supports the idea that husbands have reproductive rights, even when they conflict with their wives'. The Gallup Poll of January 2003 reported that 72 percent of those polled supported the husband of a married woman being notified if his wife decides to have an abortion. In an earlier nationwide poll conducted by the *Washington Post* in 1992, 63 percent of respondents supported a wife having to get her husband's legal permission before having an abortion. A later *Los Angeles Times* poll in June 2000 found that 49 percent of respondents favored a woman getting the consent of the "biological father" before having an abortion. These results are recognition that the husband, and to a lesser extent the biological father, have reproductive interests at stake when a woman decides to terminate a pregnancy. Whether or not his interests become a right is another matter.

I have argued that women have reproductive rights because the rights are of benefit to not just women but to humanity. Men can only have reproductive rights if it can be established that these rights too will be of benefit to humanity, not just to men. When there is not a conflict with a woman's reproductive rights, American courts recognize in theory a man's reproductive rights. However, they wrongly, in my view, use broader grounds to restrict these rights than they would for a woman, citing poverty and the potential damage to current or future children if they were to permit some men to procreate at will. When there is a conflict with a woman's rights, the courts currently give precedence to the woman's rights. The courts recognize that giving a man an equal right in effect gives him veto power over a woman's decision, and, in the context of a pregnant woman, this would mean that, if the couple could not agree on an abortion, she would give birth.

There is not much dissent currently from the proposition that a man and woman must jointly agree on becoming pregnant. However, while the law prohibits rape, it does not directly prohibit the woman from saying she is using birth control when she isn't or removing sperm from a used condom and impregnating herself. Mutual consent to pregnancy has not always been the norm. Traditional moral and religious principles said that a wife must submit to her husband in every way including sexually and in the decision to have children. Roman law required that a husband consent to his wife's abortion, on the theory that the child was his property. Roman law is one vote away in the U.S. Supreme Court from being permitted in the United States. The Supreme Court in *Casey* overturned Pennsylvania's law that required a husband's notification before an abortion is performed, but only by a five to four vote. The court noted that the vast majority of women, in fact about 95 percent, did tell their husbands and those that did not either were experiencing marital difficulties, feared violence or abuse against them or their children, or were pregnant as the result of an affair. The court stated that for women in abusive situations "a spousal notification requirement enables the husband to wield an effective veto over his wife's decision." The court added that a woman does not give up her liberty over her body and childbearing decisions when she marries.

The *Casey* court did recognize that the husband has an interest in his wife's pregnancy, but said it was not enough of one to override her interests. For example, the court said that this interest would not permit laws that would require a wife to notify her husband before she used birth control or smoked while pregnant or underwent surgery that might affect her reproductive organs. The court ruled: "A State may not give to a man the kind of dominion over his wife that parents exercise over their children."

Given that in the United States a husband's lack of legal power over his wife's reproductive decisions hangs by one vote in the Supreme Court, this issue is sure to return to the state legislatures and then to the court. Since the legislatures and the court should examine the respective reproductive interests of the husband and wife in considering any such legislation, we need to see if there is any biological basis for a man's reproductive interests to take precedence over his partner's.

Men's and women's reproductive strategies are intertwined in order to successfully propagate the human race, but they are also often in conflict. Men, who are traditionally in control of governments, have often created laws to further their reproductive interests. Have these laws been a success from the male point of view? Or from humanity's point of view? That is the issue. If not, then these laws cannot stand. To the extent that these laws harm humanity, which I submit they do, then they are wrong and immoral.

## Why Males Need Reproductive Strategies

Males, like females, need reproductive strategies in order to advance their reproductive interests. At all stages of the reproductive process, from mating to pregnancy to childbirth to parenting, they are competing with other men and for the attention of women. Men and women have co-evolved strategies, each trying to control the process.

While women and men each compete for mates and are selective, in general women set the ground rules for reproduction. Men have evolved in some ways differently than women because of this. Everything else being equal, men have a harder time getting chosen to mate than women do. Males must compete for this honor on a variety of levels. Biologist Joan Roughgarden of Stanford University argued that the social selection aspects of reproduction are as important or even more important than the sexual selection aspects: "Female choice attempts to identify males who will deliver on their promises of parental care. . . ." Thus in order to get selected by the females, males have to let the females know that they in fact have what women need, including resources like genetic fitness, family status, wealth, ability to provide, physical strength, parenting ability, and willingness to bond as a couple. Roughgarten said that women select men more for parenting than good genes. Whatever the playing field might be, men often end up competing with each other for resources and compete in demonstrating all the desired characteristics that females seek in order to get selected by them.

Not every male measures up or can win in these competitions and not every male is inclined to parent, and therefore not every male gets chosen by a female to mate. Hence not every male will parent a child. Successful men will often have successive mates and children by them, as will some successful women. More men than women will have large numbers of children, and conversely more men than women will have no children. Men who in fact have children have on average more children than women who have children. In most societies men with resources have more children than those men with fewer resources. In other words, male reproductive success varies more than female reproductive success, and higher-status males of almost every species have more reproductive success than lower-status males.

Men of different status will adopt different reproductive strategies. Professor Patricia Adair Gowaty of the Institute of Ecology of the University of Georgia described how the forces of natural selection affect the selection of strategy. Since not all males are freely chosen by females to mate, the males not freely chosen will be able to pass down their genes only by trying to manipulate or control female choice through forced copulation and other strategies of control. Natural selection will favor males who succeed in doing this, because they will actually pass down their genes. However, this strategy may lead to harm to women since they lose control over their reproduction. In this case natural selection will favor the females who resist the males' efforts to control reproduction and who reassert their own control.

The rejected males can either give up, and not reproduce, or alternatively can stay in the game. Since force or control didn't work, these men can get chosen only by trying to attract those females who successfully resisted their previous overtures by employing a fallback strategy of exchanging resources such as food, shelter, and protection in exchange for reproduction. This bargain may harm some females because they are giving up control over reproduction, and again natural selection will again favor the females who resist and insist upon controlling their reproduction. Gowaty concluded that those females who succeed in resisting these male overtures will be able to choose mates "based on honest signals of intrinsic male quality." Gowaty concluded, "Thus, within populations, mating tactics will almost always vary. . . . Mating systems variation thus can be seen fundamentally as a function of how much control of their own reproduction females have."

Under Gowaty's theory, males will engage in three types of mating strategies—the control strategy, the exchange of resources strategy, and a strategy of demonstrating their fitness. The control strategy used to be the domain of kings and tyrants who captured women and kept them as slaves or in harems. It could be reproductively rewarding. In February 2003 the first measurable example of how well this strategy could succeed was discovered when geneticists measured the Y chromosomes of men currently living in the nations comprising the former Mongol Empire created by Ghengis Khan in the thirteenth century. Geneticist Chris Tyler-Smith of Oxford University discovered eight hundred years later that:

> . . . 8% of the men dwelling in the confines of the former Mongol empire bear Y chromosomes that seem characteristic of the Mongol ruling house.
>
> If so, some 16 million men, or half a percent of the world's male population, can probably claim descent from Genghis Khan.

Few men today or in the past can attain the reproductive success of Genghis Khan. The Khan family success was due to a vast network of harems established in conquered territories. Instead of using conquest and control, most men compete in the battle of the sexes by using the other two strategies—exchanging resources or demonstrating fitness and character, or some combination thereof. There are many exceptions to and variations of these Darwinian and Gowatian rules, but in general women, if they escape the male control strategy, control human reproduction. Women control reproduction not because they are necessarily smarter, but because they have to. Natural selection has favored and does favor women who take control of the reproductive process. Women who have the traits that enable them to do this will pass these traits down to their daughters, and they will become more prevalent in the population.

Men have used a variety of strategies, short of harems, to try to take back control of reproduction from women. They seek to take control because they want to insure their own reproductive success and not leave their success up to their partners. Thus laws prohibiting abortion are an attempt by men to take control of reproduction. Men wrote laws, such as the early American abortion laws, where abortion would be permitted only when physicians, then all male, permitted it. German physicians admitted the same thing to my grandmother after World War I when they opposed laws legalizing birth control. They wanted to force women to come to male doctors for abortion and keep male control over the future of the German race. As wrong as these laws were, these men were not acting irrationally. They were trying to tilt the evolutionary scales in their favor. It was a fight over power—reproductive power.

With or without laws restricting a woman's reproductive options, men still have to compete to reproduce. They need strategies to reproduce successfully, just as women do. Not all men will be chosen, and in general high status men have more reproductive success than low status men. Men therefore compete for status and resources. Even so, women have evolved to control the process of choosing a mate, and men have responded with a variety of strategies to try to level the playing field and even to tip it in their direction. Natural selection has favored women who control reproduction since they give birth at times and with partners who will help them and their child.

Natural selection also favors men who control their reproduction. What gives men evolutionary fits is the fact that they have never been able to be sure that the children they are parenting are theirs. This is the problem of paternity uncertainty.

## Male Reproductive Strategies
## As a Response to Paternity Uncertainty

Why do males feel it important to control human reproduction? Not just their own reproduction, but women's reproduction too? Males don't have health issues with pregnancy, childbearing, and nursing, but they do have another evolutionary issue. Natural selection will only favor men who insured that the children they were parenting were theirs. Women know that their children are theirs, but men don't. If a man spends the time and resources to unknowingly parent a child of another man and in so doing forgoes having another child, his genes will not be passed down to the same degree that they would if he had parented his own child. Males have evolved to try to ensure paternity certainty. Those men who did not have this trait failed to pass down their genes. Those men who had this trait did pass it down.

Statistically somewhere between 5 and 10 percent of the time a man is cuckolded and is raising a child that is not genetically his. Even though this may seem like a small number, it is a risk sufficient to raise paternity fears in every man. It is the man's fears that we must address. It is a fear recognized in our earliest writings. Aristotle said in Book IX (7) of the Nicomachean Ethics written in 350 BCE: "Mothers are fonder of their children than fathers; bringing them into the world costs them more pains, and they know better that the children are their own."

For all of human history, until recent scientific developments in DNA testing, a woman, but not a man, knew for sure who her children were. Even if she was not entirely certain who had fathered them, she knew 100 percent of the time that she was the mother. A man has not been able to know whether he is the biological father of the child his partner has just given birth to. This state of affairs is called "paternity certainty," or more accurately, "paternity uncertainty." It is an indelible part of the sexual selection battle between the sexes.

What is the extent of the paternity uncertainty problem from the male point of view? Studies in various cultures worldwide are remarkably consistent and show that about 5–10 percent (the range is enormous and varies from under 2 percent to about 30 percent) of children are not the genetic child of the father who is raising the child as his own. The studies range from Iceland to England to the Yanomamo Indians of Venezuela. In one respect 5 to 10 percent seems like a low figure, but from a male evolutionary perspective it is extraordinarily high. It is a figure that represents evolutionary/genetic death for the non-father at least with respect to that child. It is as if in jumping out of an airplane with a parachute there was a one in ten or one in twenty chance of the chute not opening. In such as case few would take the risk. The downside risk, death, is too great at 5 to 10 percent. Why should males take the risk of evolutionary, genetic death with female infidelity or cuckoldry even if in percentage terms it is so small? A man does not want to devote time and resources to unknowingly parenting a child that is not his; he wants to conserve his resources for his genetic children. It is in a male's best evolutionary interest to know who his offspring are and presumably to parent them, if male parenting is needed to get them to adulthood safely.

Men's fears of female infidelity are entirely justified. Cases like that of Morgan Wise, a railway engineer of Big Spring, Texas, are not anomalies. Wise's youngest child was born with what doctors thought was cystic fibrosis, a genetic disease carried by both parents. In seeking confirmation, in early 1999 doctors tested Wise to see if he was a carrier of the disease. When it was determined that he was not, the issue of paternity was immediately raised, and after further testing it turned out that not only was Wise not the genetic father of his youngest child, he wasn't the genetic father of two of his other three children as well. Wise and his wife had divorced by this time, and, when Wise tried to reopen the proceedings to avoid paying child support for the children who were not his, alleging fraud by his wife, the court refused, saying the divorce decree was final. The court would not accept the paternity testing as evidence of the wife's fraud in the divorce proceedings. The prior court decree, which ordered Wise to pay child support for all his "children" and which also denied him visitation rights, was left in place, even for the one biological child that he had with his former wife. Two legal principles adverse to the interests of the cuckolded male intersect here. The husband is still the presumed father of the children born to his wife, and courts like their orders to be considered final and not subject to future reopening. Cuckolded men are the evolutionary losers in this game of two-card monte.

Anthropologist Sara Blaffer Hrdy in her book *Mother Nature* described the interlocking nature of male and female sexual strategies and why men get cuckolded. Male-male competition in the animal kingdom sometimes ends with a larger and stronger male driving off or killing a rival in order to mate with a female. The female's children by the now-deposed male are at great risk of being killed by the new male, who wants the female to devote herself to raising his children and not someone else's. Among some primates, researchers have estimated that up to one-third of all infants born are killed by the new male in the house. A man succeeds in this system we evolved in by not only being strong and a good fighter, but also by staying by his mate, guarding her and thus protecting his own position. A woman similarly succeeds if the male does this, since her children would thereby have a better chance of survival. This does not mean that a female's best strategy is monogamy. Hrdy went on, "However, if her mate dies, or is driven off by another male, she would be better off if she had associated with several males, thereby improving the odds that there will be several candidates in the neighborhood who classify her offspring as possibly 'kin.'" By having multiple partners, females can make use of inherent male paternity uncertainty to increase the survival chances of their children. It may conversely not be in her best interest to do this if all the males end up deserting her because they do not have enough paternity confidence. She might be left to raise her children alone. Females make use of male paternity uncertainty for their own reproductive benefit by, as Joan Roughgarden said, spreading "the probability of paternity among males to assure offspring safety."

It is difficult for men to solve the problem of paternity uncertainty by preventing a woman from having sex with others while she is ovulating, because a man does not know when a woman ovulates. Mate guarding is difficult enough for primates and other animals even when ovulation is clear. It is near to impossible for humans when we don't consciously know when a female ovulates. To solve this problem, men have evolved to be especially concerned about the sexual faithfulness of their mates. Those who took steps to assure fidelity or who were more attuned to their mate's moods and feelings were more likely not to have their mate be unfaithful and thus succeeded in passing on their genes and not parenting someone else's children. A past history of sexual activity with others would serve as warning for males to be extra careful.

As psychology Professor David M. Buss of the University of Michigan stated:

> Men who were indifferent to the potential sexual contact between their wives and other men would not have been successful at passing on their genes.
>
> Our forebears solved this uniquely male adaptive problem by seeking qualities in a potential mate that might increase the odds of securing their paternity. At least two preferences in a mate could solve the problem for males: the desire for premarital chastity and the quest for postmarital sexual loyalty. Before the use of modern contraceptives, chastity provided a cue to the future certainty of paternity. On the assumption that a woman's proclivities toward chaste behavior would be stable over time, her premarital chastity signaled her likely future fidelity. A man who did not obtain a chaste mate risked becoming involved with a woman who would cuckold him.

Males evolved two strategies to deal with the vagaries of female behavior and paternity uncertainty—guarding their mates and being promiscuous themselves. On the promiscuity front David Oakley and Luther Crawford are the evolutionary equivalent of Genghis Khan, but without the harem. Sara Blaffer Hrdy stated:

> Given the situation as we find it, females mate with more than one male. This leaves males little choice. They must mate with as many females as they can, or else find themselves at a relative disadvantage vis-à-vis their rival's efforts to transmit their own genes to the next generation. Like mothers, males make trade-offs of their own. Males must choose between parenting offspring they may have sired, and seeking to mate with additional females and possibly siring more.

The evolutionary benefit and risks are clear. Male paternity uncertainty is the opposite side of the coin from female infidelity or cuckoldry. It is in a female's evolutionary advantage to mate with different males. She can do this by engaging in infidelity, or by divorce and remarriage. The evolutionary advantage under the Red Queen theory is that the woman has a variety of genetic fathers for her offspring, thereby producing children with the best chance of resisting pathogens. Furthermore, under Gowaty's and Roughgarten's social selection theory, she gets support, assistance, resources, and protection from multiple fathers in order to bring up the children. Infidelity is the female way of hedging her reproductive bets. Lifetime monogamy may be one way to attain reproductive success, but it is not the only way. It is most certainly not the exclusive rule for reproductive success in any part of the animal kingdom. Animals, even those who theoretically bond for life, secretly mate with a whole series of suitors. Anthropologists have termed human society one of serial monogamy; that is to say, we tend to have more than one mate, though generally not at the same time. As anthropologist Helen Fisher pointed out, humans tend to divorce and remarry with frequency.

During the time when a man is in a monogamous relationship, as David Buss pointed out, it is in a man's interest to ensure his wife's fidelity. A man will try to ensure paternity certainty by mate guarding to insure that only he is having sex with his partner. Chastity belts, virginity tests, sequestering of females, chaperoning, not to mention laws against adultery which often punish the woman more than the man, the sexual double standard, cliterodectomy (removal of the clitoris in order to reduce the woman's sexual pleasure) are all methods devised by husbands to try to insure their wives' fidelity and to preserve their exclusive sexual access. These systems of control may also be strategies to reduce the incidence of sexually transmitted infections that can cause infertility in women, thus preserving them for men to impregnate. While chastity belts are out of fashion, all the other methods are alive and well today somewhere on the planet.

Successful cuckoldry (from the female point of view) forces a man to take the time and resources to unknowingly raise a child who is not his biological child. It diverts him from making himself available and competing to find a new mate with whom to have a child of his own. It is by no means a personal dead end since millions of men knowingly raise non-genetic children via adoption and step-parenting. This altruism is itself an evolutionary benefit since it increases the chances of all children being cared for to some degree. But from a genetic point of view the concept of paternity certainty and its inverse, cuckoldry, have been important determinants of male behavior and male feelings about women's reproductive rights. Not that the man is not conflicted by imposing restrictions on female sexuality. These restrictions make it more difficult for him to have a successful affair whereby he impregnates another woman. By enacting these laws husbands are placing their evolutionary bets on the progeny produced with their wives.

Paternity uncertainty is a major driver of male and female sexual behavior. In 5 to 10 percent of cases in some societies the father is unknowingly raising a child that is not his. This is not to his evolutionary benefit. Men only benefit evolutionarily when they raise their own children. Men have evolved to select women who show fidelity and to jealously guard their mates. Men have also put legal and other prohibitions on female sexuality in an effort to keep them from having affairs. Women have evolved to get around these prohibitions and to have multiple potential fathers for their children. Men too try to father children by other women. Each strategy carries risks for the male and female—risks of disease, risks of violence to themselves, their mates and their children, and risks of bringing up a child that is not their own. The evolutionary benefits may be worth it for some men and women.

## Why Banning Abortion May Help Males Pursue Their Reproductive Strategies

Polls indicate that support for reproductive freedom declines as one's income declines. Men of lesser status have less chance of reproductive success and want to insure childbearing in the relationships they have.

The male attitudes towards birth control and abortion will be dependent therefore on the status of the male and the particular reproductive strategy he is pursuing in his life. Sexual and reproductive behavior will change depending on the extent of reproductive freedom available. Sex during courtship or outside of marriage carries more risk of childbirth if birth control and abortion are not available. That could lead women to engage in less infidelity, thereby increasing a man's paternity certainty. Some men, depending on their circumstances, can be expected to oppose reproductive freedom for women.

Laws restricting reproductive freedom restrict the freedom of women more than men. Without birth control women are essentially helpless to prevent pregnancy if they have sexual intercourse; males can use withdrawal. Only women need abortions. Beyond this, cultural norms in most societies have long had a double standard whereby women's sexuality and sexual freedom were considered more threatening to society than men's and thus were punished more severely. The double standard is alive and well today in Africa and the Middle East, where women are stoned for adultery or have acid thrown in their faces, while their male partners are left unpunished and unscathed. Laws restricting reproductive freedom are an attempt by men to level the reproductive playing field and to gain some measure of control in the battle of the sexes.

While reproductive freedom has been in my view an essential element of human evolution and survival, it is not always viewed that way by males. Males often view reproductive freedom as opening more doors for women than for them. I have argued that reproductive freedom is of benefit to men and women and that every human benefits when humanity has control over its reproduction. The problem is that reproductive freedom is not always of direct benefit to an individual male, or female, in the particular circumstances in which they find themselves. In fact, reproductive freedom may, depending on circumstances, harm a particular individual's reproductive strategy and chances for reproductive success.

A man's reproductive prospects depend on his status vis-à-vis other males, his economic and social circumstances, his desirability as a potential mate, and the reproductive strategy he is pursuing at that moment. Lower-status males with fewer prospects for mating generally have less opportunity to get chosen by a female to mate. Giving their mate the means to avoid pregnancy or childbirth may not be in their immediate interest. Taking away reproductive control from the female gives the male more control over pregnancy and childbearing.

A man's status, his desirability as a mate, and the reproductive strategy he is pursuing are all interrelated. There are two classes of men at any one time—those married or in a stable relationship and those unmarried and not in a stable relationship. The two classes of men may be engaged in different reproductive strategies: the former is parenting or preparing to parent the children he has or will have. The latter may be looking for a new partner and may be more episodic in parenting the children he may have. Men are not locked into either category and will move from one to the other during their life span.

Men who are engaging in a control type of reproductive strategy or a strategy of exchange of resources for reproduction will in general not be in favor of a pregnancy's being terminated without their approval. The bargain they demand for devoting their time and resources to protect and provide for their mate is a successful pregnancy. The pregnancy, assuming it is his, represents his reproductive success. The same is true, but to a lesser extent, for a man who has been chosen by the female for fitness reasons. The reproductive bargain between them is more equal in power, and part of the bargain may be the female's retaining control over her childbearing. In fact, it is in the female's interest to make her continuing control over childbearing part of the mating bargain since natural selection favors her if she does. Men will have to accept this in order to get the chance to reproduce at all with the female who has chosen him.

Male, and female, support for legal abortion may depend on the status of the relationship and economic circumstances of each party at the time of pregnancy. Why would those males who are less likely to mate and father children be supportive of female-controlled contraception and abortion? Surveys reveal that the most common reasons women give for having abortions is that it is not the right time for a child, they want to continue their education, they cannot afford the child, and they don't want to raise the child alone. For males who have status and resources and who are more likely to have multiple mates, there would appear to be additional opportunities to have children if their current partner did not want to. A woman's ability to "control" the abortion decision would have less impact on these men than on those less economically fortunate. Thus higher-status males are generally more supportive of legal abortion than low-status males are.

In most cases the male and female interests do coincide in that it is in their joint interest to have the child survive, be healthy, and eventually reproduce. High- and low-status males will share this interest, but economic and other circumstances may be such that the male and female jointly or separately may decide that the time and environment are not right for reproduction. Adverse circumstances may include poor economic conditions and uncertainties, poor health, family opposition, unavailability of food, instability in the society, and war. Other adverse circumstances can include the necessity for caring for other children or other family members. In 2000 61 percent of women seeking abortions had already had at least one child. Over half of those seeking abortions (52 percent) said that they planned to have children in the future. There is much competition for a parent's time, health, and resources, and parents have to allocate them. It may be better to have a child in the future. Timing is all.

The high cost of raising a child when combined with a man's low current income can lead some low-income males to support having legal abortion accessible for his female partner in order to have his children at a better time in the future. If, however, a man is determined to be a deadbeat dad like Luther Crawford or David Oakley, then he probably won't favor giving women any control over their childbearing. Young people engaging in sexual experimentation may be having sex for pleasure and not thinking much about reproduction. While young men and women may be at or near the peak of their sperm and egg's health genetically, they are probably not anywhere near their peak earning capacity and may not want to make a lifetime commitment to their current sexual partner anyway. The obligations to support a child may not be feasible for a young couple. They will not want their child brought up in poverty, if they believe their prospects are brighter in the future. Legal abortion helps a couple sort all this out.

The mating challenge for low-income men and women was unveiled in a startling fashion in a graduate anthropology seminar at Rutgers University a few years ago when one of the female students in the middle of a discussion of DNA testing for paternity was heard to utter: "It's getting very hard to have sex in New Jersey." Professor Lionel Tiger, who was teaching the seminar, stopped the discussion to ask what she meant. The woman was referring to the new welfare regulations that required a woman requesting benefits for herself and a child to identify the father of the child. The woman reported that this requirement was a significant deterrent to courtship, or at least the sexual aspects thereof, since the young men in her circle were less than thrilled with the prospect of supporting an accidental child for eighteen-plus years.

Abortion creates a conflict for low-status men. In the reproductive dance it is the men who get chosen by the women. The men at the bottom of the economic totem pole are generally the wallflowers—the last chosen and the first to be cut in on. They have the fewest resources. Low-status men in the Western world find marriage and family formation increasingly out of their control. For males it would be in their interest to have legal abortion available so that they could determine which children they want to have when they can afford them. The problem for men is that abortion is a woman's decision, not theirs. The availability of female-controlled contraception and abortion put reproductive decisions firmly in a woman's hand. For low-status males the problem is that the woman's pregnancy may be their only shot at reproduction, and it can be terminated without their knowledge or consent. But in a case where a man's partner is pregnant, where they decide that it would be better to have a child later, and where it is likely that the man will actually have the opportunity to father a child later on, then the man will see legal abortion as being in his interest.

However, some females, depending on their status and desirability as a mate, may be just as opposed to abortion being legal as some males are. The reason is that the availability of legal, female-controlled abortion may change female, and thus male, reproductive behavior. Males and females may end up with fewer opportunities of family formation and parenting. A male's options when his partner is pregnant are greatly circumscribed by the obligations of child support. He can neither disavow the child nor demand an abortion. Because the woman has the power to have an abortion, or to have a child, the male's only countervailing power is to refuse to marry her. He can refuse the shotgun because having the child was her doing, not his. To the extent that a female wants the option to demand marriage and to the extent her right to seek an abortion is a cause of his reluctance to marry, then the legality of abortion may not be in her interest. Her interest in a commitment from the man who has impregnated her may override her interest in starting over with a new man. Her calculus (and thus her opinion about the legality of abortion) may depend on the availability of suitable males now and in the future.

Male/female cooperation and competition are both present in the reproductive game. Kristen Luker pointed out the strategic aspects of a pregnancy in getting a partner. Married males may look for other partners, but so can and do females. In so doing, this does not mean that either or both sexes want to dissolve a relationship or a marriage. Other partners may bring excitement and spice to a relationship and may result in a pregnancy. This brings a decision point. It is not always in the male's interest to know of his wife's pregnancy by another man. In order to preserve the relationship, a woman who has had an outside relationship and wants to terminate the pregnancy caused thereby must have the power to do so on her own. She thereby can preserve their marriage. Has the man been "deceived"? Yes. But has a greater good resulted? Yes. A family is preserved for the benefit of both the couple and their children. This is the compassionate result. It is sometimes better to keep jealousy, "the green-eyed monster" as Shakespeare called it in *Othello*, in check. The Supreme Court in *Casey* recognized this as a good enough reason to overturn the requirement that a wife inform her husband about an abortion.

It is not in a man's interest to have his wife succeed at cuckoldry. If he finds out, it is in his interest to have legal and safe abortion available to her, should they agree on an abortion. It would even be in his interest to require her to have an abortion. For the husband who is at risk of being cuckolded, legal abortion gives his wife the option to terminate his pregnancy as well, leaving her available to get pregnant with another male. Reproductive freedom can enable a woman to plan and space her pregnancies no matter who the father is. Reproductive freedom is a two-edged sword. Sauce for the goose may be sauce for some other gander.

Just as there is no one perfect reproductive strategy, there is no time when reproductive freedom is always of benefit to every male and female. The differing biology of males and females has led to the evolution of a reproductive system full of cooperation, competition, contradiction, and discord. Cooperation is important, even vital, for the protection of a pregnant and nursing mother and for the upbringing of a child (though many women do all this alone). A female is the best judge of the best time and circumstances whether and if to give birth. Despite this, many males do not permit female choice and power over reproduction. Males also often engage in strategies to control females and to maintain exclusive sexual access. Attitudes towards legal abortion, which is the ultimate in female control of reproduction, depend on male circumstances and the environment, including the status of the parties, the status of the relationship, and the reproductive strategies being pursued.

The male need for control or reproduction comes, as I have argued, because of male paternity uncertainty. If men and women can take steps to eliminate paternity uncertainty, then men and women can enter into reproductive bargains as equals. Under these circumstances most decisions about childbearing can be mutual but females can properly assert that, if there is a conflict, they should control the pregnancy and abortion decisions. In exchange, males need not worry that a child will be born that is not theirs.

Now for the first time men have the means to ensure paternity certainty other than by restricting a woman's reproductive freedom. How then can men reduce or eliminate their paternity uncertainty? Two ways—by taking control of contraception through condom use and, secondly, by making DNA testing for paternity routine.

## Condoms and the Reduction of Paternity Uncertainty

If it is so clearly in men's interests to take control of human reproduction and eliminate paternity uncertainty, why don't they use condoms? In part, men, like women, see pregnancy as an integral part of courtship. But in addition men are more than willing to cede responsibility for birth control to women because condoms interfere with their pleasure and because women now have a multitude of effective birth control options that they can use. The introduction of the birth control pill and the legalization of abortion led to a massive cultural change where women were expected to take control over pregnancy prevention and avoid unwanted childbearing. The undesirable consequences to men of having given up their involvement and even their control of pregnancy by reducing their condom use have been enormous (condoms used to be the number one method of birth control; now they trail sterilization and the Pill). The increase in sexually transmitted diseases and resulting infertility for both men and women are directly related. Men have less confidence in their paternity because they do not know if they are potentially impregnating their partner. This has led to less willingness of men to parent and to form lasting bonds with their partners for the benefit of their children. Men need to take back control of pregnancy and thus paternity in order to alleviate these negative social consequences.

There are important reproductive reasons for a couple to have sexual intercourse as part of courtship before deciding whether or not they will either marry or have a child, even though in so doing each risks pregnancy and sexually transmitted diseases. If a pregnancy, in the words of Kristen Luker, "connotes fertility, femininity, adulthood, independence and a wide variety of other meanings" for a female, it connotes similar meanings for a male—fertility, masculinity, adulthood, and independence. A pregnancy confirms that the couple is fertile and will be a successful reproductive pair. This after all is what they are biologically supposed to do. A pregnancy, even if the man does not want a child, thus has positive benefits for a man as it does for a woman. The man gets these benefits without the health risks of a pregnancy, so there is even less reason for him to use contraception.

While the epidemic of HIV/AIDS and other sexually transmitted infections should make condom use by males almost mandatory, condoms are still not used in all sexual encounters between unmarried persons. Sexually transmitted diseases are a leading cause of infertility and, by definition, are transmitted by sex. The more unprotected sex a person has with different partners, the greater the likelihood of disease transmission and resulting infertility. Humanity has evolved and survived by men and women remaining fertile. It is not in humanity's or men's interest to have rampant sexually transmitted diseases. It is in men's interests to have widespread condom use to prevent this. Even so, contraceptive responsibility falls today on the female, and it appears that males are content with this state of affairs. Before 1960 the condom was the most widely used contraceptive. When the Pill was introduced in the United States, it rapidly took over as the preferred "choice," and condom use plummeted along with the notion that males were primarily responsible for contraception. Reported sexually transmitted diseases have since skyrocketed.

It is no secret that men don't like condoms. Sex is more pleasurable for men without them. But the risks of non-use of condoms would seem so high that condom use would be the only rational alternative. Of course, we are not dealing with a rational world when it comes to reproduction. Some men clearly dislike condoms so much that they are willing to cede reproductive control to women to avoid having to use them. By ceding birth control to women, men never know if they are potentially impregnating their partner. They thereby increase their paternity uncertainty. Female reproductive freedom, that is to say birth control and abortion, is a license for males to avoid condom use. Reproductive freedom also becomes a license for males to avoid responsibility for a pregnancy.

In America, and in much of the Western world, the pressure to legalize abortion came after the introduction of the Pill. Shouldn't the Pill have obviated the need for legal abortion? The Pill was supposed to eliminate unintended pregnancy. Instead, the increase in Pill use coincided with an increase in abortion being used to eliminate unwanted childbearing. The legalization of the Pill led to a change in attitude. Fertility was something that could be controlled, and women were the ones doing the controlling. The legalization of abortion under female control led to a further decline in male control over his reproduction. The woman now had the power to legally terminate the pregnancy without his knowledge and even over his opposition. Men supported and enacted the changes in the law to make the Pill and abortion legal.

Kristen Luker argued that "the advent of legalized abortion ironically makes it easier for men as well as women to escape the consequences of the decision not to use contraception." Because women are made to feel accountable for contraception, it is "unlikely that a man will be pressured either by social norms or by the woman herself into taking on the major part of the financial costs of the abortion." Even though men had the ability to retain control of pregnancy through condom use, they didn't. Luker argued that because of the new social norm of female control of pregnancy, men were denied "both the means and the motivation" to avoid unintended pregnancy. Thus, men had the motivation to grant women full reproductive rights, including full access to birth control and abortion, in order that they might avoid the financial and other costs that would be imposed on them to help bring up children they did not want.

Professor Lionel Tiger of Rutgers University based his 1999 book, *The Decline of Males,* on the hypothesis that male acquiescence in female-controlled contraception brought about by the advent of the Pill has inadvertently caused men to lose even more confidence in the paternity of their children. By letting women take control of contraception, the man could never be sure the woman was on the Pill and hence whether he was potentially impregnating her. When the Pill replaced the condom, contraception was no longer necessarily a mutual activity. With the excuse that sex was better without a condom anyway, men turned over the responsibility for pregnancy prevention to women. Tiger argued, along with Luker, that, when a woman got pregnant, it was deemed by society to be her fault, and it was she alone, not the man and woman together, who had to remedy the situation—hence the pressure for legalized abortion. But, as the polls indicate, there is also substantial support for the proposition that the father should have a veto over the abortion decision. This would indicate that in their haste to legalize abortion, many men feel that they went too far too fast and eliminated more of their power over reproduction than they should have. Tiger also argued that reduced paternity confidence brought about by less condom use led to undesirable social consequences, including lower family formation and a rise in children being brought up by single women.

Can't men take some power and control over reproduction without infringing on women's reproductive freedom? If they did, there would be fewer conflicts over reproductive rights. After all, a male can refuse to have vaginal intercourse or, if he does, all a man has to do is use a condom when he does not wish to father a child. By failing to use condoms men put themselves at greater risk of sexually transmitted disease and at greater risk of having a child they do not want. But men don't. Only 25 percent of couples in the U.S. use a condom as their method of birth control. Condom use among non-monogamous is especially sporatic. Why aren't men taking control of the situation, especially since under Professor Tiger's theory their perceived lack of control leads in part to their relative "decline"?

There are countervailing pressures against condom use—greater pleasure, a culture that makes women responsible for contraception, and the psychic and other benefits of a pregnancy for the man. While these countervailing pressures lead many men to support women's reproductive rights as way of ending their responsibility for an unwanted pregnancy, this does not mean that men don't want control over that decision.

Men need to have a positive reason to support women's reproductive rights. Male support for reproductive rights that is based on the notion that legal abortion will get them out of a bad situation is based in quicksand. There are too many dangers to men when women have reproductive rights and when men don't use condoms as a result: there are sexually transmitted diseases and infertility; there is increased risk of pregnancy; there is the threat of infidelity; and there is less paternity certainty. Condom use can solve or alleviate the disease problem. The risk of an unintended pregnancy is greater if only the woman uses a birth control method, than if the man also uses a condom. Nothing will alleviate the fear of infidelity. The unique male problem of paternity uncertainty can, however, be eliminated completely, and then men can have a positive reason to support women's reproductive rights because men won't be hurt by them and the chances of their reproductive success will be increased.

Men have a conflict about reproductive rights for women since these rights make infidelity less costly for women. To be precise, reproductive rights make non-marital vaginal intercourse less costly. Reproductive rights have no effect on the costs or benefits of other forms of sexual expression that humans have engaged in since time immemorial with people of the same or opposite sex. Reproductive rights enable women to prevent pregnancy and terminate unwanted pregnancies. Reproductive rights enable women to select with more certainty when and with whom they will become pregnant. Men have evolved to be especially selective for women who will remain faithful. Evolutionary pressures discourage men from giving women reproductive rights that permit unfaithfulness, or that make unfaithfulness "easier." The male fear is not just that their partner will stray; their fear is that they will spend the time and effort to raise someone else's child to the detriment of their own children. Men lost sight of these instincts when they allowed the Pill and abortion to become available. They probably didn't know what they were getting into. These fears of infidelity and paternity uncertainty now lead many men to want to take back control over contraception, pregnancy, and childbearing by not only criminalizing abortion but also by restricting contraceptives to male-controlled methods—condoms, withdrawal, fertility timing, and periodic abstinence—and by opposing legal abortion.

Men don't need to restrict female access to birth control or abortion to achieve their goals of avoiding sexually transmitted diseases, reducing their fears of infidelity, and eliminating paternity uncertainty. They can start by using condoms. But they have to do more to make fear of infidelity and paternity uncertainty non-issues. They have to make sure their children are theirs by DNA testing. Then women and men can come together to support reproductive freedom.

## Solving the Paternity Uncertainty Problem — DNA Testing

For the first time in history the new technology of DNA testing enables men to determine conclusively whether or not they are the father of a particular child. As I have argued, the dual problem of cuckoldry and paternity uncertainty has been and is a major concern, if not the major concern, biologically for males. It is a major detriment to a male's reproductive strategy to unknowingly spend time and resources supporting a child that is not genetically his. When he raises another man's child, he is spending time and resources to facilitate the transmission of another man's genes. In many cases, a male will do this knowingly and willingly as part of a bargain to gain the confidence of a female and to partner with her to produce progeny of his own or for other reasons, including to guarantee companionship. But when the male does not know that he is not the only male on the female's reproductive horizon, he loses biologically.

The female and her children presumably gain. This is the biological trade-off. A family unit is formed. Children with variation in their genetic makeup are born and cared for because resources and parenting are provided. The male may or may not benefit from this arrangement. If he gets to have children from the female, then it is a win-win for all. If he does not or if his current children get less care, attention, and resources, then he and they lose. The mother and her children are the clear beneficiaries of cuckoldry, if she can keep it secret.

But cuckoldry is also a risky strategy for the woman and her child and is becoming riskier. There are serious risks to the woman and child of abandonment and death. The man may find out about the infidelity and leave her. Risk of violence is real. The most dangerous time for a female to be a victim of domestic violence is while she is pregnant. Medical experts have recently discovered that the leading cause of death for pregnant women in the United States is not embolism or hemorrhaging, but murder. This type of gender violence sometimes may occur because the man questions the paternity of the child she is carrying. Statistics also show that there is substantially more risk of violence to children from stepfathers than from fathers, even though the overall risk is low. Given these risks, it may be in the woman's interest, as well as the man's, to insure that the man has paternity certainty.

Women used to be protected by the law against unilateral abandonment by her husband if he had suspicions of infidelity. Historically the law did not make it easy for a man to avoid supporting a child that was not his. Ever since Roman times, the law conclusively presumed that a child born to a married woman was fathered by her husband, unless the husband could prove he was sterile or impotent, or at the time of conception was beyond "the four seas bordering the kingdom." This rather quaint formulation was designed to preserve the family unit from unfounded and unprovable accusations of infidelity. The law served to protect the mother and child from being thrown out onto the streets on the man's say-so. The law protected marriage, and the child would not be tainted by accusations of bastardy or illegitimacy, words that have now largely gone out of use.

In those pre-technology days the only proof that could be offered of non-paternity was physical impossibility. While the law was humanitarian since it viewed the children, both legitimate and illegitimate, as equal until proven otherwise, from a biological point of view, the legitimate child got the short end of the paternal stick, because he had to share time and resources with his or her illegitimate half-sibling. This law and the principle behind it have lasted for almost two millennia. But the law has now come up against cultural, social, economic, and scientific forces that are unraveling it. Defective or not, the law had the effect of providing for familial and economic stability and protection for the mother and child. For the last two thousand years at least, husbands have been living in an environment where their wives could cuckold them at will and the husbands would have to pay for it.

The advent of DNA testing is nothing short of revolutionary in terms of its potential to change the rules of the legal and biological game. But will it? DNA testing may provide refutation or confirmation of the theory that paternity uncertainty is a major, if not the major, driving force in male reproductive strategy. Whether this will take a few years or millennia to evidence itself is not known. I believe that the use of DNA testing for paternity will change male and female reproductive behavior and strategies and will lead to more male support for reproductive freedom.

DNA technology has now given males and females the ability to test for paternity with the genetic material contained in a few strands of hair or in the saliva. Samples of blood or sperm are not required. The procedure can be done by mail, and the test results are available within a week. The procedure has become so easy that daytime television talk shows now feature paternity testing as a regular staple on their entertainment schedule. Some shows go beyond the voyeuristic thrills and try to give a public service message. As one host, Jenny Jones, said to a contestant who was upset that the DNA test proved that he was the father, "It's very easy to put on a condom and not be on a show like this."

Despite all the publicity, males are not stampeding en masse to get paternity tests. The cost is not inexpensive, beginning at about $200. Still, this is less than a first trimester abortion and is far less than the cost of raising a child for eighteen years or more. DNA testing companies are openly advertising for business, and business is growing. One company put up a billboard above a Baltimore expressway with a photograph of a very pregnant Mona Lisa with her enigmatic smile asking "Who's the Daddy?" Another company put a smiling baby with a Pinocchio nose on a billboard asking, "Is his mother a liar?"

The American Association of Blood Banks (AABB) reported about 300,000 paternity tests in accredited labs in the year 2000, with the number increasing every year and the price falling. This might seem a large number until one notes that there are 4 million children born in the United States a year. The paternity testing rate is therefore just under 10 percent, within the estimated 5 to 10 percent cuckoldry rate. Perhaps only the men who have a real, concrete reason for suspicion are seeking testing. The AABB reports that in 28 percent of the cases in 2000 the man tested was not the father. In 72 percent of the cases his suspicions were unfounded. If we assume that the cuckoldry rate is 5 to 10 percent, this leaves half or more of the cases of mistaken paternity undiscovered and perhaps unsuspected. It is not clear why a man might suspect but not procure testing to confirm or alleviate his suspicions.

Even though testing can be done entirely in secret (using a child's hair or saliva is sufficient), perhaps there is a psychological barrier that the man does not want to cross. He may not know what he would do with the bad news. The potential disintegration of a marriage and a relationship with children that he has raised as his own may be too great to contemplate and risk in a confrontation.

If a man has sufficient paternity fears and has the child tested it would seem a routine legal matter at the time of the birth of a child for courts to establish paternity (or lack thereof) using the evidence of genetic testing, much as courts admit this testing in criminal cases for rape, murder, and other crimes. A quite different problem arises when the DNA testing is done years after the birth of a child where the man has been, in every respect but genetically, the father of the child. At that point the courts rule that the interests of the child and the mother to continued economic and paternal support from the man are so important that the court will not permit the man to submit evidence that he is not the father. At this point genetics becomes irrelevant.

While it would seem an easy matter for the court, or the mother, to find the other paternal suspect and get a DNA test, courts often do not permit this. From an economic point of view the other man, the genetic father, might presumably in many cases have resources and the inclination to support his genetic child. But he may not have known he had a child or seen the child for years, if ever. The mother may not want contact with the other man for many reasons. The genetic father may have other children to support. There are many variations in the human dynamic, but all the while there is a child in need of parenting and support. For this reason courts have tended to fall back on the person who has been providing it, in many cases for years—the husband. This is understandable and from the child's point of view often the best result.

But what of the cuckolded husband? What is the extent of his reproductive rights? The evolutionary damage has been done. This cannot be undone. But the husband, who is likely to divorce his wife when he gets the bad DNA results, has some evolutionary future, almost no matter what his age. The mother may not, depending on her age. This is a major conflict in male/female reproductive strategies. The mother's interest, even where she is self-supporting, may be to seek resources to supplement her own in supporting the child. The soon-to-be ex-husband's genetic interest may be to preserve his resources in order to form a new family and to support his genetic children that he has or will have.

The law is slowly evolving to recognize this. It is moving from "the four seas surrounding the kingdom approach" or "once you act like a father, you are to be treated as one no matter what the genetic facts," to "let's find out who the genetic father really is." Some states have enacted laws that permit the introduction of paternity or non-paternity evidence into divorce and child support hearings within a certain time period after a child's birth. The time periods mostly range from up to two years to five years after birth, but some states have revised their law to permit the introduction of paternity tests at any time after a child's birth. In permitting DNA test results to establish non-paternity, state legislatures are trying to balance the man's and woman's interests with what might be in the best interests of the child. Given the built-in conflicts it is hard to be fair to all the parties and to give to each due process of law. Lawmakers have to recognize that, while parenting is more than genetic, the amount and quality of parental investment is based on a genetic connection. Lawmakers are trying to find a happy medium between acknowledging a father's interests and avoiding to the extent possible the risk of damage to children who may lose a father without gaining a new one.

What will fathers do, given all this? Non-payment of child support by males has been a major issue for decades. There are now extensive federal and state programs to collect unpaid child support and to punish deadbeat dads. Since there is up to a 5 to 10 percent chance of a man's not being the father of his children, and a much higher percentage of cases in which the man has suspicions (and a still higher percentage where there is an unconscious fear), it seems logical that a man would seek to minimize the chances that his time, effort, and resources would be devoted to non-genetic children. Supporting non-genetic children diverts resources from the genetic children the man may already have or will have. It makes him less desirable as a mate for another woman; supporting another man's children inhibits family formation and the birth of children who would be genetically his. The extent of male paternity uncertainty before DNA testing, combined with the male desire to only support children that are theirs genetically, explains many of the reasons males avoiding child support payments after divorce. Men, like women, also have a reproductive strategy of having children with different women in order to have genetic variety in their children. Men with limited resources might seek to preserve as much of these resources as possible for their own use and for their future relationships and children. If paternity uncertainty is leading men to avoid paying child support, nowadays it would seem a biological no-brainer for males to seek confirmation of paternity as often as possible after a child is born.

The prospect is real that paternity uncertainty will be relegated to the rest of the animal kingdom. But if human males can now eliminate paternity uncertainty by universal DNA testing, then don't female reproductive strategies have to change, since a woman's infidelity could no longer be kept secret if she has a child thereby? If we assume that seeking diversity in the genes of one's offspring is still a valid biological goal for men and women, then doesn't it now have to be pursued differently? The essence of successful cuckoldry for women was secrecy. The female had offspring by a second mate and had her first mate raise them as his own. In a world where DNA testing is the norm this won't happen unless in the unlikely case that the husband consents to it. Paternity testing will become the norm now in divorce proceedings and, within the time limits set by states, it seems likely that men will seek it at the first signs of discord. Should DNA testing become routine at birth? If men no longer fear infidelity, doesn't the biological foundation for what are viewed in some quarters as patriarchal practices crumble? Males after all have gone to great lengths to restrict female sexuality and to preserve their sole sexual access to females. DNA testing could lead to the elimination of these practices and to reduced male opposition to a woman's reproductive freedom.

While a woman pregnant from an affair may have little biological reason to terminate the pregnancy, the cuckolded husband does have a biological interest in pressuring her to do so. Depending on her circumstances the female might find it in her interest to terminate the pregnancy as part of a strategy to try again with her husband or to try to find a new one. Here the divergent reproductive strategies of males and females hit the abortion debate. The role of abortion in family preservation and formation is real. It may keep a family intact where there are other children. It may let the infidelity be kept secret. When paternity testing is done after birth and used in a divorce proceeding, then all secrets are out no matter how strictly the courts enforce secrecy orders. The other children will find out someday, if not immediately. The devastation can be real and serious for all concerned. The interests of males and females may coincide here to have the early DNA testing and abortion option available.

Theoretically everyone should benefit from secure knowledge of paternity and from women's having reproductive rights—men's fears would be reduced. Men would have less biological, and perhaps less emotional, need to impose cultural and legal controls over their wives' sexuality. These controls, legal and cultural, including restrictions on birth control and abortion, were created in part to maximize men's paternity certainty, but also to preserve marriage and male status. With DNA testing there would be less need for these controls. Birth control and abortion would still be needed for couples to regulate their own fertility, but would not need to be restricted to minimize infidelity. Cuckoldry will be discouraged by the existence of DNA testing. Men and women can enter in relationships knowing this in advance and can use reproductive freedom to further their joint reproductive interests. The father, free from paternity doubts, will invest more in the family unit. Family formation should increase. There should be fewer children being raised in single-parent homes. Spousal and child abuse should lessen in cases where paternity is confirmed but may increase where it is disproved. Cuckoldry should decrease, along with to some extent the genetic variation of our species. Will women and men divorce more and resort to serial monogamy in order to achieve genetic variation in their children? How far along this road will our biological tendencies take us? Conversely, will DNA testing weaken, rather than strengthen, societal institutions like marriage since these institutions are no longer necessary for the male to control his wife's sexuality or the genetic parentage of her children? These are all unknowns, but DNA testing will give males an unprecedented opportunity to level the reproductive playing field and may give women new reproductive freedoms.

## What Men Need To Do

Reproductive freedom is a both a blessing and a curse for men—it can help males attain reproductive success or it can thwart them. Reproductive success is measured individually, not by couple. The sexes battle for control over reproduction, and, since reproductive freedom gives more control over pregnancy and childbirth to women than to men, women have more to gain and men more to lose from reproductive freedom. Natural selection favored women who controlled their reproduction since they and their children were more likely to survive and the mother's genes would be passed down. The threats to a man's genes being passed down do not come from the dangers of childbirth, and therefore reproductive freedom is of no direct benefit to men. Rather the threats to man's reproductive success come from being duped into parenting children that are not his to the detriment of his own children. Men who took steps to ensure their paternity were more likely to have their genes passed down via their own children than those men who did not insure their paternity.

It has been in women's interest to have genetic variety in their children. Having multiple sexual partners provided this and also provided additional potential male protectors for themselves and their children. The men who thought that they might be the fathers of these children would, even though they were not certain, thus provide some degree of protection and parenting to the mother and child.

Men sought to control women's sexuality and to prevent outside sexual opportunities in order to prevent their raising someone else's child unknowingly. Laws banning birth control and abortion were the latest in a long series of cultural and legal restrictions on women's sex lives. This imbalance in the battle of the sexes (or equilibrium, if you are a male) was upset by the advent of female-controlled contraception, the Pill, and by legal abortion, each of which a woman could avail herself of without her partner's knowledge or consent. These developments have had immense social and reproductive consequences in terms of increased sexual freedom for women and a relinquishment of birth control responsibilities by men. Paternity uncertainty increased as a result, as did the number of women giving birth outside of marriage and the number of children being raised by single parents. I believe that support among men and women for unfettered reproductive freedom is so low because these unintended consequences are viewed so unfavorably by both men and women. Support among men, at least, for reproductive freedom will increase when men take back control of their reproduction, eliminate paternity uncertainty, and become more interested in their family. How will this happen? Can men change?

Men and women have evolved over millions of years with paternity uncertainty being a constant fixture in the reproductive firmament. Men now have the power to change this and remove paternity uncertainty as a force in human evolution and behavior. Condom use and DNA testing to eliminate paternity uncertainty will right the reproductive balance between men and women. For starters men can take control of their own contraception, and they don't have to wait until a male pill is developed to do so. The solution is to use condoms. Use them carefully, correctly and throw them away with certainty. This ought to be simple. While issues of pleasure interfere, men have to balance this against the potential benefits.

What is the benefit for the man of reducing the pleasure quotient a little and using a condom? The main advantage is certainty, within the breakage percentages (for adults the failure rate is about 14 percent), that he is not impregnating the woman. Paternity certainty can be further increased if the man and woman actively discuss contraception and, preferably, each uses a method. Having the male know that the female is also using a method, leads to almost 100 percent contraceptive protection and vastly increases paternity certainty, since if the woman gets pregnant, then the man can safely assume the baby is not his. Will men do this? Will they put on the condom every time? Will they refuse to have sex unless they are certain that the woman is also using a method? Unlikely. The threat of getting AIDS or another sexually transmissible disease with their risks of infertility and death hasn't made them use condoms yet with any regularity. If biological death for a man from AIDS hasn't led to universal condom use, it is hard to imagine that evolutionary/genetic injury or death, in terms of supporting a child that is not his, will do so either.

The second way to increase paternity certainty is to use the technology of DNA testing. At prices beginning at about $200 a test, it is in the price range of almost every male. The man can test for paternity secretly. Given the inflexibility of the courts on the issue, the man had best do it immediately after a child's birth. This seems callous in the extreme. But so is not paying child support for children that actually are yours.

The widespread use of DNA testing will lead to new reproductive strategies, or at least less secretive ones. Cuckoldry, and thus paternity uncertainty, could become extinct. In evolutionary terms, this is a major development. But one suspects it will not lead to lifelong monogamy between couples. Nor from an evolutionary point of view, need it. Humanity has benefited by having the genetic variety brought about in part by men and women having different sexual partners, sometimes through serial monogamy and sometimes through infidelity. Just because the human race may have gained from these strategies, this doesn't mean that individual men and women have.

The importance of planning for one's children is as important in the modern world as in the ancient world not because of the dangers to mothers and children from childbearing and disease but because the costs after child "survival" are so high. Men and women face huge economic pressures and need to balance childrearing and work. It is much harder to raise a child on a single income. A father's support and parenting are as vital today as they ever were. With reduced rates of childbearing and increasing cost of raising children, it is in the man's best interests to be a father in every sense of the word. If male parental investment was ever a luxury after a child was weaned, it is no longer; it is a necessity.

Can men and women do anything before beginning a relationship to strengthen the chances of successful childrearing? Some states, like Louisiana, have enacted a more restrictive form of marriage, called covenant marriage, in order to make it harder for couples to divorce. The theory is that if a couple thinks about divorce issues ahead of time and agrees to make divorce more difficult, then it is more likely that they will work harder at the marriage and stay together for the benefit of any children. Whether or not this works is open to debate and relatively few couples have opted for it, preferring the flexibility of current state divorce law.

But is there a model here that might work for couples when they start dating? Before a pre-nuptial agreement, there could be a pre-sex agreement. What would it cover? For starters, any agreement to have sex. Some colleges have codes about dating practices in order to assure consent of both parties to any sexual contact or touching. While widely derided, the codes may be of some benefit given the proclivity for human passion to overwhelm reason and decorum, especially when alcohol or drugs are available. Of course, passion may be evidence of a reproductive strategy in action, and I doubt that a piece of paper will stand in the way. But if some thought is given in advance to contraceptive use and the methods to be used by both parties, then the pre-sex agreement might have some usefulness. Healthy communication is not a panacea for our reproductive and sexual ills. But in some circumstances the communication opportunity can be helpful if men and women would seize it. It could make men partners with women in the mating game instead of competitors or antagonists.

If men and women could make themselves partners, then men would see that use of birth control and abortion are as much in their interest as they are for women. After all, the birth of a child is almost as much of a life-changing event for men as it is for women, or it should be. The goal should be having a child when both parents can support the child and give the child the best chance to survive, be healthy, and in turn to reproduce. Postponing and timing childbearing is thus as urgent for men as for women, if the men are going to be fathers rather than just inseminators. Men need to finish their education, get job training, and get a job, just as women do. They need to take care of their own health, just as women do. With new reproductive strategies, they can be sure they are the genetic fathers, and they can time when it is best for them and their partners to be parents. Now all they have to do is act accordingly.

It is ironic that any recommendations for men relate to their behavior before sex: communicate, negotiate, take control, and use a condom. Be prepared for the consequences if you don't. Think about the diseases you might catch. Think about the consequences for your life if your partner were to have a child in nine months. Think about the child support and parenting obligations, as well as the joys. After you have sex, reproduction is out of your control. The woman decides whether to have a child or not. This all sounds suspiciously like advice from a pro-life advocate. But it's the biology. It is neither fair nor unfair. It is. The effects on men can only be ameliorated if men and women ahead of time understand them and try to find a way together through the thicket of possibilities.

# CHAPTER SIX

# Defending Reproductive Freedom from the Dangers of Reproductive Technology

*Barbara is a lawyer in her thirties. She has worked hard and is a success. She was married in her early twenties but is now divorced. She got pregnant during her marriage, and she and her husband decided they were too young to have a child and had an abortion. After her divorce and throughout her late twenties and early thirties she had an active dating life and was on the Pill. Most but not all of the time her partners used condoms. She got one sexually transmitted disease, chlamydia, which, after it was diagnosed, was cured. She decided to have a child on her own and had in vitro fertilization with donated sperm. She selected female embryos to be implanted, and after several tries got pregnant and now has a three-year-old daughter.*

Even though rudimentary reproductive technologies have been available to humanity for eons, new fertilization and genetic engineering technologies and new contraceptive and abortion technologies now allow women to get pregnant and give birth to healthy children when they would otherwise be unable to. Women also have unprecedented control over when they get pregnant and when they give birth. All these technologies are steps forward in enabling women like Barbara to better plan and control their childbearing to meet whatever their reproductive goals may be. Technology would seem to help both women who want to be mothers and those that do not. Technology may, however, not be on the side of reproductive freedom.

## The Dangers That Reproductive Technologies Pose

While the introduction of new reproductive technologies may initially expand women's and men's reproductive options, it does not always lead to an expansion of reproductive rights. Technological advances in controlling or advancing reproduction throw off the balance of power in the battle of the sexes in their fight for control of reproduction. Reproductive freedom is threatening to men in many ways; so too are reproductive technologies that enhance that freedom. The nineteenth-century discoveries of how to prevent pregnancy with rudimentary IUD's, the diaphragm, and synthetic condoms were unsettling to men on a variety of levels and were followed almost immediately by the Comstock laws, which outlawed the sale and distribution of birth control. Even though technological developments in abortion safety and antibiotics have made abortion safer than childbirth all throughout a pregnancy, abortion is viewed by its opponents as profoundly threatening to the social order, as well as being intrinsically immoral. And no sooner had the first scientific steps been taken to clone humans than there were laws passed to outlaw cloning for both reproductive and research purposes. The lesson to be learned from these examples is that no reproductive technology will be permitted by society unless an ethical and moral framework is laid down for its use and unless both men and women benefit from its use. The danger in any new reproductive technology for pro-choice advocates is that whatever threat it poses to the established social order can be used by opponents of reproductive freedom in the political realm to try to curtail not just the particular technology, but all reproductive freedom. If this happens, then, contrary to the intent of the inventors, reproductive technologies can reduce, rather than enhance, reproductive freedom.

Reproductive freedom and reproductive technologies should enable women to take better control of their childbearing. Natural selection favors women who take this control because it is more likely to lead to healthier children being born who will survive and in turn reproduce. Society should therefore favor reproductive rights and technologies. But no technology provides benefits without drawbacks. The collective use that some people make of reproductive technologies has unintended consequences for society. I will explore in this chapter whether sometimes new reproductive technologies may hurt, not help, humanity's biological goals and its survival.

There have been three major technological innovations in human reproduction in the last half of the twentieth century—the Pill, safe abortion, and assisted reproduction, including genetic engineering. These technological developments have done more than any others to enhance a woman's ability to control her childbearing and, with the possible exception of the advent of antibiotics, more to make childbearing safer and to make child survival more likely. These technologies are not an unmixed blessing, however. Their use may lead to undesirable health consequences for women, men, and children; their use may result in harmful reproductive and sexual behavior; and as a result their use may have negative biological and evolutionary consequences. These negative consequences need to be balanced against the benefits that the technologies bring by enhancing control over reproduction.

There are a few truisms about technology: New technologies will always be developed; they will always be used; they will change human behavior; and every new technology in every field is introduced and used before its unintended consequences are known. Some observers argue that undesirable social and biological consequences are now becoming evident for each of the new reproductive technologies. For example, female hormonal contraception has led to a simultaneous increase in sexual activity and reduction in condom use, thereby facilitating an exponential increase in sexually transmitted diseases and infertility. Some argue that abortion, since it has become safer and more available, has, when used with prenatal ultrasound technology, led to an increase in discrimination against girls in Asia through prenatal sex selection abortion of female fetuses. And some argue that the new reproductive technologies that permit genetic engineering and cloning will bring about serious biological harm to humanity when we try either to reproduce without sex or to determine the genetic makeup of our children.

All these challenges need a thoughtful and persuasive response from advocates of reproductive freedom. Do reproductive technologies lead to bad individual choices that collectively lead to bad results for society? Does the harm caused by reproductive technologies outweigh their benefits? If so, then must these technologies, and by extension reproductive freedom, be curtailed? If we permit some restrictions on reproductive technologies and choice, then do we slide down a slippery slope towards the elimination of reproductive freedom? Will a law banning cloning lead inevitably to the return of the Comstock laws and the overturn of *Roe v. Wade*? The allegations that reproductive technologies bring about undesirable social and biological consequences represent the biggest challenge today to reproductive freedom because they undermine the traditional arguments for choice.

My grandmother and her successors framed the arguments for birth control and abortion rights in one or more of the following terms: women's autonomy and bodily integrity, women's rights and equality, the promotion of children's and family health by encouraging wanted children, and the promotion of public health by the elimination of the negative health consequences of unsafe abortion. But arguments based on choice do not provide sufficient moral underpinnings to support the exercise of individual choices that may result in harmful social and biological consequences for humanity, including increases in sexually transmitted diseases, in infertility, and in anti-female gender discrimination. The unintended consequences of new reproductive technologies force us to answer why society should permit unfettered human, especially female, autonomy, choice, and rights if it is possible that there is more harm done than good. The collective use of these technologies may have such devastating consequences that perhaps society cannot permit them. If, for instance, a technology increases infertility instead of allowing more control over childbearing, then the technology is, to say the least, counterproductive. Human dignity, rights, and choice are powerful moral values. But the requirements of human evolution and survival may trump them.

I don't believe that society can permit its citizens to choose their way to biological disaster. The issues raised by new technologies go beyond choice. Some uses of reproductive technologies are unwise and biologically counterproductive. A biological framework can give the pro-choice movement the means to concede that not all exercises of reproductive freedom are wise and perhaps can not be permitted without undermining the moral basis for that freedom.

## Does Hormonal Contraception Hurt Reproductive Success?

The estrogen and progestin hormones contained in modern birth control pills alter a woman's body chemistry and prevent her from ovulating. A woman taking hormonal contraception appears to be chemically pregnant. But is that all the hormones do? Do the biological and chemical changes wrought by hormonal contraceptives also cause conscious or unconscious changes to the woman's, and her partner's, sexual behavior? Do they lead to changes in reproductive strategies and, if so, what is the evolutionary impact of these changes? There is evidence that hormonal contraception alters our criteria for mate selection and, secondly, that it causes changes in sexual behavior that may increase the rate of transmission of sexually transmitted diseases, with the result being an increase in infertility.

## *Hormones Change How We Choose Our Mates*

Mating does not occur by chance. The process of sexual selection is a complex system that has evolved over human history for the propagation and survival of the human race. Natural selection favors those men and women who select mates with a compatible, that is, dissimilar, major histocompatibility complex (MHC), because their children are more likely to have a stronger immune system to ward off pathogens. There is increasing evidence that humans, like other animals, send out genetic information relating to their MHC that is detected by our sense of smell and by a sixth sense that picks up chemical signals or pheromones from a potential mate. The mechanism for how this works is unknown, but some scientists believe there are hidden receptors in the nasal passages that can detect pheromones. There is some recent evidence that the use of hormonal contraception interferes with the functioning of the sense of smell and the ability to detect pheromones and thus with the normal mechanism of sexual selection as reflected in MHC preference. This may have adverse effects on mating behavior and mate selection.

There is evidence from studies of one of our closest primate relatives, the stumptail macaque, that hormonal contraception does alter sexual selection. An extended series of experiments on the effects of hormones on the sexual behavior of a colony of stumptail macaques were conducted by scientists at Rutgers University, led by anthropology Professor Gary Linn and psychiatry Professor Horst D. Steklis. In one study some, but not all, of the female macaques were given a hormonal contraceptive, in this case the same progestin as found in Depo-Provera. Females significantly outnumbered the males in the colony; in fact there was only one dominant male and one sub-dominant male, and so, in this study, the males had an unrestricted choice of females to mate with. In this species the males usually initiate sex and so dominate the females that they are generally able to have sex with those they choose.

After over a year of observations, the researchers concluded that not only did the females macaques' sexual behavior change, the *male* macaques' sexual behavior changed also. Normally the male macaque is polygamous and has sex with every available female he can. Before the injection of some of the females with progestin, the males had an equal amount of sex with every female. After some of the females got the progestin injection, the amount of sex the males had with the treated females was markedly reduced if not eliminated entirely. In fact, researchers observed no sex at all between the males and the treated females for much of the time. The males' sexual activity appeared to occur exclusively with the females not taking hormonal birth control. Presumably, the males sensed via the female's odor or pheromones that the females treated with Depo-Provera were not ovulating and were chemically pregnant, and they preferred to direct their sexual energies to the untreated females where a pregnancy could possibly result.

Further studies of this colony showed that in the instances when the males had sex with a female who had been treated with birth control the amount of the male's ejaculation was markedly reduced. Since the amount of male ejaculation in many animals is considered an important indicator of female sexual attractiveness, the researchers concluded that the use of progestin led the males to see the treated females as less attractive sexually. In addition, the treated females themselves demonstrated a reduced libido by initiating sex less and by rejecting the few sexual advances they did get.

The tentative conclusion, at least with respect to stumptail macaques, is that the presence of contraceptive hormones, in this case a progestin, caused the males to shift their sexual attention to the females who were not taking hormonal contraceptives. The treated female appeared pregnant to the male, even though the female did not overtly act like she was pregnant. The females on birth control appeared less likely to get a mate or to want to. This may be another part of the explanation for why the males had sex elsewhere. Do these conclusions apply to humans? Do men have less sex with women on the Pill or who are pregnant? Do hormones affect how males sense sexual attractiveness and availability, and, if so, what does this mean for the male and female's mate selection and reproductive strategies?

Part of the sexual selection process is to get males and females with compatible, i.e. dissimilar, major histocompatibility complexes to mate, because, when they do so, it appears that they have a better chance of a successful pregnancy and of having a child with better immunities to resist pathogens. In the University of Bern, Switzerland, study of t-shirts that tried to assess whether female preferences for male human body odors was dependent on the MHC similarity or dissimilarity between the males and females, the women were selected to smell the males' t-shirts as close as possible to their estimated time of ovulation, when the scientists believed that their sense of smell would be at its peak.

Some women in the study were taking hormonal contraceptives and some were not. The women who were not on the Pill favored the odor of the males who had a dissimilar, that is to say compatible, MHC to their own. They were not attracted to the odor of men whose MHC was similar to their own. Interestingly, this preference was reversed for the women who were taking hormonal contraceptives—women on the Pill preferred the scent of men who had a similar, or incompatible, MHC to their own.

The Swiss scientists concluded that:

the contraceptive pill seems to have a strong influence on odour preference.

. . .

This indicates that steroids which are naturally released during pregnancy could change body odour preferences, leading to a preference for odours which are similar to those of relatives. This preference is probably not related to mate choice but may be comparable, to a certain degree, to the observation that female mice prefer MHC-similar individuals for communal nesting . . . *Therefore, the contraceptive pill seems to interfere with natural mate choice.* If the pill changes preferences for familiar as well as unfamiliar body odours, then starting with the pill could have an influence on the stability of an already existing pair bond by influencing odour preference. (Emphasis added)

There is a significant body of research showing that MHC incompatibility between a couple increases the likelihood of an unsuccessful pregnancy. Studies have shown that couples having trouble getting pregnant with in vitro fertilization share a greater number of HLA antigens, meaning their MHC is similar, than do couples who had less trouble getting pregnant. Couples who have recurrent spontaneous abortions also tend to share a higher proportion of HLA antigens than do couples who do not experience spontaneous abortions. These unsuccessful pregnancies could be natural selection mechanisms to prevent the birth of a child that might have less resistance to pathogens.

The Swiss study concluded:

> Our findings show that some genetically determined odour components can be important in mate choice. The observed mate preference could be a means to efficiently react to pathogen pressures. If so, the negative consequences of disturbing this mechanism, by the use of perfumes and deodorants or *by the use of the contraceptive pill during mate choice*, need to be known by users. (Emphasis added)

Hormonal contraception may unconsciously alter the sexual selection process. It may alter male and female mating preferences, which may lead to more unsuccessful pregnancies or less healthy children. The potential problem with hormonal contraception is not that it may lead a woman to favor one man over another, the problem is that it may lead her to favor one class of men over another class, with the class being favored having from her point of view the "wrong" kind of MHC. This problem is not confined to women. Male behavior and choices may be affected, and they aren't even taking the hormones. The resulting failure to conceive or produce a child will lead to less reproductive success for men and women. The problem is that this is something that men and women don't have a choice about when a woman is on the Pill—it just happens. For this reason the arguments in favor of hormonal contraception based on choice are not relevant because there is no choice to defend and the unintended consequences may be indefensible.

From a biological point of view, since hormonal contraception enables women to control their childbearing, hormonal contraception is supposed to lead to reproductive success, not reproductive failure.

None of the numerous side effects listed in the patient literature that comes with birth control pills hints that hormonal contraception may lead to changes in the sexual selection process and reproductive failure. There is increasing evidence though, and the patient literature does list it as a risk, that some women will experience a loss of libido when on the Pill. From a health point of view hormonal contraception has been shown to prevent some diseases, including ovarian cancer, and it is used in the treatment of some gynecological conditions. Hormonal contraception is generally considered remarkably safe and, more importantly, provides major health benefits by enabling women to control when they get pregnant and by allowing women to avoid the many medical risks that are inherent in any pregnancy. But we cannot ignore the negative side effects of hormonal contraception that disrupt natural biological and evolutionary processes, and we must balance them against the evolutionary benefits that accrue to women from being able to control pregnancy.

Further research is clearly needed about the effects of hormonal contraception on mate and MHC preference as they affect reproductive success. Primate studies are not sufficient, and the limited human studies that show potential Pill interference with MHC preference need to be refined and expanded. Which way the scales tip is not clear given that there are alternatives to hormonal contraception for women to use to control pregnancy, even though they are less effective and have their own drawbacks. While educating women about these risks is the least we should do, this does not solve the problem that men and women who take the Pill are taking reproductive risks that cannot be seen or measured.

## The Pill, Reduced Condom Use, and the Increase in Sexually Transmitted Diseases

The use of hormonal contraception may hurt not help reproductive success. Hormonal contraceptive use since its introduction in 1960 may have led to an increase in sexually transmitted diseases, which can cause infertility, premature death, and bad birth outcomes, and in general thwart successful reproduction. If hormonal contraception in fact leads to these outcomes, women and men may be turning reproductive success into reproductive failure.

Dr. Willard Cates of Family Health International, in *Contraception, Contraceptive Technology and STDs*, stated the problem:

> The choice of contraception is furthered complicated when considering its longer-range reproductive implications. Contraceptive use has an influence on not only the acute risks of STDs and unplanned pregnancy but also on the eventual reproductive capacity of those making reproductive decisions.

Before 1960, the chief methods of birth control were condoms, diaphragms, the IUD, withdrawal, periodic abstinence, the natural family planning or rhythm method, spermicides, and douching. The condom was the number one contraceptive. The introduction of the Pill in 1960 led directly to a reduction in condom use. Professor Andrea Tone of the Georgia Institute of Technology in her book, *Devices and Desires*, cited the fact that in 1958 before the pill was introduced, "Condoms were a $150 million business and the most frequently used contraceptive in the country. But the Pill displaced the condom, whose U.S. sales had plummeted to $85 million by 1963. In 1968, Americans were twice as likely to use the Pill as they were condoms."

The major downside of hormonal contraception is that it provides no protection from sexually transmitted diseases (STD). The risk of contracting a STD if no condom is used varies by disease from less than 1 percent per act of intercourse for HIV to about 50 percent on average for gonorrhea. For most STDs the risk of contraction is greater than the pregnancy risk. In the 1960s though, men and women acted as if pregnancy were the greater risk and relied on the Pill, since it provided better pregnancy protection than condoms. At that time many STDs could be cured with antibiotics, while legal abortion was largely unavailable to "cure" an unintended pregnancy.

By relying on the Pill and foregoing condom use, women were taking a bigger STD risk than men. For instance, females have a 60 percent to 80 percent chance of contracting a case of gonorrhea with each act of intercourse with an affected man, whereas men only have a 20 percent chance, or three to four times less risk, with each act of intercourse with an infected woman. With just two acts of intercourse a female is almost certain to get gonorrhea from an infected man. This risk is unacceptably large even though gonorrhea, when discovered, is curable with a single dose of antibiotics. The health risks of gonorrhea for women, if undiscovered, include pelvic inflammatory disease, cancer, infertility, and harm to the children born while the mother is infected. If left undetected, and gonorrhea and other STDs often are, they cause serious health damage.

Sexually transmitted diseases cause infertility by damaging a woman's fallopian tubes, thus preventing conception or implantation of the fertilized egg and increasing ectopic pregnancies. STDs can also cause birth defects and life-threatening infections in the children born to an infected woman. Studies estimate that pelvic inflammatory disease accounts for one third to one half of the cases of female infertility. A World Health Organization report from 1987 estimated that "Almost two-thirds of infertility in African women was attributed to infection (by STDs). . . . "

It is difficult to pinpoint the extent to which women changed their sexual practices, the amount of their sexual activity, and the number of their sexual partners when they changed from condoms to the Pill. There is, however, fairly reliable data on the results of these changes, all of which show a rise in most STDs over the years. Researchers believe that, after two decades of decline, condom use began to increase in the mid–1980s in response to the AIDS epidemic, but even today condom use is by no means universal (about 25 percent of couples use condoms as their method of birth control), or even used in the majority of acts of sexual intercourse even by non-monogamous couples. Documenting the actual fall and rise in various STDs is complicated by improved detection and reporting systems, which means that more STDs get reported to the government. It does not necessarily mean that there has been an absolute rise in STDs.

Reports from the Centers for Disease Control and Prevention indicate that gonorrhea increased during the 1960s until the mid–1970s and has been in decline since; syphilis also increased during the 1960s until about 1990 and has since decreased; and HPV increased until the late 1980s and has decreased since. On the other hand chlamydia and herpes have continued their increase throughout the 1990s to the present. The difference in these disease patterns can be explained by many factors, including reporting differences, the infectivity and virulence of a particular STD, the cures available for each disease, the evolution and mutation of each bacteria or virus in response to each "cure," the rates and kinds of sexual activity among risk groups, and different patterns of contraceptive use among at-risk populations. One cannot put all the blame for the increase in some STDs on declining condom use in the 1960s and '70s or give credit for the reduction in other STDs on the increase in condom use since the mid–1980s. Since this increase did not lead immediately to a reduction in all STDs, either condoms are not equally effective against all STDs or there are other overriding factors fueling the STD increase. Despite the irregular pattern in the rise and fall of STDs, health experts agree that contraceptive patterns are a major factor in the transmission of sexually transmitted diseases and that condoms are the best way to prevent the transmission of STDs if one is going to be sexually active.

The use of hormonal contraception carries its own risks, not just because it does not prevent the transmission of STDs, but in some cases may increase the risk. The effect of hormonal contraceptives on STDs, HIV, and resulting infertility is "unsettled," according to Dr. Willard Cates. Studies have found both an increased risk of chlamydia and gonorrhea among Pill users as compared with non-users, but at the same time a decreased risk of being hospitalized with PID. It was not clear why the Pill increased the risk of some STDs but did not aggravate others. Another study found that users of high estrogen pills had a greater risk of infertility than non-users. A recent 2003 study of women taking oral contraceptives published in *The Lancet*, the leading British medical journal, found that "long duration use of hormonal contraceptives is associated with an increased risk of cervical cancer." Women who had human papillomavirus (HPV) and used the Pill were at even greater risk for developing cervical cancer.

Some scientists believe that use of hormonal contraception increases the chances of HIV infection. Dr. Cates in "Contraception, Contraceptive Technology and STDs" stated: "The effect of hormonal contraception use on HIV transmission, acquisition, or disease progression remains unsettled." Human studies so far are conflicting and inconclusive. In 2003, at the same time as studies in Uganda found no evidence that oral contraceptives contributed to the risk of acquiring HIV, a long-term study in Kenya among sex workers "provided support for the hypothesis that use of hormonal contraception could facilitate HIV acquisition." Dr. Ludo J. Lavreys, of the University of Washington, who is based in Kenya, and his colleagues found that the rate of HIV–1 acquisition was 1.8 times higher for those women using Depo-Provera and 1.5 times higher for women using oral contraceptives than for women using no contraception or who had been surgically sterilized. Dr. Lavreys said that his research team adjusted the results for any differences in condom usage or in sexual behavior because of different methods of contraception the women used, as well as for different sexually transmitted infections the women might have contracted. Dr. Lavreys said he believed that both Depo-Provera and oral contraceptives bring about certain biological and physiological changes to the vagina and cervix that might increase the risk of contracting HIV.

Even with the recent increase in condom use, there is still a STD epidemic in the United States and the rest of the world. In 2003 in the United States there were 65 million people currently infected with a STD, out of a population over the age of fifteen of about 230 million people, with 3 million new cases being reported a year. This figure represents almost 30 percent of the adult population. There are also about 3 million reported unintended pregnancies a year (about half of pregnancies are reported as unintended). It is clear that new contraceptive technologies have not gotten us as far as we might have hoped in solving the twin problems of preventing unintended pregnancy and sexually transmitted diseases. But have they made it worse?

Did men and women's perceptions of the risks from engaging in sexual activity change when female-controlled contraception was introduced? Does the perceived risk differ for men and women since the evidence suggests that it is easier for a sexually transmissible disease to be transmitted during intercourse from a male to a female than vice versa? Whether or not the woman or her partner desires a pregnancy, neither party wants to contract a STD. How can a woman get pregnant without risking the latter? Since both pregnancy and disease risks are greater for women than men, women are at a greater risk than men when they pursue their reproductive goals. A woman's risk level for pregnancy is under her control, but her risk level for a STD depends on the level of STDs in society at large. Women wanting to have a child are at risk because other men and women have taken risks and have contracted STDs. When men and women fail to use condoms and a disease is transmitted, then the other women and men they have sex with are at risk even though they have been careful about condom use. The problem is that a man or woman's individual choice about condoms does not affect just them. It affects every other person in their or their partner's sexual universe. And in order to have reproductive success, which virtually everyone wants, you have to have unprotected sex, and the risk-taking of your partner and the people your partner had sex with becomes your risk.

In response to the AIDS and STD epidemics, public and private health organizations have campaigned to reduce sexual behavior among teens and the rate of teen pregnancy and to increase condom use. Recent evidence, as of 2003, indicates that the campaigns have been successful, since there is a reported delay in commencing sexual activity among teens and a reported increase in condom use. It is not clear if there was a decrease in teen sexual activity, and reduced teen pregnancy rates may be a result of teens switching from the Pill to the more effective Depo-Provera. However, the idea of the male and female both using contraception did not take hold during the 1990s. The percentage of teen males who reported that they and their partner used both a male method and a female method of contraception during intercourse remained level at 17 percent. It appears that the use of condoms, which increased, was substituted for female methods such as the

Pill, which decreased. One study during this time period found that teen girls reported that their use of oral contraceptives fell from 43 percent to 25 percent from 1988 to 1995.

In the United States today, given that 65 million people are infected with a STD, virtually anyone who is sexually active with another person who has also been sexually active is at risk of contracting a STD. For instance, up to 50 percent of sexually active men and women have been infected with human papillomavirus (HPV) at some point in their lives. Women and men are also always at risk of pregnancy. Even with these dual risks, relatively few couples use dual methods to prevent both pregnancy and disease. In studies done in Baltimore and Philadelphia of women who were sterilized, only 6 percent and 12 percent respectively used condoms to prevent STDs. In general, the more effective the method of pregnancy prevention that a woman used, for example, sterilization or hormonal contraception, the less likely she was to use condoms for STD prevention. For instance, Norplant users were less likely to use condoms than Pill users.

Another study reported that teenage girls using Depo-Provera as their birth control method were less likely than girls using the Pill to also use condoms: 63 percent of girls on the Pill said they also used a condom in their last intercourse, while only 52 percent of the girls using Depo-Provera did. The girls using Depo-Provera reported that they were less likely to believe that condoms prevented sexually transmitted diseases and that they were less likely to believe that their partners would use a condom. The difference in results may be because the girls who were on the Pill, which needed to be taken daily, were more activist in general and felt more in control over their health and sexual activity. Or, perhaps, the more technologically advanced method of contraception, Depo-Provera, gave a false sense of power and control to the woman using it. Another study reported, in contrast to many other studies, that women who were given instruction on proper use of condoms had an increase, not a decrease, in STDs. This is inexplicable, except when one considers that the women receiving the instruction may have felt more at ease with sex and thus had more sex without always using condoms, despite all the instruction they received.

One would hope that the experience of having a STD would lead a young woman to modify her behavior so that she would not become infected again. This is not always the case. In a study of sexually active fourteen- to eighteen-year-old girls in Birmingham, Alabama, who were getting treatment and counseling at clinics, the infected teenagers had a *greater* risk of "having unprotected intercourse, using condoms inconsistently and having sex when either they or their partner were drinking." These women were less motivated to use condoms than those who had never been infected with an STD.

A variety of explanations are proposed for the pattern of reduced condom use the more one knows about them or when more effective and technological pregnancy prevention methods are used. These explanations range from the extra cost of condoms, wishful thinking about the non-risk for STDs, a false sense of security and power, and an exclusive focus on pregnancy prevention as the greater risk to the difficult human and gender dynamics of each sexual event. Whatever the explanation, it is clear that men and women do not have sex and mate in an entirely rational world. The world of sex and reproduction is not logical; it is "bio-logical," as Professor Lionel Tiger has said. Based solely on efficacy of preventing pregnancy and on the efficacy in preventing STDs, a couple would use two methods of birth control—a condom (male or female) as well as a method for the woman, hormonal or otherwise. This generally does not happen. When women use a more effective hormonal contraception, men are less likely to use a condom. As a result, Dr. Cates concluded: "Epidemiologic studies are equivocal regarding the value of either recommending dual methods of contraception or relying on condom use alone to prevent both unplanned pregnancies and STDs." In other words, the uncertainties and unpredictability inherent in human sexual and mating behavior make it difficult or impossible to design public health programs to urge people to use dual methods to reduce unplanned pregnancies and STDs. This is in contrast to the success that the United States had in the 1990s in delaying the age of first intercourse for teens and in increasing condom use.

One solution to this dilemma, which is increasing in the United

States and elsewhere, is the promotion of the exclusive use of condoms for both pregnancy prevention and STD prevention, with the backups of emergency contraception if the condom breaks and of abortion if a pregnancy ensues. Condom use, with abortion as a backup, would prevent unwanted childbearing and could reduce the incidence of STDs, barring any changes in sexual practices that would result in an increased risk of STDs. Condom and abortion use would eliminate the misplaced confidence in hormonal contraception as a protector for all the risks that men and women face from sexual intercourse.

Can supporters of reproductive freedom justify the choice of hormonal contraception as an exercise of reproductive freedom? We support education about contraceptive methods and informed choice. While we can educate about the direct medical benefits and risks of hormonal contraception, it is harder to educate about the indirect risks, those that result from unconscious behavior change and from the behavior of others. The individual choices that women and men make about their contraceptive and sexual behavior can have a collective society-wide impact. Can we permit technologies that simultaneously enable women to control their fertility and yet damage it? Sexually transmitted diseases can spread so rapidly and easily that, like other communicable diseases, they can spread even to those who are taking all reasonable precautions. Since the majority of women want to get pregnant and have a child and thus must have some unprotected intercourse, they are at risk from the past sexual behavior of their partners and of the other men and women that their partners have had sex with. The biological consequences are so severe that saying that these outcomes are fully justified by "choice" is not sufficient because they aren't the choice of the woman affected.

I believe we can still justify reproductive technology on the basis of the biological benefits that the technologies offer, which in most cases exceed the biological risks. In the case of hormonal contraception, while the negative evidence is troubling, I believe that the biological benefits for women being able to control their childbearing still outweigh the negatives. If a community had full and complete access to emergency contraceptives and abortion services for all women, as well as widespread male and female condom distribution, then I would discourage hormonal contraception for most women. This would require women accepting abortion as a method of regulating their fertility, which is something that by no means all women accept. Until that happens, hormonal or other equally effective female-controlled methods of contraception will be necessary. Women will always have the option of getting a potential mate tested for STDs and HIV before consenting to unprotected sexual intercourse in order to have a child. It is an option that should be used more frequently. Scientists are also working to develop different versions of microbicides that when applied topically would prevent the transmission of HIV and other STDs but which would not kill the sperm. If and when these microbicides are developed, they would permit unprotected intercourse that would lead to pregnancy but not to a disease. The research has proven very difficult and success is not assured.

Arguments based on choice become even less persuasive as a justification for reproductive freedom when we examine the unintended consequences to society of another exercise of reproductive freedom—sex-selection abortion.

## Sex-Selection Abortion As a Social Disaster

The ability to select the sex of one's children enhances individual choice and perhaps also reproductive success. People want reproductive success, meaning children who will survive, be healthy, and in turn reproduce. The chances of reproductive success may vary by the sex of one's children, depending on the environment in which the family finds itself. Reproductive success may also vary by the amount of parental investment allocated to a child, which may vary by the degree the parents want the particular child. It is normal for parents to desire a certain sex for a child. While nature, or God, provides an almost equal chance of a boy or girl being born (boys have a slightly better chance), nature does not give every family their preference. Some couples want a certain sex balance in their family, even a particular order of sexes. This, to me, falls under the rubric of reproductive choice. From a biological point of view, parents will attain more reproductive success the more they have the children they want and can allocate resources to them. The problem with choosing the sex of one's children is not that it "designs" the children or treats them as a "commodity." The problem is that women often are discriminated against and in some societies the sex ratio becomes so skewed favoring males that it becomes a social and political time bomb.

Sex preference has long been a part of human reproductive strategies. While in the past (and still) infanticide after birth has been used for selecting one sex (usually male) over the other, there have also been for centuries folk remedies that allegedly increase the likelihood of conceiving one sex or another, including special diets, different sexual positions, and sex during different times of the menstrual cycle, or during different phases of the moon. Aristotle recommended that the man tie off his left testicle to ensure the fathering of a son. The Talmud advised that the woman should have an orgasm before the man if they wanted a boy.

Even my grandmother got into the sex selection advice business. In 1933 the royal family of Japan was desperate to produce a male heir to inherit the throne. Emperor Hirohito and his wife Empress Nagako had produced three consecutive daughters and no sons. My grandmother, who was friends with some members of the Japanese parliament, gave her friends the recipe for a special diet that could increase the likelihood of a male being conceived. A Universal Service news story of the time said: "A diet of carbohydrates for six weeks before and six weeks after conception, with lots of alkalis, no acids, no cigarettes and no alcohols, is the basis of the formulas for women desiring male babies." My grandmother got this diet from a Viennese doctor who had prescribed it to the Czarina Alexandra of Russia, who had given birth to four daughters before, with the aid of the diet, giving birth to a son. The Sanger diet made its way to Emperor Hirohito and his wife. In December 1933 the Empress Nagako gave birth to a son, the current Emperor, Akihito.

Various assisted reproduction technologies, such as in vitro fertilization, can now be manipulated to "ensure" the sex of the fertilized egg, either male or female, by selecting for chromosomal characteristics in the sperm. A sperm with an X chromosome will create a female, and a sperm with a Y will create a male. If sperm sorting is not used and embryos are randomly created, then the embryos themselves can be tested to select the sex to be implanted. But since relatively few couples use assisted reproduction technologies, most people must rely on chance to get the sex they want in their children. That is until pre-natal sex diagnosis came along. Earlier and earlier in a pregnancy, prenatal testing, mostly the use of ultrasound or sampling of genetic material from the embryo or amniotic fluid, can now tell a mother the sex of the embryo or fetus she is carrying. These tests carry risks of miscarriage, and so new techniques are being developed to instead test the mother's blood rather than the embryo or her amniotic fluid to pick up genetic indicators of the fetus's sex.

Around the world couples are making use of prenatal ultrasound and other tests to determine the sex of the fetus. If the fetus is of the undesired sex, usually female, they can and often do abort it. One's reproductive success, and that of one's children, can vary by sex depending on the environment. Shelly Lundberg, a professor of economics at the University of Washington in Seattle, found that, for unmarried couples, having a son made it 35 to 40 percent more likely for the mother to marry the father than having a daughter would. Other research by economists Gordon B. Dahl and Enrico Moretti of the University of California at Berkeley found that parents of girls were more likely to divorce than parents of boys. Whatever the explanation for these differences, the increased parental investment the father brings to his son can only help the chances of both parents having reproductive success with their sons at least.

The future reproductive success of children also varies by their sex. Under the Trivers-Willard theory, first set forth in 1973, a poor male is less likely to have reproductive success than a poor female because he is less likely to succeed in the male-male competition for mates, whereas a poor female will still be able to find and choose a mate no matter how poor she is. Under this theory a high-status male is likely to have more reproductive success than a high-status female because he will have more reproductive opportunities. The Trivers-Willard theory states that natural selection will favor parents who select the sex of their offspring and allocate parental investment accordingly. Under this theory wealthier families should favor male children since it is more likely that these male children will have more children than their sisters will, and poorer families should favor female children since they are more likely to have more children than their poor male siblings will. All this is relevant to a parent's reproductive success because the reproductive chances of their children represent their own reproductive success. If your children don't have children, or have fewer than they might otherwise, then you have failed in the reproductive sweepstakes, or have not succeeded as much as the next person.

The forces of natural selection vary by sex in each particular environment. Recent studies trying to prove or disprove the Trivers-Willard theory have concluded that parents will allocate their parental investment among their children according to the marginal reproductive benefit to be achieved. Therefore other factors, especially economic and cultural ones, will intervene to alter the Trivers-Willard calculus. We see poorer families, especially in agricultural parts of Asia, favoring the male child to do the heavy work on the farm and to take care of the parents in old age (daughters tend to become part of their husband's family and there is no Social Security). Because of this cultural and economic preference for male children, sex-selection abortion, and to a lesser extent infanticide, are used against female fetuses and female children, especially in India, Korea, and China. Even if these methods of sex selection are not used, many parents in poor families will allocate scarce resources, including food and medical care, in favor of their male children, leaving their female children more vulnerable to disease and early death. The result is an imbalance in the sex ratio between males and females in society.

These cultural patterns demonstrate that one may have to choose between supporting women's rights and reproductive rights. In Asia reproductive freedom and new reproductive technologies are being used not to increase the status of women but to degrade it. While there are instances around the world of cultural preferences for girls—for instance there are reports that women in Japan increasingly favor having daughters—for the most part, where there is gender discrimination or preference, it favors boys, not girls. Does permitting sex-selection abortion constitute an endorsement of this gender-biased view of the value of women? If so, does that not fly in the face of one of the philosophical tenets of reproductive rights—to enhance the status of women? Does the allowance of abortion rights in general, which allows sex-selection abortion, lead ironically to a diminution in the status of women?

As with hormonal contraception, the unintended consequences of sex-selection abortion are not just felt by the woman who terminates a pregnancy; they are felt by society as a whole. On a society-wide basis, a preference for males leads to an imbalance in the male/female ratio, which is far from a benign occurrence. Mother Nature, when left to her own devices, provides an imbalanced sex ratio at birth of between 105 and 106, that is to say, for every 100 girls who are born, about 105 boys are born, except that in tropical climes proportionately fewer boys are born, and the sex ratio is closer to 103, or less in some areas. Mother Nature does this because boys die more than girls as infants and in their youth, because of some inherent biological weaknesses and because of their greater risk-taking behavior. Because of this pattern of early male death in the Western world at least, the sex ratio soon evens out, and then some. In the United States the sex ratio for the entire population is 98, meaning 98 males are alive for every 100 females alive.

Nature is not allowed to take its course in Asia. Sex-selection abortion and infanticide immediately after birth in Asia have led to a recorded sex ratio at birth of 115 or more in some areas. China provides the most egregious example of a distorted sex ratio. For the last two decades China has had a one-child policy in an attempt to lower its population growth rate. Aided by a surge in economic growth, the increasing cost of children, the wide availability of contraceptives, and some forced abortion and sterilization, this policy has worked. But it has worked at the expense of girls. The one-child policy, combined with China's cultural preference for males, has led parents to ensure that they have at least one male heir by employing prenatal sex selection abortion that targets female fetuses and to a lesser extent female infanticide. The unsurprising result is a growing imbalance in the sex ratio both at birth and the sex ratio of the population as a whole. The reported sex ratio at birth in China in 2000, rather than being the norm of 105, was about 117, that is to say 117 males were born for every 100 females. Estimates for 2002 are that the sex ratio at birth is 120; that is to say 120 boys are born for every 100 girls born. There is certainly an underreporting of both female births and of female infanticide, but experts believe the reported figures accurately reflect the sex ratio imbalance. This imbalance persists and is growing even though sex-selection abortion is specifically forbidden under Chinese law.

The result of substantially more boys being born and surviving than girls is that over the next decades estimates are that about 30 to 40 million young Chinese males will be unable to find a bride, marry, and settle down. Chinese families are pursuing various strategies to get their sons married, including early, arranged marriages. The kidnapping of girls for marriage is on the increase. Still, many young men are permanently excluded from the marriage market. With a reduced prospect of finding a bride in a home village and with a continued life of poverty stretching in front of them at home, poor young men are migrating to the cities in search of better paying jobs, in part with the hope of being a more attractive spouse. Migration from the country to the city has skyrocketed in China, as it has in much of the developing world. Estimates are that there are 125 million migrant workers in China. Some migrants get official permission to move and live in cities or at the site of public works projects, but many others do so without permission and live a shadow existence in the underground economy. Estimates are that urban unemployment totals about 30 million workers. The unemployed are mostly male, poor, uneducated, unmarried, and migrant. For society's point of view they are not just a wasted resource, they are a danger. Urban crime is on the rise, and experts believe it is perpetrated by the migrant male workers living on the fringes of urban society.

It is the young, unemployed, migrant, unmarried males who are trying to survive and improve their competitive position vis-à-vis other males who engage in lives of crime and violence. It is these unattached males who cannot find a partner who, along with married men, frequent prostitutes, with the result of the rapid spread of HIV into the entire population. HIV is also spread by intravenous drug use and needle sharing among migrant men living together in cities. Given the demographics of China for the foreseeable future, the country can look forward to more socially disruptive behavior from its young men, as well as more AIDS. There are reports that China is co-opting some of its unattached males by increasing the size of its police and military forces. This is worrisome to say the least. Military authorities worry about their ability to discipline and control these unattached males who are now armed and trained in combat.

None of this is a prescription for the eventual liberalization of China's authoritarian state and the building of democratic institutions. As researchers Valerie Hudson and Andrea Den Boer pointed out in their article "A Surplus of Men, A Deficit of Peace": "There is only one short-term strategy for dealing with (this) problem (excess males): Reduce their number. There are several traditional ways to do so: Fight them, encourage their self-destruction, or export them." One might be tempted to argue that the cause of China's less-than-robust response to its AIDS crisis is that AIDS lessens the problem of excess males. The problem is that AIDS will also spread into the young female population, killing off those who could bear children. Ignoring AIDS is not a sound health or demographic policy. The combination of AIDS and fewer women is that the China's population growth rate will in all likelihood continue to decline.

Longer term, the only solution for China is to reduce its sex ratio imbalance and that means reducing discrimination against women before and after birth. At the moment, there are laws banning sex-selection prenatal screening and abortion in China and India, places where it is widely practiced. Do laws like these make any difference? Given the strong cultural bias against females, these laws are probably unenforceable. Because women need not give their real reason for abortions, sex-selection abortion will continue. Even if the law is enforced, unless the Chinese culture is changed, Chinese parents will shift their discriminatory practices from before birth to after birth, with the same end result—girls not living to adulthood. Laws preventing prenatal testing and abortion will also result in abortion being done illegally and unsafely, with consequent damage to women's health.

There are no laws prohibiting sex-selection abortion in the United States. There have been bills introduced in Missouri and elsewhere to prohibit the practice of sex selection in choosing which embryos to implant after in vitro fertilization. While the American Society of Reproductive Medicine says it is acceptable to use sperm sorting to determine the sex of one's offspring, the use of embryo sorting "should be discouraged," because it involves the destruction of already created embryos. In a cultural twist the Arkansas legislature passed a law in 2003 that requires a doctor before performing an abortion to tell the patient that she can view her ultrasound. While this law is motivated by an urge to dissuade women from having abortions, a similar law in China would facilitate sex-selection abortion since the ultrasound would reveal the sex of the fetus.

There is no problem with an unbalanced sex ratio in the United States, yet. There are no adverse societal consequences from women having the choice of sex-selection abortion in the United States, and thus there is no need for a law prohibiting it. Except that sex selection might reflect a skewed view of gender, I believe there is nothing inherently wrong with it. Some parents will desire a balance in the sex composition of their families, or some may want all of one sex or the other. Some parents will find it easier to raise one sex or another. It is in the child's interest to be wanted in all respects and to be well brought up. Children of different sexes will have different reproductive value at different times and circumstances, as well as value in many other respects, to their parents. Under these circumstances some parents will try to select the sex of their children. In my view this is a valid exercise of reproductive freedom which can lead to increased reproductive success, family happiness and child welfare.

There is, however, a difference between individual gender preference and societal gender discrimination, even though one might follow from the other. I am arguing, as the example of China shows, that there is serious societal harm done when parents collectively demonstrate a preference for sons and against daughters that goes beyond whatever inherent harm there may be in individual gender discrimination. Sex-selection abortion in Asia, which leads inevitably to having tens of millions of unattached males loose in society, will bring about dangerous societal, political and national security consequences. Under these circumstances, proponents of reproductive choice cannot say that sex selection is just another exercise of reproductive autonomy when the massive gender disparities that result may also result in serious societal harm to all. To protect itself a society is justified in forbidding sex-selection abortion, until it can be shown that abortion is not used extensively to discriminate against girls. A society can take reasonable steps to protect itself from the serious consequences of collective individual reproductive choices, even when it means limiting human freedom. That being said, since laws banning sex-selection abortion will probably not work in China or elsewhere, government efforts should be directed at changing the nation's culture and economic system in order to elevate the status of its women. Since this is almost as impossible as enforcing abortion laws, one can only hope that females, as they become scarcer, will become more valuable and that Chinese parents will no longer want to discriminate against them. When there are so many excess men, a daughter may represent the best chance of reproductive success for Chinese parents.

## Genetic Engineering and Cloning Threaten Evolution

Conceiving and giving birth to healthy children is difficult. Many parents are infertile and many carry genes for inherited diseases that can affect their children. Genetic screening can detect whether or not an embryo carries a defective gene and the parents can choose to have the child, have an abortion and try again, or try to have the defect corrected in utero. Genetic screening at the beginning of a pregnancy offers the hope of a healthy child to those who might not otherwise have a chance to have one. But genetic technology can do more. There is rapid scientific progress being made that would give the ability to eliminate, add, or manipulate certain genes in an embryo via genetic engineering. What does this mean for the human race? Genetic technologies on the one hand may increase the health and wantedness of children, thereby increasing their chances of survival, but they may also be doing harm to these same individuals and society at large. There are increased birth defects in children conceived with in vitro fertilization. There is no certainty that a gene carried by a parent will result in a disease or attribute in a child. We don't know what every gene does and manipulating a gene may have unintended consequences to the child. The dangers of eugenics are present when we permit genetic engineering. We have to move cautiously and examine all the pros and cons of new reproductive technologies before we use them widely.

When we talk of genetic technologies we must be careful to distinguish between the various kinds. The President's Council on Bioethics, chaired by Leon Kass, wrote a report entitled, "Beyond Therapy: Biotechnology and the Pursuit of Perfection" in October 2003. The report stated:

> We concentrate instead on various powers that depend upon precise genetic knowledge and technique: (a) the ability to screen and select fetuses, embryos, and gametes (egg and sperm) for the presence or absence of specific genetic markers; and (b) the ability to obtain and introduce such genetic material in order to effect a desired genetic "improvement." The first, by itself, leads to two powers that merely select from among genetic endowments conferred by chance, the difference between them being the stage at which screening is done and whether selection is "negative" or "positive." Prenatal diagnosis during an established pregnancy (using amniocentesis or chorionic villus sampling) permits the weeding out, through abortion, of those fetuses carrying undesired genetic traits. Preimplantation genetic screening and selection of in vitro embryos, in contrast, permits pregnancy to begin using only

those embryos that carry desired genetic traits. In contrast to both of these, a third power, directed genetic change (or genetic engineering), would attempt to go beyond what chance alone has provided, improving in vitro embryos directly by introducing "better" genes.

## Genetic Technologies – The Hope and the Danger

Genetic technologies have given reproductive choice a whole new meaning. The era of designer children may not be far off. Do these technologies carry the same or different dangers for society as sex-selection abortion? Pre-implantation genetic diagnosis and sex-selection abortion can both be used to select the sex of one's children. With pre-implantation genetic diagnosis, sex selection can, for biological as opposed to social reasons, more often than not, favor females. While males and females have different susceptibility to various diseases, there are over 500 X-chromosome diseases that are passed only from mothers to sons. These include Duchenne muscular dystrophy and hemophilia. Parents carrying these defective genes and wanting to avoid the chance of these fatal diseases in their children can use sex-selection technologies to produce daughters, not sons. Thus sex-selection abortion can be sex neutral and have uses that society may favor or disfavor.

Genetic screening can be used to further human reproduction and to overcome the twin problems of infertility and birth defects. Reproductive success does not come automatically. There are pitfalls, conflicts, and dangers throughout the entire mating and child-rearing process. Between 15 and 20 percent of couples in the United States suffer from infertility. There is a definite connection between the rise in sexually transmitted diseases and rising infertility. But even for those who are fertile, successful reproduction is not guaranteed. There are estimates that up to 75 percent of conceptions either do not result in a pregnancy or miscarry. The fertilized egg either self-destructs or does not implant in the uterus. Mother Nature takes a lot of life before birth, but does not always take those with defects of one sort or another.

According to the March of Dimes, birth defects are found in about

150,000 babies born each year in the United States, representing almost 4 percent of births. Some babies born with birth defects will survive to adulthood and will be able to reproduce, and some will not, depending on the disease or defect. For this reason and others, many parents in planning their children will seek any way possible to conceive and insure the birth of healthy children who in turn can have children. This is why parents who can afford it use pre-implantation genetic diagnosis (PGD) that screens out embryos with a gene for an inherited disease and implants embryos without it. Some reports indicate that PGD can increase the success of in vitro fertilization rates by up to 50 percent. Increased chances of a successful pregnancy are also why, for instance, many parents have responded to the March of Dimes recommendation that women take folic acid early in their pregnancies in order to help a baby's brain and spinal cord develop properly and thus to prevent neural tube defects.

While some birth defects can be prevented—for instance, bringing a pregnant woman's diabetes under control reduces the risk of birth defects—few genetic diseases can be prevented with better prenatal care. Modern genetic science can now help some parents who are carriers of abnormal genes and give them a better chance of reproductive success. For instance, some Jewish families use genetic screening to prevent carriers of Tay-Sachs disease, a fatal disorder seen mainly in people of European Jewish heritage, from marrying each other. For carriers of other genetic diseases, pre-implantation genetic diagnosis permits fertilizing multiple embryos in the laboratory and then selecting and implanting an embryo without the defective gene. Genetic diagnosis after a pregnancy commences permits parents to abort an embryo that carries a suspect gene, or in a few cases to employ in utero surgery to correct the genetic defect.

Opponents of PGD argue that this technology will change the parent-child relationship, make children a commodity, and undermine parents' unconditional acceptance of their children. These opponents need a dose of biological reality. Those parents struggling to conceive and to have healthy children see the issue quite differently. It's a matter of seeking biological success and avoiding failure if you can. Eve Rubell, age forty, of Los Angeles, who carries a gene for Fabry's disease, said: "It's not about eugenics or designer babies. Certainly if I have a child with a disability or a health problem, I'm going to love that child like any other. But if it was something I knowingly could have prevented, I would want to do that, and I would feel guilty if I didn't at least try."

Pre-implantation genetic diagnosis is quite different than genetic engineering. In the future the science of genetic engineering holds the possibility of permitting parents not only to discard certain harmful genes but also to add to their children's genetic makeup certain genes that would translate into what the parents would believe to be favorable characteristics. For those who are infertile there is the promise of cloning, which would permit a person to have a child alone. Genetic engineering and cloning represent the ultimate steps in taking control of one's reproduction. They are attempts to take the one random element in human reproduction—which DNA molecules from each parent come together in the fertilized egg—out of the reproductive process. To opponents of genetic engineering, these technologies represent the bottom of the slippery slope that begins when genetic technology is permitted for worthy reasons. I have argued that controlling one's reproduction is generally of biological benefit for women and men. But despite the natural instinct of parents to use whatever science can provide to better their chances of reproductive success, the question remains, should society permit these exercises of reproductive freedom? Or are the biological and social consequences so harmful that society must discourage them?

Leon Kass, a bioethics professor at the University of Chicago and the chair of the President's Council on Bioethics, said when in vitro fertilization was first developed and the first test tube baby was born: "At stake is the idea of the humanness of our human life and the meaning of our embodiment, our sexual being, and our relation to ancestors and descendants." Over a million babies have been born using in vitro fertilization (IVF) since Kass made those comments and expressed his objections to IVF. Kass is, in my view, asking the right questions. I disagree, however, with some of his answers.

When parents use PGD or genetic engineering to improve the genetic make-up of their children or even to determine their sex, they are saying that those children who result are truly wanted. To the extent that "wantedness" will increase the parental commitment to and investment in that child, it is a good thing. Starting prenatal care early, for instance, will increase that child's chance of good health and survival. Genetic screening allows parents to affirmatively decide whether a particular child should be born and to plan accordingly. A potential birth defect, disability, or disease in the child will have biological, familial, and societal consequences that parents have to weigh. Pre- and post-implantation genetic screening can test the embryo for genetic or chromosomal diseases, abnormalities, or disabilities. While the tests can reveal conditions for which remedies can be attempted during pregnancy, often the tests reveal conditions for which there are two choices: The child can be born with the condition or can be aborted. Some have argued that permitting or encouraging abortion of fetuses with birth defects will lead to increased discrimination against those born with disabilities. They argue that those with disabilities will be rarer (and thus less politically powerful and easier to discriminate against) and that since their birth was the conscious choice of their parents, the parents, not society, should bear the burden of caring for them. The issue here is not that permitting testing and abortion in these circumstances will lead to discrimination against the disabled. Abortion for reasons of fetal defect was permitted in many states long before *Roe* and is now permitted nationwide under *Roe*. During this time discrimination against the disabled has decreased and health care treatment options for them increased, and the disabled are more incorporated into the life of America. The issue, rather, is one of allowing parents the best chance of biological success and of family happiness.

Genetic screening and in vitro fertilization, however, are not panaceas for reproductive success and can raise more questions than it answers. First of all, recent research has found that babies conceived through in vitro fertilization (IVF) are two and a half times more likely to be of low birth weight than those babies conceived naturally. Furthermore, IVF babies are twice as likely to have multiple serious birth defects compared to naturally conceived children. Secondly, carrying a gene indicating a disposition for a disease or disability is no guarantee that the carrier will ever contract the disease. Some diseases, including cystic fibrosis and Down syndrome, are amenable to genetic prediction with some degree of certainty. Other conditions are less predictable: whether they will occur at all, the age at which they might strike or how severely remains unclear. If the suspect gene indicates a propensity towards breast cancer, for example, the cancer may occur at age forty-five, age seventy-five, or never, and, if the cancer does strike, it may not be malignant. Genes express themselves in their environment, that is, our bodies, and to a large extent we cannot control the environmental factors to which our genes react. For some genetic diseases such as alcoholism, there is a large element of human control over whether the disease will strike and the extent to which it can be overcome. But for most genetic diseases, it is a roll of the genetic dice as to whether we contract a certain disease and the extent to which it will affect our health and reproductive capabilities. Given these uncertainties, there is a risk that parents will abort pregnancies of children who might have turned out to be healthy.

The specter of eugenics hangs over any discussion of genetic screening. We must remember that eugenics was a government mandate against reproduction by certain classes of people with disabilities. At that time there was a broad cultural but inexact definition of disabilities, both social and medical, that were thought to be both dangerous and heritable and a justifiable basis for sterilizing potential parents. Genetic screening differs in that the parents, not the government, decide what a disability is and whether or not to have a particular child. But is the societal effect the same? Genetic screening makes it more likely that those with potential or actual disabilities will not be born. In some cultures girls will more likely not be born, and in a few boys will not be born.

While some have expressed concerns that genetic engineering may harm those women who undergo experimental genetic treatments or procedures, on the other hand genetic screening may aid women wanting to be pregnant who would no longer need to be implanted with as many embryos in order to have a successful pregnancy. There will also be a class differential—until genetic screening is covered by health insurance or Medicaid and available on a routine basis, it will be used more by the wealthier members of society. Does genetic screening that enables parents to select their future children on the basis of their genes lead to a devaluation of and discrimination against those who have diseases or disabilities? I have argued that this has not happened. Although genetic screening permits parents to define disability for themselves, they are doing so in a cultural context. Is parental judgment about preventing the birth of a child with a disability any less worrisome than a governmental judgment? Will these technologies lead to the commodification of children with, for example, parents having a child for the purpose of that child being a tissue or organ donor for an already-born sibling with a genetic disease? Parents in England recently sought permission to do just this.

In England where genetic screening is tightly regulated, the authorities sometimes grant and sometimes refuse permission for preimplantation genetic diagnosis (PGD) depending on the individual disease sought to be cured. Michelle and John Whitaker were refused permission to use PGD to obtain an embryo for implantation that would have been a perfect tissue match for their son Charlie who suffered from Diamond-Blackfan anaemia, a rare blood disorder. By contrast Shahana and Raj Hashmi were granted permission to use PGD to obtain an embryo that would be a perfect tissue match to cure their son Zain of beta thalassaemia, another rare blood disorder. The UK Human Fertilisation and Embryology Authority (HFEA) explained that Zain's condition was hereditary but Charlie's was not. The Cardiff Centre for Ethics, Law and Society explained that, "This meant that any child conceived by the Hashmis was itself at risk of developing the relevant disorder, whereas it was extremely unlikely that any child conceived by the Whitakers would suffer from the relevant disorder." Because the child the Hashmis wanted to conceive would be at risk, the PGD was granted, but because the Whitakers' child would not be, permission was denied. The Whitakers went to the United States where there is no authority regulating PGD, had the PGD and had a son James who is a perfect tissue match for his brother. As of the end of 2003 the Whitakers are awaiting their doctor's decision about the timing of the tissue transfer from James to Charlie.

Whether parents are motivated by a desire to give their children the best start in life, by a desire for perfection, or by a inclination to see their children as a reflection of themselves, some will use whatever technology permits with little thought as to the consequences to society. Professor Francis Fukuyama of Johns Hopkins University, in his book *Our Posthuman Future: Consequences of the Biotechnology Revolution*, said: "Scientific knowledge about causation will inevitably lead to a technological search for ways to manipulate that causality." Fukuyama illustrated the dangers inherent in genetic engineering by asking whether society should permit the research into the hypothetical "gay gene," a gene that might cause homosexuality. What if science discovers such as gene and finds a way to manipulate or eliminate that gene using genetic engineering that would minimize the chances of child being gay? Assuming this can all be done in the privacy of a doctor's office, would parents make use of this technology and should society allow it?

Fukuyama supposed that many parents would, assuming that there were no other side effects (a rather major assumption). Many parents would view homosexuality of their children as a "less-than-optimal condition that, all other things being equal, one would rather have one's children avoid. (The desire of most people for descendants is one guarantee of this.)" Fukuyama raised the important issue about the effects of this "private" form of discrimination on the gays left in society. "Wouldn't this form of private eugenics make them more distinctive, and greater targets of discrimination, than they were before? More important, is it obvious that the human race would be improved if gayness were eliminated from it?" Should we remain indifferent, Fukuyama asked, that this form of reproductive choice, or eugenics, is made by parents as a free choice?

Fukuyama raised three separate issues. His opinion on the discriminatory effect of genetic engineering is unpersuasive. For the last several decades, as our society has moved to expand genetic screening, it has at the same time expanded the rights and treatment of people with disabilities. Secondly, Fukuyama raised the issue of whether parents are entitled to define their reproductive strategy as they see fit or whether society can set limits? How we define a problem, such as what constitutes a disability, is often very much determined by the goals we as parents have for our children. Virtually all parents share one common goal—to be grandparents. This is basic human nature. Homosexuality is not a bar to having children, but it is a reality that fewer homosexuals have children than heterosexuals. Can't parents play the reproductive odds as they see them? In theory they can and will, and society should permit it unless there is an overriding societal reason not to, as in the case of sex-selection abortion in China. In the unlikely event a gay gene is uncovered that can be manipulated by genetic engineering, I would agree that the societal discrimination would be so severe that it would be dangerous to permit it. However, I believe that the better solution, as with sex selection in China, is not a ban on the technology, but a change in culture that embraces homosexuality as a sexual preference that nature has given us.

Parents naturally want children who are healthy, who will survive, and who will have children of their own. When genetic screening indicates that the potential child will not be able to do any of these, there is a powerful incentive to terminate the pregnancy. But some parents don't. They might have other children already or will have some in the future to carry on the genetic line. The fact that many parents continue pregnancies even when the evidence indicates a severe disability of the fetus and an inability to reproduce shows the limits of a purely genetic approach to human reproduction. Many parents are willing to make extensive parental investment even when there is no genetic payoff. Humanity demonstrates its altruism in many ways. When altruism conflicts with biological goals, altruism sometimes gives way. Parents are entitled to pursue the biological path with the best chances for reproductive success.

Genetic screening is both a sword and a shield for those with disabilities. The same technology that permits the discovery of abnormal genes before conception or birth also permits corrective surgery in some cases. New reproductive technologies should soon permit those with some defective genes to themselves reproduce without the danger of passing on the disease or disability to their children. This would eliminate one of the greatest worries of many parents as they grow older—that their child would be unable to reproduce. Genetic technology could thus be a boon and a bane for those with disabilities, just as sex-selection technologies can be used to select for both and against females. I would argue that the best way to allay the fears of those with disabilities that genetic screening will be used against them is to use it for them, to increase their ability to become parents should they want to.

Fukuyama's third objection, that no one knows whether society would be better off if the gayness gene were removed, raised the essential biological dilemma that we do not fully understand the human genetic code and its functioning. Here I agree with him. Scientists do not know exactly what every gene does and which genes do more than one thing. It is well known that the sickle cell gene also protects the carrier against malaria. Do other "defective" genes protect against other diseases or serve some other genetic or evolutionary purpose? Parents may think that by manipulating, adding, or deleting genes with genetic engineering they are increasing their chances of giving birth to a healthier child, but they may not be. The affected gene may have other unknown purposes. The changes made to one gene not only affect that child, they affect that child's descendants. Changes to genes may unknowingly harm the health of one's descendants and may lead to decreased not increased reproductive success.

I seriously question whether it is safe to use genetic engineering to put the genetic future of the human race in our conscious (as opposed to subconscious) hands. Until now sexual reproduction has been the key to our evolutionary success. Sex between males and females and the process of sexual selection has likely evolved in part as a way to create genetic variety and to mix genetic material to create offspring who can better ward off pathogens. I am enormously skeptical of any human attempt to improve upon that process through genetic engineering. Our knowledge of the human genome is limited and to think that we can manipulate one part of it without affecting another part is idiotic. As Edward O. Wilson, the distinguished Professor of Science at Harvard, once warned: "in heredity as in the environment, you cannot do just one thing. When a gene is changed by mutation or replaced by another gene, unexpected and possibly unpleasant side effects are likely to follow."

## Cloning—Repealing the Laws of Sexual Selection

Wilson's warning is equally true for genetic reproduction that transmits only one person's genes to the next generation—cloning. Cloning is counterproductive from an evolutionary perspective under the Red Queen theory, which tells us that we are in an evolutionary race against pathogens and that sexual reproduction, where two person's genes are combined, leads to the development of new human genetic combinations in our progeny that enable them to better ward off pathogens.

The main problem with cloning, other than that it does not yet work in humans, is that there is no mixing of two parents' genes in the conception of the child; rather it is the duplication of the genes of one parent. We may never know if cloning really "works," even though the process may result in the birth of a live organism. There may be hidden defects and mutations in the cloned child that do not become evident for generations. Cloning does not make an exact copy. This was demonstrated in 2002 when scientists cloned a cat to produce "CC," a kitten. CC turned out to have different colored fur than her "mother." It may also have other different attributes and behaviors as it grows older. Dolly, the first cloned sheep, aged faster than normal and died quite young. Research on cloned pigs by Dr. Jorge Piedrahita, a professor of molecular biological sciences at North Carolina State University, found that "the DNA is often modified during the cloning process in such a way that it affects the activity of certain genes." In addition, under the Red Queen theory, by passing on only one person's genes and by eliminating sexual selection and reproduction, cloning makes it easier for pathogens to survive, grow, and overcome the host. If the cloning process is repeated for generations, the cloned line will be less likely to survive. Even if the cloned child reproduces sexually, we do not know the effect on those children of having one ancestor that was not the product of sexual reproduction.

Cloning is asexual reproduction. Humanity has evolved quite successfully with sexual reproduction. Sexual reproduction accelerates evolution by leading to a "more rapid generation of a wide array of variants" and by "removing deleterious mutations," as Michael E. N. Majerus argued. Human cloning is an attempt to rewrite the laws of evolution. Is there any possible benefit?

One arguable benefit of cloning is that cloned children in all likelihood will not have genetic abnormalities that are not present in the ancestor. Since there is no genetic recombination through sex or assisted reproduction, there is little or no risk that an abnormal gene will appear. There may be more chance of a mutation in a gene however, as with CC's fur gene; we simply do not know. It is possible that birth defects will occur with less frequency in cloned children, if the cloning can be done properly. A cloned child is, as has been described by Princeton biologist Lee Silver, a "later-born identical twin."

Will there be a demand for human cloning? In 2002 a group of activists from the Center for Genetics and Society, who described themselves as longtime advocates for human rights, the environment, social justice, and reproductive rights, urged Congress to ban reproductive cloning: "There is no unmet need that requires the creation of genetic duplicates of existing people." Is this so? What of the enormous rise in infertility, much of which cannot be cured? Mightn't the infertile want to try cloning as a last reproductive option? Or what of the increasing number of families that only have one child? What if that child dies before reproducing and the parents are unable because of age or disease to reproduce again? Parents may have entirely valid reasons to want to try cloning. One woman who saw her child die as a young adult said to me that she would "clone him in a minute" if she could. She knew that the cloned child would be different, but that didn't matter. To her, both she and her son would have another chance.

Reproductive cloning, to the extent that it would work, is beneficial in that it enables a person who otherwise has not had reproductive success to have a chance of success. This success, however, may be limited and a danger to others. Cloning is a bad idea biologically because it removes the benefits to humanity of sexual selection and sexual reproduction and may therefore hurt humanity in its evolutionary race against pathogens. There is enormous diversity in the human population because of sexual reproduction. This is a good thing. We don't know enough to say which genetic variations are good or bad. It is a normal human instinct for parents to try to eliminate birth "defects," however defined, from our children. The danger is that in so doing we eliminate defenses against pathogens and retard our evolutionary progress. Sexual selection and reproduction, as imperfect as they are, have gotten humanity to where it is. We should not discard them even in the face of the compelling personal tragedies of those who cannot reproduce sexually. We do not know enough about biology to interfere with its inner workings. The sexual selection and reproductive process are the products of millions of years of evolution. We discard them at our peril.


## Should We Evolve Out of Evolution?

Humanity has always been a major force in its own evolution, and technologies of every kind have enabled humans to evolve more rapidly. Humans evolved to have the ability to create and use tools for certain activities, such as agriculture, making clothes, and building homes, which themselves have been a major influences on human evolution and survival. I have argued that reproductive technologies that permit the planning and spacing of children are another example of tools essential for human evolution and survival. Modern reproductive technologies in the form of hormonal contraception, prenatal ultrasound and safe abortion, and genetic screening and cloning all provide benefits to human health, well-being and survival. These benefits, however, do not come without costs and unintended consequences. The consequences of reproductive technologies don't just impact those using them and their children; they impact the other members of society who didn't use them, both individuals and society at large.

With each technology parents are trying to maximize their reproductive success through timing their offspring or through selecting their offspring's sex or their genetic makeup. This is natural. The problem is not that parents are making poor individual choices, even if we could define what a poor choice is. The decision to have a child at a particular time or of a particular sex or without a gene for a fatal or debilitating disease are decisions that I believe parents are uniquely entitled to make, and should make, under the rubric of reproductive choice, just as the number of children one has is also a unique decision for parents. Some decisions that parents make may be wrong or unwise biologically. Some decisions we won't know whether they are right or wrong, wise or unwise, until some point in the future, if at all. I believe, for instance, that parents should be entitled to genetically engineer an embryo to delete a gene for sickle cell anemia even though it may lead to a greater health risk for the child if they contract malaria in the future. Parents should be permitted to do this only with the understanding that our medical and genetic knowledge is still limited in its ability to evaluate the medical trade-off when we alter genes to eliminate the certainty of having one genetic disease while increasing a future risk of contracting another.

Parents do not, however, have carte blanche to do what they want with their children either before or after birth. This is the major moral problem with abortion in general, and also with genetic engineering. There is another party with an interest in the parent's decisions—the child, whether born or unborn. In 2002, one deaf lesbian couple, Sharon Duchesneau and Candy McCullough of Bethesda, Maryland, used pre-implantation genetic diagnosis to select an embryo to be implanted that had a deafness gene so that their child would have a chance to be deaf like them. By way of contrast, a married couple won the right in 2003 from the Victoria Australia Infertility Treatment Authority to genetically screen their embryos in order to exclude any that had a deafness gene that they both carried. So far the IVF has failed. Which of these children, if they are born, will have a greater chance at success in life, including reproductive success, will not be immediately known. Society can hope that parents, as they generally do, will make the right decisions for their children before, during, and after they are born. Parents do this because they want reproductive success.

The main problem I have raised in this chapter is not whether using reproductive technologies has consequences for the individuals using them or for their children but rather whether the collective use of technology by individuals leads to unintended consequences that harm society's collective reproductive success and human survival. For instance, a parent's decision to have two children rather than four, or four children rather than two, is a decision that has only indirect consequences on other members of the community. Collective family size decisions, for instance, will affect the capacity of the environment for better and for worse to sustain its population and as such will indirectly affect the well-being of the entire community. But the individual childbearing decisions made possible by new technologies are of a different qualitative order because they may directly and unknowingly affect the behavior and health and reproductive success of others.

A theoretical framework arguing for reproductive freedom based on the notion of women's autonomy or on the rights of the individual does not fully answer the question of why society should permit this autonomy or this freedom. Any right that leads to more harm to humanity than benefit cannot long stand. Abortion opponents argue that legal abortion harms humanity by killing its children and by promoting callous behavior and a disrespect for human life in general. I have argued in opposition that reproductive freedom is good for humanity because it promotes human health and survival and that there is no direct evidence that it contributes to callous behavior or to a disrespect for the life of those born.

When any right or freedom harms humanity more than it helps it, then society is justified in curtailing its exercise. No right is absolute. The right to freedom of speech can be curtailed when there is direct societal harm, including, for instance, prohibiting speech that can incite a riot. Traditionally, reproductive freedom was based partially on the notion that the decisions made affected only the parents and their family. These decisions were seen as uniquely within the province of individual conscience, much like the decision about whether and how to practice one's religion, and not within the province of the government. We have now seen that some exercises of reproductive freedom can adversely affect everyone in a community. How can we balance the potential harms of these technologies against their benefits? Biological analyses are needed to weigh the pros and cons and to justify these exercises of reproductive freedom.

If attempting reproductive success through the use of hormonal contraception, sex-selection abortion, or genetic enhancement, is theoretically harmful but cannot be proved, why not let evolution run its course and see if it favors or disfavors the children and their descendants? By definition, natural selection will not favor those who have become infertile because of a sexually transmitted disease and therefore in the long run condom users might have more reproductive success. I would hazard a guess that there will be less reproductive success in the Asian families that produce only boys, since they will have relatively fewer options to reproduce. Evolution, as we have seen, is a process whereby the genes we pass on to our children are selected for or against by their ability to adapt to our environment. Won't the same happen when we select certain genes to be passed on to our children? Won't the forces of evolution acting through our environment select for or against them? Is this so bad?

Given the varieties of human experience, conditions, and resources, some humans will make use of these technologies and some won't. Each will make a somewhat different use. In this sense variation in the human species will remain. The laws of evolution will select those who will survive and reproduce. Should we allow children to be experiments in testing the laws of natural selection? In a sense every child tests these laws because each is born with a unique genetic code in a unique environment. When faced with a new disease, we don't wait to see if the disease will decimate us or if our immune systems will defeat it. We search for cures and vaccines to prevent the disease from killing us. In that sense we are trying to manipulate the forces of natural selection. If we can see the potential for reproductive harm, why wait until it becomes a reality? Why not stop the harm in any way we can?

I have argued that at the moment there is insufficient evidence for government intervention restricting the use of these technologies, at least in the United States. The negative effects of hormonal contraception need much more human research beyond the disturbing studies that I have cited. Sex-selection abortion is not a problem in the United States, although it is in Asia, and in that case I support the bans on sex-selection abortion that China and India have enacted. Pre-implantation genetic diagnosis and in vitro fertilization provide measurable health benefits to children, and I support their use. Genetic engineering to alter genes and cloning either do not work yet or do not pose a provable threat to society. But what of the future when genetic engineering and cloning may actually work? At that point, if the societal threat can be established, I would support a ban on them.

All the technologies discussed in this chapter will enable humans to take, if we wish and if the science works, total control of our reproduction and our own evolution. We will be able to eliminate the mating of males and females, the sexual selection process, and the mixing and mutation of genes. As one observer, George Ennenga, Director of the think tank GXI, said in his article "Artificial Evolution," we have the power to "evolve out of evolution." Is this the final nightmare of eugenics or is it a form of salvation? Is this wise or unwise, and if the latter, what can or should we do about it? Can we rely on our culture to deter unwise decisions, or do we need to resort to the power of law? The disaster of eugenics was that bad science was followed by bad laws enforcing the science. Eugenics teaches us to be cautious about believing science and about passing laws to enforce scientific theory. Preconceived notions and ideologies that try to fit science into a pigeonhole lead inevitably to disaster.

One's position on when life begins is not necessarily determinative about one's moral position on the issues raised in this chapter. Those who consider themselves pro-choice or pro-life may have a variety of opinions about new reproductive technologies. Some who are pro-choice oppose human cloning, and some who are pro-life support genetic engineering. This divergence of opinion from rigid ideology may give our society the opportunity to find new bases for discussing reproductive issues in their broader context beyond the abortion issue. For the advocates of reproductive rights, the reproductive choices available because of new technologies may bring consequences we do not like. Technology forces us to face the reality that individual reproductive options are not only increased but are changed by technology, and that the individual consequences of reproductive choices affect not just the user but others and society as a whole. Under these circumstances, it becomes more difficult to say that all reproductive choices are private and should be beyond the purview of culture or society's laws. The problem for those of us who are pro-choice is that the notion of choice is not just part of the solution; it is part of the problem. Reproductive freedom, including new reproductive technologies, can be best defended when its use is in alignment with human evolution and survival, as I believe it usually is. Technology has broadened choice, but some of its unintended consequences make its defense harder. I alluded earlier to the nineteenth century experience where new birth control technologies were seen as a threat and were quickly followed by the Comstock laws restricting reproductive freedom. To prevent a recurrence of this, pro-choice advocates must make a compelling argument as to when, if at all, human reproduction should be regulated by the government.

# CHAPTER SEVEN

# Ought There Be a Law?

*In early 2003 the North Dakota legislature considered legislation that would have made it a felony to kill a "preborn child." The proposed law applied both to the physician performing an abortion and to the woman having the abortion. The Catholic bishop of the Bismarck Diocese, Paul Zipfel, testified against the bill, stating that the church "for pastoral, moral and prudential reasons" opposed abortion laws that made women criminals. Zipfel testified that women were "abortion's second victim" and often pressured, coerced, or driven by fear into having abortions. Abortion is a "grave moral wrong," he said, but "not every moral wrong . . . demands a corresponding penalty in civil law."*

When does a moral wrong require a law to enforce it? Governments throughout history have enacted laws and policies attempting to promote marriage, to restrict sexual activity to marriage for purposes of procreation, and in general to promote public morality. In addition to laws against contraception and abortion, there have been laws prohibiting adultery, fornication, rape, non-procreative sex, homosexuality, and incest. The law has disfavored children born out of wedlock. While laws against rape and incest remain, the laws against homosexuality, adultery, fornication, and illegitimacy have slowly faded away in many countries. Birth control is legal almost universally. Abortion is legal to save the life of the woman and for various other reasons in almost every nation on earth. Why should governments intervene in some sexual and reproductive behaviors and decisions and not others? Whenever there is a sexual or reproductive behavior that society thinks should be discouraged, ought there be a law?

## The What, the Why, and the Ought of Laws on Sex and Reproduction

Many societies now and in the past have believed that a large and growing population was necessary to attain their national objectives, be they military, political, economic, or social. Today some societies believe that, on the contrary, a large and growing population will prevent them from attaining whatever their national goals might be. Citizens don't necessarily cooperate with their nation's demographic plans. They have their own childbearing goals. And all too often nations fear, sometimes quite correctly, that individual sexual and reproductive behaviors in the aggregate can threaten the biological, social, economic, and political order. For these reasons governments often do not leave sexual and reproductive matters entirely to the discretion of their individual citizens. There is not always a clear line of cause and effect between a particular sexual practice or reproductive decision on the one hand and its ramifications to the public on the other. Nonetheless, governments often intervene extensively into the sexual and reproductive lives of their citizens with only a hazy understanding of the actual biological or social consequences of their laws.

Governments have some legitimate interest in the sexual and reproductive lives of their citizens because governments were established in part to help their people survive and reproduce safely and successfully. The size of a tribe or nation's population often determined the ability of the community to defend itself, conquer the environment, and thrive economically. Rulers and governments encouraged childbearing and frequently restricted what we now call reproductive freedom in the service of population growth. While some nations still encourage childbearing, other nations now view excessive population growth as a threat to national stability and economic growth and actively discourage it. Government attempts to manipulate childbearing in the modern age range from draconian measures trying to limit family size, as in China, to encouraging contraceptive use, as in many developing countries, to banning both contraception and abortion, as in Romania in the 1980s. Most governments currently use more indirect methods of fertility regulation, including tax benefits or direct grants as an incentive to increase childbearing or providing voluntary family planning programs as a means of decreasing it. Most of these incentives, with the exception of family planning, have been found to be a waste of money, affecting only the timing of childbearing rather than changing the number of children a family desires. It turns out to be extremely costly for a society to purchase its own descendants.

Family planning programs have been found to be effective in reducing absolute family size and in promoting maternal and child health. Tragically, some governments don't want to wait for voluntary family planning programs to work or don't want to provide sufficient incentives for childbearing and instead get into the business of coercing their citizens to either have or not have children. Bans on birth control and abortion are in the short run effective in increasing childbearing but are extremely damaging to both maternal and child health. Romania, which banned birth control and abortion, and China, which forced their use, provide object lessons of why governments should tread lightly when it comes to trying to control the reproductive decisions of their citizens—the coercion did not work and in many cases women and children suffered the consequences.

Governments frequently justify their laws regulating sexual and reproductive practices on the basis of promoting a common morality and community values. A common morality is important for the functioning of society and to make society conducive for the bearing and raising of children. However, the definition of what is moral and the decision as to what morality is necessary to attain these goals are problematic issues that pit individual freedom against the goals of the community. Any reasoned argument for and against adopting morality legislation should examine the biological consequences of these laws. Since many of these laws purport to defend life, we have to define what is important about "life." I agree with the pro-life movement that promoting life is the most important value when we are discussing reproductive laws, but my definition of life includes the ability, indeed the necessity, of life to reproduce itself. If life fails to do this, it ceases to exist. Reproductive freedom is vital because it permits and enables life to reproduce itself successfully.

Some laws that ban such practices as incest are entirely justified because incest damages children and makes them less likely to survive and reproduce. Programs to reduce the incidence of sexually transmitted diseases are also legitimate since these diseases can lead to increased infertility. Abortion involves a trade-off for parents—do they have this child or wait until later to have a child (or even not have any more children at all and devote themselves to the children they have)? A strictly moral analysis, without being informed by biology, is not adequate to answer these questions for parents or for society. There is, in my view, no seamless web of morality relating to sexual matters. We can permit abortion without concern that certain other immoral behaviors will increase. Morality changes over time. Certain things long thought moral, such as slavery, are now immoral. A blanket rule that a pregnant woman must give birth makes no biological sense and is not moral. It does not necessarily help the woman attain her reproductive goals, nor does it help society attain its goals. Restrictions on abortion access only make a woman's ability to attain her reproductive goals more difficult. The proscription of the so-called partial birth abortion procedure had no biological justification. Its basis in morality was undercut by the fact that the law left in place another abortion procedure that the law's proponents conceded was equally distasteful to them.

The legitimacy of government trying to enforce a moral code, as opposed to encouraging one, must recognize the fact that laws trying to change the laws of human nature, especially as they relate to human reproduction, are not only bound to fail, but are dangerous. Legitimacy should depend on whether the laws are trying to support or contravene humanity's innate biological tendencies. I believe the Supreme Court understood that trying to interfere with humanity' ability to reproduce as it sees fit was dangerous, and therefore, for this and other reasons, decided that there was a right to privacy embedded in the Constitution's Bill of Rights and that it encompassed birth control and abortion. While generally in a democracy the majority in the legislature can set the rules that enable society to function, the Supreme Court has long ruled that in the United States the Constitution sets some outside limits on what the majority can and can't do. These limits prohibit the government from interfering with its citizens pursuing their own reproductive strategies, as they think best.

Nonetheless, even for those of us who generally oppose government intervention in sexual and reproductive matters, there are some legitimate reasons for governments to do so. One can be pro-choice and support some government intervention in human reproductive affairs. The limits on government must be set on biological grounds. Only those measures to protect humanity's ability to reproduce are justifiable, and then only if they can be shown to be effective. Otherwise the presumption must be for human freedom. There is a difference between laws enacted to preserve the biologic function, which must be encouraged, and laws that take away an individual's reproductive options, which cannot.

The constitutional right to privacy is a bulwark against over-zealous moralists trying to rewrite the laws of biology and human evolution. While some moral legislation in general can still be permitted, it needs to have some positive justification other than that the majority thinks it is good for society. The Texas sodomy law recently declared unconstitutional by the Supreme Court had no other justification other than that the legislature did not like homosexuality. Without a right to privacy, a government could pass any law it wished relating to human sexuality and reproduction. Humanity cannot let the majority try to redefine the laws of nature by trying to change how and why and with whom we have sex and reproduce. Reproductive freedom has gotten humanity to where it is today. It is essential for our well-being and survival that we keep it.

## Why Governments Insist upon Entering Our Bedrooms

Advocates of reproductive freedom more often view the government as the enemy rather than as a friend. Governments at their best should exist to provide for a stable, prosperous, and peaceful society that allows its citizens to have the children they want and to raise them as they see fit. The requirements of the community to preserve everyone's ability to reproduce successfully sometimes must override individual freedom. This does not mean that society can and should take it upon itself to make reproductive decisions for its members.

Governments, laws, and legal systems have evolved over time to enable the biological survival of humanity. Humans discovered that they survived better when they lived in large groups and cooperated in providing each other the basics of survival, such as food, warmth, shelter, and protection from enemies. As early humans coalesced into larger groups and societies, rules evolved that set out the minimum standard of behavior that was expected of all members of the group as a condition of being a member of the group and of getting these benefits. These rules, which we now call our social or cultural norms or moral code, enabled the group to function in a more cohesive fashion and to survive. They included things like honesty and reciprocal altruism. As human groups grew in size, they needed a more formal system of rules to insure the social cohesion and collective effort necessary for survival. Thus, governments and laws were created that did two things: They set forth rules on how the government itself would be constituted and govern, and they also codified some, but not all, of the cultural and behavioral norms into law and provided sanctions for breaking them. While there are political, economic, cultural, and social aspects to legal systems, for instance tax laws, property laws, and contract laws, the fundamental reason for a society to be governed by law is biological. As population grew, law became necessary for human survival.

Anthropologist E. Adamson Hoebel of the University of Minnesota summed up the reasons why humanity created civil societies with formalized legal systems:

(1) to maintain the biologic functioning of group members; (and)
(2) to reproduce new members of the group. . . .

Humanity is no different from other organisms in that its biological function is to convert resources into further organisms. Humanity differs from the rest of the animal kingdom in that it developed the ability to create a common morality and a legal system that would make a society conducive to human reproduction. Law and morality create an environment where, biologically speaking, resources can be more easily converted into further organisms, or, in common parlance, families and children can thrive. This is not to say that civil society does not have other functions, including enabling humanity to attain spiritual, economic, and other goals. But these goals are not attainable unless humanity reproduces itself.

A society will succeed biologically only when its members succeed biologically. This happens when its individual members succeed in passing their genes to the next generation, and have children who in turn survive in good health to reproduce and so on through the generations. The Darwinian process of natural selection means that those with the attributes, traits, or genes that best enable them to adapt and survive in a particular environment will in fact survive and reproduce more than those without these genes. Reproductive success is therefore measured at the gene or individual level. But an individual's reproductive success may not be due entirely to his own efforts and skills. It may depend not only upon the state of the environment but also upon help received from his family or from the community. If there is plentiful food, if an individual feels safe in his community, and if there are no external threats to the community, it is probably more likely that the members of community will have children. While a system of law and morality constrains individual freedom and may even put individual reproductive success at risk, the evolutionary benefits of civil society and a common morality in general outweigh the individual costs.

This does not mean that freedom can be restrained whenever civil authorities see some societal or public safety justification. On the contrary, I believe that maximizing individual freedom should be the presumption and should be preferred over community safety and societal harmony unless there is a compelling case made for restricting freedom. A well-ordered society balances freedom with community safety and harmony to makes it easier for members to attain their biological as well as other goals in life. The restrictions on human freedom should only be those necessary for society to attain those goals. When we err, it should be on the side of freedom. There is a major difference between laws enacted to preserve the biologic function, on the one hand, and laws trying to make reproductive decisions on behalf of the citizenry, on the other. Governments should be doing the former and not the latter.

A central threat to a community's biologic function is infertility. Individual sexual behavior can cause an increase in sexually transmitted diseases and infertility that makes it more difficult for others in the community to reproduce. Personal sexual behavior thus has public, biological consequences. Since governments have as one of their purposes "to maintain the biologic functioning of group members," they can legitimately try to forestall the adverse effects of sexual practices that impair the biologic functioning and reproductive abilities of the group. Just as war is too important to be left to the generals, there are times when reproduction is too important to be left to the troops. There is a built-in tension in society because reproductive freedom both helps and hurts individual members of society. Individuals have reproductive success when they control their reproduction and when they have the freedom to reproduce as they think most advantageous. For this reason, I believe that it is a legitimate and necessary function of government to provide the family planning, reproductive health care, and abortion services that women and men need to control their fertility and child-bearing. At the same time it is the role of government to minimize the negative consequences of individual sexual behavior on the reproductive environment. This can mean adopting laws that restrict certain individual sexual and reproductive options.

To act legitimately, governments must establish some causal connection between the laws they enact and the results to be achieved. The goals of preserving the biologic function and creating an environment in which citizens can reproduce successfully are so elastic that they could justify virtually any government policy. One traditional justification of laws regulating sexual activity and promoting marriage was to channel sex into marriage for the production, protection, and well-being of children. As Professor Lionel Tiger of Rutgers University has stated, marriage was created to strengthen the bond between the father and the mother for the benefit of their children. Many believe that marriage is essential for the promotion of family life, community harmony, and social stability. Therefore, many believe that laws banning adultery, incest, homosexuality, fornication, and any sexual activity other than between a married man and woman can be justified because they strengthen marriage and therefore society at large.

As we have seen, though, limiting sex to within marriage is not necessarily in accord with the reproductive strategies that men and women have evolved to use, and for that reason laws attempting to do this are unenforceable and are doomed to failure. This does not mean that these laws do not serve a purpose. It does mean that society has to find some other way of supporting marriage as an institution if it believes that marriage helps society to function and helps people reproduce successfully. Sometimes governments go over the line into trying to control, rather than enhance, our reproduction. I would argue that lines are drawn wisely when they support humanity's reproductive strategies, not when they dictate them. It is entirely within the purview of government to enact policies to create a society conducive to reproduction. It is not within its purview to make reproductive decisions on behalf of its citizens. But that hasn't stopped governments from trying.

## Why Governments Try to Manipulate Our Childbearing

Nations have long believed that a certain population size and growth rate were necessary for the nation to defend itself, grow economically, and conquer its environment. For these reasons, governments have frequently gotten into the business of encouraging or requiring certain childbearing goals. In modern times some governments want to encourage decreases in family size.

Each citizen may of course view optimum family size differently than the government will. A government in trying to attain its population goals is somewhat at the mercy of the sexual practices and reproductive strategies of its citizenry—but only somewhat. Societies throughout history have established cultural norms and laws regulating sexual practices and reproductive strategies to favor population growth. Christian nations encouraged their adherents to "be fruitful and multiply." Only recently has there been a shift in this norm in countries that see population growth as a threat and not a boon to their national aspirations. No matter if a government wants to increase or decrease its population, it appears that, as Lionel Tiger has said, "Sex is politics by other means."

Advocates both for and against population growth agree that population size and composition affect most of the other matters that governments are empowered to deal with, including the economy, the environment, and the public's health. The 1994 U.N. Conference on Population and Development in Cairo stated as an underlying principle: "Population-related goals and policies are integral parts of cultural, economic and social development, the principal aim of which is to improve the quality of life of all people." The population and other policies that are necessary to improve the quality of life or to save the environment may vary by nation, but a few are universal: A nation must be protected from its enemies and an economy must grow without ruining the environment. While the United Nations did not mention national self-defense as a rationale for having a large and growing population, it is not beyond the role of government to provide "for the common defense," as the U.S. Constitution says. In pre-technological times, generally the larger a nation's population, the more powerful and safe from invasion the country was.

Today governments rarely publicly justify their population policies in military terms, one exception being the island nation of Sri Lanka, with a fertility rate of 2.0 children per woman, which has been torn by a civil war for many years. In 2001, the prime minister called for an increase in the population to provide more troops to fight Tamil rebels and to provide more monks and priests for Buddhist temples. The government, which has in the past actively encouraged smaller families as a means to speed development through its voluntary family planning program, announced that it would now pay bonuses for bigger families.

Governments also intervene in a nation's population size and composition in order to insure economic growth and prosperity, even though there is an unresolved conflict among economists as to whether the size of a population, or its growth rate and composition, has a direct relationship to general prosperity in a country. There is some consensus that too many young people and too many old people in relation to those of working age are not beneficial to the economy. And there is some arguable justification for government intervention to encourage or discourage childbearing under certain demographic conditions.

One observer, Michael Prowse, wrote in the *Financial Times* about the population stagnation in Western Europe: "The failure of a society to reproduce itself is as great a sin, in its way, as a rodent-like tendency to overpopulation. . . . Politicians must also attempt to counter the graying of Europe with policies designed to stimulate indigenous population growth." Prowse's population proposal for Western Europe should be contrasted with another expert's population plan for the developing world. Onora O'Neill, a prominent British academic, suggested that population control policies should be a necessary condition for receiving foreign aid. If non-coercive population policies fail, O'Neill said, "and just productive and redistributive measures too cannot meet needs, direct coercion of procreative decisions would not be unjust."

Thus depending on the demographic situation and the level of economic development in the nation one is talking about, some advocates and policymakers are ready to institute incentive-laden or even coercive governmental policies designed to attain specific childbearing outcomes. The level of individual fertility is assumed to be a legitimate state matter. Simone Veil, a French human rights advocate, a Holocaust survivor, and the first president of the European Parliament, declared: "Avoiding a long-term weakening of a country brought about by a dangerously low birth rate and, inversely, avoiding excessive population growth when it becomes an obstacle to economic development and to the well-being of the population must certainly be among the basic goals of all governments." There is no doubt that fertility "is consequential for societies. . . . Fertility is generally too high during development, too low after it: a problem for public policy."

Population size and economic growth also affect the natural environment of a nation. A nation's natural resources are common resources, be they the water supply, clean air, or open spaces. While development pressures and consumption patterns can act independently of population growth, the expansion of a nation's population has an immediate impact on a nation's natural resources. In pre-industrial days, the natural environment was perhaps the deciding factor in reproductive decisionmaking. Would it be a cold winter? Was there enough food and water? Did the family have to migrate in search of a more hospitable environment? Given these life or death variables, a family would need the power to decide on having a child now or waiting for better times.

Thus governments have a variety of interests in controlling or influencing the sexual behavior of their citizens and the size, rate of growth, composition, and health of their populations. Depending on the circumstances, governments may want to increase or decrease their absolute size or at least their rate of growth. Governments all prefer a healthy population. To attain these goals governments can institute economic incentives or disincentives for having children born, or legal prohibitions on contraceptives and abortion, or criminal penalties against certain sexual behaviors that are thought to retard population growth or to be damaging to the public health and its ability to reproduce.

## Is It Too Expensive for a Nation to Purchase Its Own Descendants?

While there is little evidence that governments can change their citizens' sexual practices, it can sometimes change the number of children their citizens end up having. Some governments, for instance, directly subsidize childbirth through additional benefits for parents and tax deductions for children. These nations are in the business of "collectively purchas(ing) their descendants," as Geoffrey McNicoll of the Population Council, a demographic research organization, has said. Is the transfer of tax dollars from those who already have the children they want to those who don't a legitimate government function and an efficient use of government resources? Rarely. A government is, in general, not terribly effective when it intervenes in sexual, reproductive, and population matters.

While a government may have an overall view of what its population should be or look like, it is quite another matter to make it happen. People have their own reproductive goals and strategies, which may result in quite different levels of population growth, size, and composition than what the governing authority may think is optimum. A governmental childbearing policy may conflict with or may support the individual preferences of its citizens. With the exception of China, governments have usually adopted noncompulsory incentives and disincentives to affect population size and childbearing rates. These steps include economic and social regulations that make childbearing financially easier or harder. Governments can mandate parental leave from employment or provide child-care subsidies, cash bonuses for each child born, tax credits for children, or subsidized education and housing for families with children. Since these types of policies only encourage a certain outcome rather than require one, they will by definition have uncertain effectiveness. The law of unintended consequences is also likely to come into play.

Some countries in Europe and Asia have taken the lead in modern times to try to use social and economic incentives to increase their birth rates. France currently believes that encouraging population growth is an important, indeed vital, function of the government. Family Minister Christian Jacob stated in 2003: "Of course the state must step in and help. The more children that are born, the better it is for our pension system and for our economy in general." The French policies to encourage births include providing children's allowances with a premium for a third child and subsidizing day care. While the total fertility rate for French women reached new highs in 2000 and 2001, rising to 1.9 children per woman, demographers do not know if the government's policies had any influence. The central cause of the increase appeared to be that women who had reached their thirties without having had children were finally beginning their childbearing. The average age for a French woman to have a first child is twenty-eight, up from age twenty-three twenty years ago. There did not appear to be an increase in the desired family size. At the same time that France was pursuing its policies to increase childbearing, the government further liberalized its abortion law and made emergency contraception easier to access for adults and minors. By so doing France recognized the continuing importance of women's having control over their childbearing and did not sacrifice this principle to its goal of increased childbearing.

Because of the multitude of factors that enter into individual childbearing decisions, it is hard for researchers to quantify the effect that governmental policies have. One study of childbearing trends in Canada from 1921 to 1988 found that a combination of three separate incentives—a personal tax exemption for a child, a child tax credit, and family allowances for each child—had "positive and significant effects on birthrates," but that the "elasticities of fertility . . . seem to be rather small." The three transfer tax benefits for each woman of reproductive age totaled $389 annually in 1988. At the time the cost of raising a child to age 18 was probably in the neighborhood of $100,000, not to mention the time, effort, and other costs required. The economists from the University of Western Ontario doing the study, led by Professor Junsen Zhang, estimated that the three programs would have to be increased over five times, to $1,982 annually, to bring the fertility rate up to 2.1, the replacement rate, from its then level of 1.7. Interestingly, this latter dollar amount approximated the amount of the transfer tax subsidies to childbearing in various Western European countries, including France, that continued to have replacement levels below fertility rates. The economists did not explain why their proposal would work in Canada when it did not work particularly well in Europe. Even when Canada's birth rate increased in 2001 after an expansion of the government's benefits for parents, experts could not say whether this was a result of the government's program or whether people who had deferred childbearing in a poor economy finally were having their children as the economy improved.

In looking at the effects, or lack thereof, of government programs on fertility rates therefore, a certain amount of skepticism is in order. First, the mere existence of a government, even if it has no specific fertility policies, probably has an effect on fertility by virtue of its efforts to establish a stable civil society and assist economic growth. Geoffrey McNicoll of the Population Council has noted: "By virtue of its mere existence the state cannot *not* influence fertility" (emphasis in original).

In making and timing their childbearing decisions, citizens of a nation will assess what the future bodes for themselves and their children. This will depend on the parents' status in society, their social and economic prospects, and the prospects of their children. All these are in turn affected by their race, ethnicity, class, sex, geographic location, education levels, health, and opportunities and prospects for advancement, if any. All these factors may affect not only the timing of births, but also the number of children desired. Childbearing decisions are not made in isolation from the society in which the parents find themselves or from their history and cultural tradition. The dismal environment of inner city teens in the United States can often lead them to early childbearing. Both economic opportunities for women as well as economic uncertainty can lead to declining birth rates. The plummeting birth rates in the United States during the great depression in the 1930s, and their recovery into a baby boom after the Second World War ended, are examples. The transfer from a communist society to a market society in Russia and Eastern Europe in the 1990s and the entry of women into the economic marketplace in America and Western Europe are others. Governments make changes to their social and economic systems with purposes other than fertility management in mind. Nevertheless, when these changes occur, they often have profound effects on fertility.

When governments, as in France and Canada, decide to get involved in fertility management, either to increase it or decrease it, the changes induced may be miniscule. When a government gets involved in fertility management, McNicoll noted, its response "is typically hesitant, clumsy, and often, no doubt, futile." With monetary incentives to influence the birth rate, McNicoll has observed: "Apparent effects are sometimes detectable, more often in the tempo of fertility than in lifetime births, but overall the impact of such measures has been fairly marginal." As we observed earlier with respect to the Canadian analysis: "Against the actual costs of children, the kinds of monetary incentive offered to parents in most pro-natalist programs are trivial."

Despite the evidence that governments are wasting their money, they persist in trying to purchase their descendants. I can only say that the evidence indicates that the cost of effective economic incentives needed to influence childbearing rates in a significant way would be so large as to be unfeasible, as would the political costs. Furthermore, there is no apparent reason at least in developed countries for government to do anything. As Judge Richard Posner concluded in his book *Sex and Reason*: "I conclude that at present in wealthy nations there is no strong economic argument for either pro-natalist or anti-natalist policies . . ." This is not to say that politicians will not conjure social, economic, or moral justifications for political intervention in matters of sexuality and childbearing, and it is not to say that courts might not defer to these legislative judgments as a constitutional matter no matter how flimsy the arguments might be.

## Does Providing the Pill Reduce Population Growth?

During the latter half of the twentieth century governments in developing countries addressed their perceived over-population problem by increasing access to modern contraception through subsidized clinical services. Additionally, many governments urged their populace to use family planning and tried to alter their people's traditional preference for large families and to establish the small family as the cultural norm. Only a few governments, as in China, used coercive methods to reduce birth rates. Most other programs were voluntary, even though there were often incentives to adopt the small family norm. Voluntary family planning policies have helped people have the number of children that they actually want to have. Coercive policies to increase or decrease childbearing, while they may work in the short run, are a human, political, social, and medical disaster. China and Romania are the prime examples of what governments should not do in trying to control their nation's fertility.

By way of contrast, for over fifty years India has had an official government population policy, which in its latest iteration has economic incentives to encourage late marriage, late childbearing, and sterilization after two children. India has recognized that childbearing decisions do not occur in a vacuum and over time has adopted programs to reduce infant mortality and to increase literacy rates and economic opportunity for women. The current population policy sets a target birthrate of 2.1 children per woman by the year 2010 and offers economic incentives to government health workers to reach this goal. While there is justifiable concern that these incentives would lead to a return of the coercive sterilization practices that marred India's program in the 1970s under Indira Gandhi, the policy officially calls for better and more accessible voluntary reproductive health programs for women and men. Under its population policies, the birth rate in India has been cut in half since 1952, from about six children per woman to about 3.3 in 2000. During that same time, the population of India has tripled through a combination of there being more women of reproductive age having children, even though they were having fewer children, and a lower death rate. As we saw in China, when family size declines, the law of unintended consequences kicks in. Sex-selection abortion, even though it is illegal, and a resulting skewed sex ratio are on the increase in India as Indian families attempt to insure a male heir in their smaller families.

Despite the evidence that family planning programs have enabled millions of couples who otherwise would not have been able to voluntarily use modern contraception and evidence that family size is decreasing throughout India, as it has throughout the world, there is considerable debate in academic and political circles about whether the latter state of affairs is the result of the former. Did family planning programs lead to a reduction in family size? It is difficult for researchers to figure out what would have happened if there had been no family planning programs. For instance, during the nineteenth and twentieth centuries, family size declined in United States and Western Europe without modern contraception and family planning programs.

Couples seeking to implement whatever their conscious or subconscious reproductive strategy might be are hardly at the mercy of their government or of the society or environment in which they find themselves. Couples, as we have discussed, can and will find ways, though imperfect, to manage the timing and number of their children without resorting to "modern" contraception. Nonetheless, the most recent research indicates a direct relationship between the use of modern contraception and a declining fertility rate. Amy Ong Tsui, a professor at the Johns Hopkins School of Public Health, published a study in 2001 that showed that for every 15-percentage-point increase in contraceptive use (the contraceptive prevalence rate) there was a reduction by one child in the total fertility rate, for example a decline from 4.5 to 3.5 children per woman. Her conclusion was that "although family-limitation behavior might have increased without modern contraception and the services of public programs (as indeed occurred in Western Europe), such behaviors would likely neither have been as effective as afforded by safe contraceptive technologies nor gained widespread use as quickly."

But, Tsui noted, "One should not overemphasize the role of supply-oriented policies and programs in recent fertility declines and disregard the forces that raise demand for those public goods and services." The factors that increase demand for family planning and that lead families to want to limit their size, include, under Tsui's analysis, female education, an increase in non-agricultural sectors of the economy, and more food availability. Interestingly, while increasing female education leads to a decrease in family size, increasing male education leads to an increase in the number of children men desire. Tsui found, finally, that foreign population assistance, which pays for family planning clinics and birth control methods, either from Western governments or the United Nations, had reduced birth rates in developed countries by an average 0.5 births. Previous estimates had been higher, showing a reduction on the order of 1.5 births, and suggested that organized family planning programs had accounted for half of the fertility decline in developing countries since the 1950s.

The academic consensus is that women's education, economic development, and family planning programs all contribute to fertility decline, and the more of each, the faster the decline. There is also a consensus that these social, economic, and political realities will trump whatever the government's public policy on childbearing might be and that people will pursue their own reproductive strategies whatever obstacles their government puts in their path. As a result, it should not be surprising that some nations have adopted more draconian methods to increase or reduce family size.

Laws setting a maximum permitted family size and laws banning birth control and abortion can have measurable effects, at least in the short run until the citizenry figures out how to circumvent the laws and pursue their own childbearing strategies. China's one-child policy, for example, was supposed to limit each family to one child. In response to both non-compliance and protests, Chinese authorities were forced to adopt some limited exceptions to the law. But even those who could not fit into an exception still pursued their own reproductive plans and, despite the law and its rigorous enforcement, tried to have the number of children they wanted. As a result in 2000, China's one-child policy resulted, not in an average of one child per family, but in an average of 1.8 children per family, which means that out of ten families, an average of two families had the mandated one child while eight families had two children. Thus in spite of limited exceptions to the law and punitive enforcement measures, including forced contraception, sterilization, and abortion, most Chinese families figured out a way to evade the law and have two children, and in some cases more.

Unlike China, some other nations had declining birth rate as their central demographic concern, and some of them, like France, adopted social and economic policies that tried to make having a family less stressful and less costly. These policies were only marginally effective, if at all, so some nations turned to the more drastic alternative of trying to force an increase in birth rates by banning birth control and abortion. In a study on the demographic effects of restrictive abortion laws published in 2002, economists Phillip B. Levine of Wellesley College and Douglas Staiger of Dartmouth College found that in Eastern Europe "strict limits on abortion access are associated with large increases in the birth rate, on the order of 10% or more . . . (and) we estimate that pregnancies fall by 27 to 45 percent when abortion access was very restricted (although this is most likely an over-estimate because it does not count illegal abortions)." Restrictive abortion laws not unsurprisingly affected both the pregnancy and birth rates, decreasing the former and increasing the latter.

Among the nations that Levine and Staiger examined was Romania, which in the 1980s took unprecedented pro-natalist steps to try to increase its anemic birthrate. The Communist regime, led by Nicolae Ceausescu, outlawed both birth control and abortion, but it didn't stop there. In 1986, President Ceausescu declared: "the fetus is the socialist property of the whole society. Giving birth is a patriotic duty. . . . Those who refuse to have children are deserters, escaping the law of natural continuity."

In an attempt to crack down on its fertility deserters, the government required each employed female to have a monthly gynecological examination to look for telltale signs of either pregnancy, which would be duly registered, or for signs of contraceptive use or of a recent abortion. Women who refused the examination lost their medical, social security, and pension benefits. A monthly birth quota was established for each factory, and the factory physician was paid only if the plant's women met the quota. As an added incentive to childbirth, extra taxes were imposed on unmarried men and women over age twenty-five and on married couples who were childless after two years of marriage (unless there was a finding of infertility).

As one might expect, the Romanian people did not share their leader's enthusiasm for a higher birth rate and resorted to withdrawal and rhythm (and smuggled contraceptives), as well as illegal abortion to avoid pregnancy. The birth rate quickly doubled, since pregnancy prevention was less effective and not every pregnant woman was willing to risk an illegal abortion. But within a few years the birth rate settled back from a pre-criminalization rate of less than 2 children per woman to a marginally higher level of 2.3 children per woman, just above the replacement rate and close to the 10 percent increase that Levine and Staiger found to be the norm when abortion is banned. The resulting unwanted child was frequently abandoned in a state orphanage, where it often perished under appalling conditions. Maternal mortality doubled and gynecological injuries to women sharply increased, both due to unsafe abortion. It is estimated that a half million women, or 10 percent of Romanian women of reproductive age, were left sterile as a result of unsafe abortion. Ironically, the government's policies aiming to increase birth rates ended in the involuntary sterilization of the women who were necessary to achieve this goal. After the overthrow of the Communists, Romania lifted its restrictions on access to contraception and abortion, and the birth rate soon resumed its long-term decline. In 2000 it stood at 1.3 children per woman, similar to the rate in the rest of Eastern Europe.

The evidence indicates that governmental policies to encourage or discourage childbearing will in general not be effective. Nor will laws to restrict family size or alternatively restrict access to birth control and abortion in an attempt to increase family size, at least in the long term. People have their own reproductive strategies that are not generally amenable to change when a nation adopts its own reproductive strategy. We saw this in the United States during the late nineteenth and early twentieth centuries when, even though birth control and abortion were outlawed, American family size continued its century-long decline.

The Comstock and other laws criminalizing birth control and abortion did have an effect, usually on the poor. Those who had a physician could navigate the state's therapeutic abortion exceptions and get a legal abortion, or frequently a safe illegal one. Those who could not access a physician, usually the poor, had unsafe, illegal abortions. There were those, whether wealthy or not, who were deterred by the bureaucratic process or by the danger, or even by the moral sanction that the law represented, and decided not to have abortions. One estimate by Philip Levine and others published in 1999 states that criminalizing abortions in America would reduce abortions by only one-third. As Judge Richard Posner said in his book *Sex and Reason*, making abortion criminal raised the cost, thus reducing the number, made abortions occur later, and made abortion less safe. It also makes large numbers of citizens into lawbreakers.

The criminal law in matters of sexuality and reproduction, while questionable on many grounds, is not totally ineffective. It can deter the proscribed behavior, even if law authorities make little or no effort to catch violators. But what in general the criminal law cannot do is prevent men and women from striving to achieve their reproductive goals. Men and women will find a way around the law. That is why voluntary programs can work and why coercion fails.

A government's intervention into its citizens' sex lives for the purpose of manipulating population growth is mostly futile and, if coercive, illegitimate. It is not a long road from France to Romania or from India to China. Despite the fact that governments have an interest, indeed a mandate, to preserve their citizens' ability to reproduce and to create an environment where reproduction is feasible and desired, governments all too often see the manipulation of population growth as a legitimate governmental function to attain other goals such as national defense and economic growth. What governments end up doing is establishing a national reproductive strategy to replace their citizens' individual reproductive strategies. When it does this, a government is saying that it does not trust reproductive decisions to its citizens. This is an entirely new, and I submit, illegitimate function for government. There is no justification for either Romania to require childbirth or for China to ban it. Both are equally wrong.

## Should the Government
## Be a Sunday School Teacher?

I have argued that the creation of a suitable environment for the raising of children is a legitimate function of government. This environment is created in two ways: first, by the creation of a civil society and a government with laws and a common morality, and second, by the society's supporting families. These two are frequently conflated, and governments frequently assert that it is a legitimate function to promote a common morality that supports strong families. This common morality often involves restrictions on certain sexual and reproductive practices. It also may attempt to allow more sexual freedom to males than females.

The proponents of restrictions on contraception and abortion or on certain sexual practices need to surmount several hurdles in order to maintain their legitimacy: first, that a sexual moral code, however defined, is necessary for the establishment of a civil society; second, that the moral beliefs in that code are correct, that is to say that the restrictions proposed actually relate to promoting family life or a common morality; and third, that the government ought to enforce those beliefs given the private nature of the conduct that is proscribed. Each nation must assess the extent to which its government can regulate its citizens' private sexual behavior without undermining its own legitimacy. The problem is that the sexual restrictions may run so contrary to human reproductive strategies that they cost more in evolutionary terms than whatever benefit they claim to provide. In other words, the morality may not make practical sense, and even if it does, the cost of enforcement may be too high and the negative consequences of enforcement may outweigh the positives. In other words, government restrictions on the sexual behavior of its citizens may not be moral.

I would argue that laws restricting most sexual and reproductive practices fail these tests. They also fail an important constitutional test. The U.S. Constitution rightly restricts what the majority can decide is part of the moral code. The right to privacy protects our ability to have our own reproductive strategies. This protects us from the majority creating, as was said in *Griswold*, an "asinine" moral code. There are some limits beyond which the majority may not go.

## *Is a Sexual Moral Code Necessary for Civil Society?*

Traditional political philosophers have argued for over a century about the extent of the realm of privacy, the meaning of liberty, and the corresponding role of the government in regulating and constricting, or expanding, the private sphere. John Stuart Mill and Lord Devlin argued in the nineteenth century about the extent that government could regulate private morality. Their argument is just as important today as then. While I do not believe, as Devlin did, that one immoral act necessarily leads to another, there is a societal interest in creating an environment in which citizens want to live, be happy, and have and raise children.

John Stuart Mill argued in *On Liberty*:

> The sole end for which mankind are warranted, individually or collectively, in interfering with the liberty of action of any member, is self-protection. That the only purpose for which power can be rightfully exercised over any member of a civilized community, against his will, is to prevent harm to others. His own good, either physical or moral, is not a sufficient warrant.

Mill believed in using other social measures, including public opinion, to improve the behavior of individual members of society. He argued that some bad behavior is itself a bad example and might corrupt others. Certain behaviors can be legally prohibited but only "things which have been tried and condemned from the beginning of the world until now; things which experience has shown not to be useful or suitable to any person's individuality." On balance Mill thought that society ought to refrain "for the sake of human freedom" from legal punishment of behaviors that harm only the individual. The line between public and private, as Mill recognized, is often illusory, and, even if a line can be drawn, does not mean it should be drawn. Mill's opponents and even Mill himself recognized that there are certain "private" behaviors that should be outlawed and a certain society-wide conformity that should be enforced.

The proponents of the view that government must enforce a common morality argue, as did Lord Devlin, a nineteenth century opponent of Mill's, that: "A recognized morality is as necessary to society's existence as a recognized government." A breach of a moral principle is an "offence against society as a whole." Under this view, it is permissible to outlaw certain private acts on the grounds that they cause offence to the majority's sensibilities. Devlin's successors have argued that enforcement of morality as such is a good in itself whether or not a violation weakens society and whether or not individual privacy is invaded and freedom restricted. Society is strong if a positive morality is enforced, and, conversely, society is on the road to ruin if any part of the common morality is breached. Under the Devlin view, all morality is a seamless web, a unity, the deviation from one part being likely to lead to deviation from other parts. For Lord Devlin or for his successors, like William Bennett, there is no handrail on the slippery slope to moral ruin.

If, as I have argued, the biological purpose of civil society is to better enable humanity to reproduce successfully, a moral code and a legal system that promote an orderly and safe society are essential. The issue then becomes, what kind of moral code is necessary? If we grant that there is a benefit to having a moral code, does this mean that, whatever the contents of the moral code, it is necessarily a legitimate code simply because the majority voted for it? The danger of legislating morality was pointed out by Judge Learned Hand: "If we forbid birth control in the interest of morals, is it inconceivable that we should tax celibacy?" Once we permit government action to enforce a morality, this permits government enforcement of any morality.

## *Is the Traditional Moral Code Moral?*

The moral condition of society may be a glass half full or half empty, depending on one's ideology. The study of biology may help us bridge our political and ideological differences and come up with a standard for evaluating whether laws enacted to improve the moral condition of society are actually helpful. My test is whether moral laws help "preserve the biologic function." For instance, incest laws serve a biological function since they help prevent birth defects. Other laws regulating sexual practices serve no biological function. Laws banning birth control and abortion fail this test completely. While abortion opponents argue that the taking of human life is prima facie evidence that abortion does not serve a biological purpose, I would argue otherwise. Abortion and birth control help humanity succeed in its reproductive strategies and thereby advance the human race. While abortion takes life, it enables life to reproduce itself successfully, not on nature's terms but on human terms. The unborn child is not just an innocent life. While it is the epitome of human destiny and the greatest potential joy that humanity can create, it is also a liability, a threat, and a danger to the mother and to the other members of its family. In order to survive, humanity has necessarily taken pre-born life to preserve other life all throughout its evolutionary history.

How does one measure society's moral condition? William Bennett of Empower America proposed an Index of Leading Cultural Indicators, which included a variety of measurements including levels of out-of-wedlock births, violent crime, divorce, teen suicide, TV viewing, SAT scores, charitable giving, voter participation, and abortion. Bennett left out other arguably relevant indicators of societal wellbeing, including church attendance and the infant mortality rate. He also left out gambling, perhaps because it was later revealed he was a frequent gambler. Given all these different measures, how can one measure the impact on society of citizens' obeying or not obeying various portions of the moral code? It is hard to find causation between the evolving societal approval of homosexuality (or at least decreasing disapproval) and the above measures of alleged societal health. Nor with the nation's abortion rate.

Instead, I find correlation. (There is a correlation between children's growing up in broken homes and delinquent behavior and lower educational achievement.) Nor do I see how many of these indices relate to making a society more conducive for its citizens to reproduce. Clearly a high crime rate and teen suicide do not make for a healthy and safe society. Other factors like charitable giving and participation in civic life by voting are important. But do they enhance family life so that reproduction is easier? Or are they just quality-of-life indicators?

In looking at Bennett's Index of Leading Cultural Indicators, I am struck by how few are promoted or prevented by the legal system, aside from violent crime. Abortion stands out in that many restrictions on access to abortion are in place in the states. There are few or no laws trying to change other cultural indicators such as the levels of out-of-wedlock births, divorce, TV viewing, SAT scores, charitable giving, and voter participation. For the most part there is less inclination in the United States, as compared to other countries, to try to influence these indices by force of law. Some countries require voting. Some prohibit divorce. Out-of-wedlock births can result in the death penalty for the mother in some countries today. Why couldn't a nation require tithing and prohibit TV?

What standard is used to transform a cultural indicator into a cultural or moral norm and then into a law? I believe that for sexual and reproductive matters it takes a compelling biological reason to make a sexual law legitimate. This can be either to preserve the biologic function or to create a civil society in which successful reproduction can occur. Not all sexual behaviors are equal. Fornication, meaning sexual intercourse outside of marriage, is hardly a threat, and is actually a boon, to human reproduction. But is incest, for instance, enough of a threat to the biologic function and successful reproduction that it is legitimate for government to ban it?

As anthropologist Helen Fisher of Rutgers University has said: "All human societies have some sort of incest taboo." As humans evolved, it was important for human survival to have as many adults responsible for and caring for its younger members. Two families committed to the welfare of the children of the marriage were better than the one family that would be the case if there was an incestuous union. An expanded kin network brought about by marriage among neighboring families and tribes was vital in insuring peace and cooperation among these families and tribes that could be competing for resources. An incestuous union could also weaken the relationship between husband and wife, which was vital to the well-being of children. For these social and political reasons societies would favor marriage outside the family and even outside the tribe.

Natural selection would also favor marriage outside the family and, for genetic reasons, disfavor incest. Biologists agree that genetic diversity is the key to survival; there is substantial evidence that a greater risk of birth defects exists when children are born to close relatives. If both parents have a gene such as for cystic fibrosis, there is a 25 percent chance their child will inherit the disease. While there are societal reasons for an incest taboo, there is a biological interest too—that of protecting the child. It is in the interest of children generally that they not be born of an incestuous union.

Over time, as Helen Fisher said: "What had been a natural tendency became a cultural dictum too . . . . Incest had become taboo." Why did society feel the need to make a taboo into a law? Assuming there is a biological basis to promote or restrict certain sexual and reproductive practices, why can't society do this with suasion? Perhaps in the case of incest suasion didn't work. Perhaps the biological and social stakes were so high that, if everyone disobeyed, the future of society was at stake. Incest threatens both the biologic function of the citizens and civil society in general.

There are no similar genetic concerns with the other sexual practices, such as sodomy, adultery, bigamy, and polygamy. Nonetheless, valid societal reasons exist for adultery, bigamy, and polygamy to be disfavored. A society can validly protect the institution of marriage and the marriage contract, especially when there are children involved. Each of these practices runs the risk of family disintegration to the detriment of the children. However, sodomy, or any homosexual or non-procreative sexual behavior, runs no such risk. It is not a direct threat to family or the children.

What of birth control and abortion? Can it be argued that banning them promotes family life or successful reproduction? There are societal pros and cons to an individual's ability to regulate his or her fertility. There are also, and primarily, biological benefits when parents can space and limit the number of offspring. The value of having sex during courtship and as a means of bonding a couple together without fear of pregnancy cannot be underestimated. The by-product of legal contraception and abortion—that they can be used to increase the amount of sex outside of marriage with all that this entails—can be admitted without conceding that this is cause enough to forbid them.

There are practical arguments in favor of permitting abortion. Primarily, I argue, the availability of abortion permits a couple to carry out their reproductive strategies to have healthy children that they can invest in so that the children in turn will survive to reproduce and invest in turn in their progeny. Under this argument it is not "life" that is the goal, but "surviving life that in turn reproduces surviving life." This is a fundamental distinction. Those who oppose abortion claim that their underlying concern is preserving life. This is less than fully meaningful. Those making this argument would not be alive to make it if their parents had died at an early age of malnutrition or malaria. Their parents survived to adulthood and reproduced and invested in their children. This is what life is. It is a continuum of survival and reproduction repeating itself. Assigning an absolute right to life is as biologically and morally meaningless as saying that life consists of DNA and nothing more.

Many people do not believe the fertilized egg or embryo to be anything less than a full human being and therefore do not accept that its existence can be traded or sacrificed to permit another to be born at a later time or to permit others living to survive. Under these view, the ends never justify the means. Even those who view the fetus as a potential child, rather than the moral or legal equivalent of a born child, can argue that, like bans on incest, bans on abortion protect something that will eventually be a child. The question of which beings are to be included within the scope of our laws is a question of moral definition. But even if we define an embryo as a "person" with all the inherent rights of persons who have been born, or even as a potential person who might be born, this does not end the discussion.

Abortion opponents often call the embryo or unborn child "innocent," and they call abortion the taking of innocent life. However, no pregnancy, birth, or child is "innocent." Pregnancy and childbirth each pose grave risks to the mother, and a child needs extensive parental care and investment over a long period of time. A child may be a joy forever, but it is a liability for years. This investment takes away from the care of other children born or to be born and affects their chances of survival. Parents sometimes have to choose between their current and future children in order to best preserve their chances of successfully reproducing. The timing of childbearing is especially vital. All reproduction involves trade-offs between finding a mate, pregnancy and childbearing, raising children and having the resources to survive now and in the future. All these must be balanced in a particular environment and socioeconomic situation. This is why many women defer childbearing until they have finished their education and are economically secure and alternatively why many poor women accelerate their childbearing since their life expectancy is less and their economic prospects dismal. If parents don't make these hard choices, then natural selection will and all might perish. Abortion should be legal because giving parents the ability to control their reproduction helps more of humanity survive.

Laws prohibiting abortion say that every child conceived should be born, Mother Nature permitting. Our evolutionary history says otherwise. Sometimes it is in a woman's reproductive interest not to carry a pregnancy to term. A woman and her partner must take into account their ability to invest in the child and to get the child to adulthood safely and in good health so that the child can successfully reproduce. This may mean not permitting the unborn child to be born and having another child at a later date, or it may mean the couple's concentrating their reproductive efforts and parental investment on the children they already have.

The rightness and wisdom of a moral code is measured against people's real experiences. For morality to govern reproduction, it must be in alignment with human biology. There is an almost infinite variety of conditions under which women find themselves pregnant and under which they and their partners consider childbirth. There is no call for a reproductive moral code or law requiring a one size fits all solution. Civic morality does not depend on this. Morality, contrary to what Lord Devlin asserts, is not a seamless web. There is no clear causation between one behavior on Bennett's list and another. There are not many slippery slopes. Women who have abortions and people who don't vote are no less moral than their voting neighbors or the women who give birth in or out of wedlock. The absence of sexual indicators on Bennett's list is revealing. This would seem to indicate that not only are sexual matters not a matter for legal sanction, they aren't even a cultural indicator. Clearly some amount of common sense is being demonstrated in not treating particular sexual activities as matters for the legal system, as cultural bellwethers or as a necessary part of the moral code. There are few plausible connections between some sexual and reproductive practices and the preservation of public morality.

## When Is It Legitimate for a Government To Enforce Morality?

Assuming that a moral code of some sort is a necessary component of civil society and that it should contain particular prohibitions of certain sexual and reproductive practices, are there nonetheless any limits on the extent to which the government should enforce the moral code? Should all of the moral code be written into law and enforced? Enforcement requires invasions of personal liberty. Enforcement is costly. To this extent a certain level of judgment and prudence is required. There should be an assessment of how serious the societal problem is before enforcement of a sexual law is undertaken. Authorities need to be sure there is causation between the behavior sought to be banned and the problem to be cured. And authorities need to be sure that the unintended consequences of enforcement don't outweigh whatever benefits are asserted for the law. Enforcement of a sexual law may undermine government legitimacy.

I suggest that policymakers should add a biological analysis to their political and social analysis before they enact any law regulating sex. They should remember that there is a major difference between trying to preserve the biologic function on one hand and requiring certain reproductive outcomes on the other. Laws to minimize sexually transmitted diseases and resulting infertility are legitimate. Laws outlawing genetic engineering are not yet legitimate since there is yet no evidence of widespread biological harm, and the law would prohibit parents from conceiving the children they want. Laws banning sex-selection abortion are legitimate, but only in societies where there is demonstrable harm to the society from the imbalance in the sexes. Otherwise parents should be able to have children of a particular sex. The ban on so-called partial-birth abortion served no biological or societal purpose; it was merely an expression of moral outrage by abortion opponents for political gain. A law that would require childbirth when one is pregnant would frequently not provide the best solution for that woman and her family.

Society's presumption must be in favor of liberty. In the United States the Bill of Rights and Fourteenth Amendment serve to make this presumption the law. Liberty allows people to make mistakes. Nowhere is the government granted the power to be our moral guide. Supreme Court Justice Robert Jackson said in 1950:

> It is not the function of our Government to keep the citizen from falling into error; it is the function of the citizen to keep the Government from falling into error.

The system of human reproduction grants extensive leeway for individuals to make errors. The system also makes it virtually impossible to determine if some biological, or as has been said, "bio-logical," decisions, acts, or omissions are in error or wrong. Incest at one end of the scale is universally condemned and illegal, while masturbation isn't. In between are various sexual practices, which, while they are condemned under the traditional Judeo-Christian moral code, are not universally illegal. Where is the line drawn? What standards do we use?

A legal system and a moral code regulating human affairs must recognize certain biological realities to be legitimate. H. G. Wells said in his introduction to my grandmother's book *The Pivot of Civilization*: A civilization is "a system of society-making ideas at issue with reality. Just so far as the system of ideas meets the needs and conditions of survival of the society it dominates, so far will that society continue and prosper." The conditions of survival mean that government can, among other measures, validly try to improve social and health conditions that threaten society and its ability to reproduce.

There is in the United States an epidemic of sexually transmitted diseases that has caused a rise in infertility. The use of hormonal contraception may be a contributing factor to the spread of these diseases. It is most definitely in society's interest to reduce infertility, but I would argue society should do so in a manner that least restricts the ability of its members to regulate their fertility and have the freedom to enjoy sex. Restricting hormonal contraception and requiring condom use, or even trying to restrict sexual activity, are overly broad and intrusive approaches to the problem. Hormonal contraception is remarkably effective in preventing unintended pregnancy and should not be discouraged lightly. And we must remember that sex, even unprotected sex, with multiple partners is a reproductive strategy pursued by many individuals. Public health messages on the dangers of STDs and explaining the benefits and risks of condoms, combined with early treatment programs, would go a long way to solving the problem. In addition, about half of the states have specific provisions in their public health laws that make it a crime to knowingly expose other person to a sexually transmitted disease, including HIV. Other states have more generic criminal law provisions that might apply to this type of behavior. The HIV Criminal Law and Policy Project identified only 316 prosecutions of people for exposing another to HIV during the fifteen years between 1986 and 2001. This amounts to about twenty cases a year. While increased threat of prosecution would drive possibly infected persons away from seeking testing, counseling, and treatment and would thus lead to more HIV transmission, more selective prosecutions of egregious behavior that transmits any STD may help send a serious public health message.

While genetic engineering and cloning pose serious biological questions, at present they do not represent a threat to society. Cloning enables an individual to reproduce but at a cost of foregoing the benefits that sexual selection provides. If this results in a more rapid and effective breeding ground for pathogens, then this represents a clear danger to others in society. Reproduction without sex also may weaken the progeny that the cloned child may have via sex with others. Cloning thus lessens the chances of reproductive success by the cloned child's partner, and therefore is harder to justify as a reproductive alternative. But cloning is not something that is going to be used in a widespread fashion, at least at present. I believe sexual reproduction will remain the norm. The same applies to genetic engineering. The dangers of manipulating genes by altering or discarding some in the reproductive process need to be fully explored. Genetic technologies will enable those who are infertile, those who do not want to risk sexual intercourse because of STDs, and those who cannot risk reproduction because they carry genetic diseases to reproduce. These are all good things and should be circumscribed only upon clear proof of danger to the child or others.

Sex-selection abortion, however, presents a different magnitude of problem. Sex-selection abortion, while it helps some parents pursue their reproductive strategies and leads to wanted children, is in some countries a societal disaster. The excess sons have a far less chance of reproducing than daughters would. Excess males represent a threat to the stability of the entire nation and its neighbors. There is no other way to effectively stop sex-selection abortion and the resulting imbalance in the sex ratio other than banning the practice. Changing China's or India's culture is a project that will take many years with no guarantee of success. The risks of waiting and the lack of confidence in any other solution dictate that action must be taken now. The damage to girls and boys in these countries is happening now, and the societal dangers from the imbalance in the sex ratio are too great to be ignored.

I have argued that a society will survive when its members have the freedom to have children when they decide it is best, rather than when society dictates. For me, only when reproductive freedom causes health or other damage to society is it legitimate for the government to intervene in childbearing decisions. The connections between certain sexual or reproductive behaviors, deemed by some to be immoral, and the health of society or its members are neither clear nor provable. Nonetheless, this has not stopped lawmakers from enacting abortion legislation to promote their moral viewpoint. Frequently abortion opponents propose laws restricting access to abortion under the guise of promoting public health when their real purpose is to express the view that abortion is wrong and should be discouraged. State legislatures do not possess unlimited powers to enact legislation for any purpose they want. There must be, at minimum, a compelling connection between a state law and the promotion of a legitimate state interest. Furthermore there must be not other way for the state to meet its policy goals other than by the particular piece of legislation.

During the 1990s many states, including Nebraska, criminalized vaguely defined abortion procedures that they collectively called "partial birth abortion." Proponents of the law argued that the procedure was so grotesque that it was morally indefensible, as well as medically unnecessary. The abortion procedure that the law purported to outlaw involved reducing the size of the fetal skull so that it could pass through the cervix. It was not clear where the states got the authority to enact such a law and whether the law was thus legitimate. Partial birth abortion laws, while purporting to outlaw a particular method of abortion, in fact outlawed other abortion methods as well, with the result that a woman and her doctor's choice of abortion methods both before and after fetal viability was severely restricted. The laws provided no exception for the woman or her doctor to make unfettered medical decisions and to select the medical procedure to best preserve her health. The main procedure that was outlawed, also known an the intact dilation and extraction procedure, was designed by a physician to best preserve a woman's chances of having another successful pregnancy. The abortion procedure was designed to preserve her biologic function. The partial-birth law was consciously designed to attack the basic under-pinnings of the *Roe* and *Casey* decisions. Under those cases states could not outlaw a particular abortion procedure. Secondly, states could not impose "undue burdens" on the abortion decision before fetal viability, and for any restriction on abortion access to be valid, it must contain an exception for the woman's health.

In 1999, a federal Court of Appeals in Chicago in the *Hope Clinic* case failed to find any traditional justification for the partial birth laws of Illinois and Wisconsin. The states advanced no convincing argument that they were promoting women's health, the general welfare, or public safety, the judges ruled. Judge Frank H. Easterbrook, writing for the majority, found that the only legal justification for the laws was on moral grounds:

> So long as the law does not harm women's legitimate interests, the fact that its effects are small and justified by moral rather than by utilitarian concerns does not spell unconstitutionality.

In his dissent, Chief Judge Richard Posner challenged Easterbrook's conclusion:

> I do not deny the right of legislatures to enact statutes that are mainly or for that matter entirely designed as statements of the legislator's values. Nothing in the Constitution forbids legislation so designed. Many statutes are passed or, more commonly, retained merely for their symbolic or aspirational effect. But if a statute burdens constitutional rights and all that can be said on its behalf is that it is the vehicle that legislators have chosen for expressing their hostility to those rights, the burden is undue.

The Easterbrook opinion incorporated the Devlin view that states are permitted, indeed compelled, to pass laws to advance the public morals. While there is no express prohibition in the federal or state constitutions against criminal laws based solely on morals, there is no grant of authority to do this either, except as can be read into their general welfare clauses. Posner would grant states the right to pass such laws, bounded only by the people's retained rights under the U. S. and state constitutions. Mill would limit the state's authority to enact criminal laws to instances of preventing specific harm to others.

The State of Nebraska had also enacted a partial-birth law and, sensing a difficulty here in the wake of Posner's dissent, stretched to find some legitimacy for the law other than that it advanced a particular conception of public morality. Nebraska argued when a challenge to its law reached the Supreme Court that the law's purpose was 1) to prevent cruelty to partially born children, 2) to prevent unacceptable disrespect for potential human life, and 3) to preserve the integrity of the medical profession. Nebraska Attorney General Don Stenberg argued that it was a legitimate state interest to limit the cruelty or grotesqueness that is practiced in abortion. U.S. Supreme Court Justice Antonin Scalia suggested during oral argument a fourth rationale, that the state could legitimately be concerned about society's becoming callous to infanticide. Nebraska argued also that its law still permitted doctors to use other abortion procedures to terminate a pregnancy after the first trimester and therefore that it was not compromising women's health.

Simon Heller of the Center for Reproductive Rights, a New York legal advocacy organization, arguing for the doctor challenging the law, adopted in his brief the Posner position that the state's arguments were "moral stances that the state cannot enforce at the expense of woman's constitutional rights." He thereby dodged the issue of whether or not a state can legitimately pass such a law in the absence of a violation of a constitutional right.

In rendering the decision that overturned the law, the Supreme Court justices issued almost as many opinions as there were justices. Justices John Paul Stevens and Anthony M. Kennedy faced off on the intersection between law and morals as applied to Nebraska's partial-birth law.

In his concurrence, Justice Stevens stated:

Although much ink is spilled today describing the gruesome nature of late-term abortion procedures, that rhetoric does not provide me a reason to believe that the procedure Nebraska here claims it seeks to ban is more brutal, more gruesome, or less respectful of "potential life" than the equally gruesome procedure Nebraska claims it still allows. . . . That holding—that the word "liberty" in the Fourteenth Amendment includes a woman's right to make this difficult and extremely personal decision—makes it impossible for me to understand how a State has any legitimate interest in requiring a doctor to follow any procedure other than the one that he or she reasonably believes will best protect the woman in her exercise of this constitutional liberty. But one need not even approach this view today to conclude that Nebraska's law must fall. *For the notion that either of these two equally gruesome procedures performed at this late stage of gestation is more akin to infanticide than the other, or that the State furthers any legitimate interest by banning one but not the other, is simply irrational.* See U.S. Const., Amdt. 14. (Emphasis added)

In contrast, Justice Kennedy specifically agreed with Nebraska's stated description of the interests it was furthering by the law. He went on to say:

Nebraska was entitled to find the existence of a *consequential moral difference* between the procedures . . . (the procedure's) stronger resemblance to infanticide means Nebraska could conclude the procedure presents a greater risk of disrespect for life and a consequent greater risk to the profession and society, which depend for their sustenance upon reciprocal recognition of dignity and respect. The Court is without authority to second-guess this conclusion.

. . . *The decision nullifies a law expressing the will of the people of Nebraska that medical procedures must be governed by moral principles* having their foundation in the intrinsic value of human life, including life of the unborn. Through their law the people of Nebraska were forthright in confronting an issue of *immense moral consequence.* The State chose to forbid a procedure many decent and civilized people find so abhorrent as to be among the most serious of crimes against human life, while the State still protected the woman's autonomous right of choice as reaffirmed in *Casey*. The Court closes its eyes to these profound concerns. (Emphasis added)

In the past, governments have enacted laws that have primarily a moral basis. But the state's view of what is moral has evolved over time. For instance, there have long been constitutionally valid statutes establishing Blue Laws (laws that prohibit commercial activity on Sunday) and laws prohibiting gambling. Most states now permit Sunday opening of stores and even encourage gambling with their state lotteries. In the past many states, and not just Southern states, prohibited miscegenation on moral grounds. The Supreme Court did not get around to declaring these laws unconstitutional until 1967. The legitimacy of laws can change over time as morality changes, especially with laws regulating sexuality and sexual expression. These types of laws provide the clearest conflict between the rights of the individual and the right to personal privacy on the one hand and the right of the government to enforce a majoritarian view of private morality. They also provide a warning about anyone's claiming moral certitude for their sexual laws.

Changes in abortion laws over time reflect the fact that there is no one morality; there are a variety of moral opinions on many issues, and especially as regards sex and abortion. Many Americans regard (or say to a pollster that they regard) abortion as immoral. Yet, these same Americans also have abortions, often—over a million women a year, year after year. About 35 percent or more of American women will have an abortion during their lifetimes. Women who have an abortion often consider their particular abortion to be a moral choice, if they think about it in moral terms at all. Abortion is often a solution for a failed reproductive strategy and a chance to start on a new strategy. The women having abortions who ask themselves moral questions might ask themselves: Is it right to bring this child into the world if I can't be a good mother, or if I can't afford to bring it up properly, or if the father won't be there for the child, or if it will prevent me from finishing my education so that I can contribute more to society and be better able to support that child? Few women consider adoption as an acceptable alternative. Many women balance these considerations, and more, with other moral considerations about their preventing a child from being born. The pro-choice position is that the only person who can make that judgment is the woman herself and that this should not be a matter for the law. Some who are pro-life also feel that a criminal abortion law is not the right remedy, at least as regards the woman.

When Catholic bishops testify in support of legislation criminalizing abortion, they are careful to distinguish between making a woman a criminal, which they oppose, and making the physician a criminal, which they support. They say that while a woman making the decision to have an abortion is wrong, the law should not make her a criminal, just the physician. The Catholic Church's compassion for the woman is commendable, but its willingness to make the doctor, who is only trying to help the woman, a criminal is totally hypocritical. Why does compassion stop with the woman? Women seeking abortions have good reproductive reasons for doing so. I don't believe women for the most part are pressured, coerced, or driven by fear into abortion. Women do face economic pressures and pressures from their partners, yes. That's life. Men can be unfair to women when they are pregnant. A woman seeks reproductive success, and sometimes a pregnancy, while in one sense a reproductive success, is not in the long term her best chance of success. She may have to get back in the game and start over. She may be right or wrong in her judgment. Society owes her all the support it can to help her do this. The last thing she needs is to go to jail.

Humanity benefits when individuals can make their own reproductive decisions. Humanity also benefits when its governments make society conducive for reproduction. This is the tension when governments enact laws to preserve the biologic function. Governments must tread carefully when they try to discourage practices such as sexual activities that increase infertility or allow sex-selection abortion that is biased against girls. The ban on partial birth abortion served to satisfy a political constituency without furthering any biological or social purpose. A woman in her fifth or sixth month of pregnancy has already invested heavily in that pregnancy. If she has to terminate that pregnancy for whatever reason, she does not benefit, nor does society, from being prohibited from doing so or from her doctor being forced to use some other procedure than the one he believes safest for her future fertility. Laws should preserve the biologic function, not destroy it.

But even if society cannot accept the argument that abortion should be a matter of personal conscience and not the law, society might agree that as a matter of political policy that it is not a proper role for government to be involved in the private lives of its citizens to this extent.

## The Right to Privacy As the Protector of Individual Reproductive Strategies

There is little political consistency in how Americans define the proper role of government in their lives. There is a seemingly irreconcilable conflict between the John Stuart Mill thesis that limited government is best and the natural inclinations of society to want to be hospitable to family life and of legislatures to pass laws to make this happen. By definition, every law encroaches upon some aspect of human freedom. The guarantee in the United States Constitution prevents the government from "depriv(ing) any person of life, liberty, or property, without due process of law." Liberty can be deprived as long as there is due process of law.

The word "liberty" is undefined in the Constitution. This has meant that the Supreme Court ultimately defines what is encompassed by the word. Some personal liberties seem obvious: the right to work at whatever job one wants, to live where one wants, to travel where one wants, to marry whom one wants, to have the number of children one wants, and to bring these children up as one sees fit. None of these liberties are specifically mentioned in the Constitution. But even if they are included within the Constitution's meaning of liberty, that does not make them into absolute rights. There can be laws providing for a minimum age of marriage. Zoning laws can restrict where one lives. Schooling of children either at school or at home can be required, as can vaccinations.

Into this rubric came the Supreme Court cases on use of birth control and abortion. The right to decide whether or not to get pregnant (*Griswold*) and whether or not to terminate a pregnancy (*Roe*) were found to be encompassed within the word "liberty" and to be part of a broader right of privacy, the right to be let alone by the government in certain personal matters.

In his concurring opinion in *Griswold*, Justice Arthur Goldberg explored the limits of this right to privacy. Connecticut had argued that the purpose of its birth control ban was to discourage extra-marital relations. Goldberg concluded that this state interest, which he admitted was a valid one, could be met by a more "discriminately tailored statute, which does not, like the present one, sweep unnecessarily broadly, reaching far beyond the evil sought to be dealt with and intruding upon the privacy of all married couples." Goldberg suggested that Connecticut enforce its statutes, "the constitutionality of which is beyond doubt, which prohibit adultery and fornication." The right to privacy had limits even for the majority in *Griswold*.

The *Roe* court was faced with the problem that the criminalization of abortion seemed to be the only way to advance the state's goal of promoting fetal life. The court concluded that this goal, though valid, did not override the woman's freedom not to have a child. In dissent, Justice William Rehnquist accepted that the word "liberty" included the right to marry whom one wanted, the right to procreate and the right to use contraceptives. But he made it clear that this did not mean that there was "an all-encompassing 'right of privacy.'" Abortion involved not just the woman but the fetus she was carrying: "One cannot ignore the fact that a woman is not isolated in her pregnancy, and that the decision to abort necessarily involves the destruction of a fetus. . . . The abortion decision must therefore be recognized as sui generis, different in kind from the others that the Court has protected under the rubric of personal or family privacy and autonomy."

Senator Rick Santorum of Pennsylvania is one of many politicians who go further than the Chief Justice and assert that there should not be a constitutional right to privacy for either abortion or contraception. Santorum set forth his beliefs in an interview in April 2003 with the Associated Press, which discussed the pending legal challenge in the Supreme Court to a Texas law criminalizing homosexual sodomy between men:

> We have laws in states, like the one at the Supreme Court right now, that has sodomy laws and they were there for a purpose. Because, again, I would argue, they undermine the basic tenets of our society and the family. And if the Supreme Court says that you have the right to consensual sex within your home, then you have the right to bigamy, you have the right to polygamy, you have the right to incest, you have the right to adultery. You have the right to anything. Does that undermine the fabric of our society? I would argue yes, it does. It all comes from, I would argue, this right to privacy that doesn't exist in my opinion in the United States Constitution, this right that was created, it was created in Griswold. . . .
>
> The right to privacy is a right that was created in a law that set forth a (ban on) rights to limit individual passions. And I don't agree with that. So I would make the argument that with President, or Senator or Congressman or whoever Santorum, I would put it back to where it is, the democratic process. If New York doesn't want sodomy laws, if the people of New York want abortion, fine. I mean, I wouldn't agree with it, but that's their right. But I don't agree with the Supreme Court coming in.

The Supreme Court, when it decided the Texas sodomy law case two months later, firmly disagreed with Senator Santorum in every respect. In *Lawrence v. Texas* (*Lawrence*) the Supreme Court overruled its own *Bowers* decision from 1986 and declared the Texas sodomy statute unconstitutional. The right of privacy of *Griswold* and *Roe* was affirmed. Justice Kennedy stated for the six to three majority:

> Liberty protects the person from unwarranted government intrusions into a dwelling or other private places. In our tradition the State is not omnipresent in the home. And there are other spheres of our lives and existence, outside the home, where the State should not be a dominant

presence. Freedom extends beyond spatial bounds. Liberty presumes an autonomy of self that includes freedom of thought, belief, expression, and certain intimate conduct. The instant case involves liberty of the person both in its spatial and more transcendent dimensions.

Kennedy pointed out that the sodomy laws:

> seek to control a personal relationship that, whether or not entitled to formal recognition in the law, is within the liberty of persons to choose without being punished as criminals.

> This, as a general rule, should counsel against attempts by the State, or a court, to define the meaning of the relationship or to set its boundaries absent injury to a person or abuse of an institution the law protects. It suffices for us to acknowledge that adults may choose to enter upon this relationship in the confines of their homes and their own private lives and still retain their dignity as free persons. When sexuality finds overt expression in intimate conduct with another person, the conduct can be but one element in a personal bond that is more enduring. The liberty protected by the Constitution allows homosexual persons the right to make this choice.

Even though many in society view homosexuality as immoral, Kennedy stated that:

> The issue is whether the majority may use the power of the State to enforce these views on the whole society through operation of the criminal law. "Our obligation is to define the liberty of all, not to mandate our own moral code." (Citing *Casey*)

Kennedy was careful to limit his decision to sodomy. He stated that this was not a case of gay marriage, of public conduct that might be offensive, or of prostitution. Justice Sandra Day O'Connor, in a concurring opinion, was careful to state that there were other rationales to support a state's limiting marriage to persons of the opposite sex.

Justice Scalia disagreed with the majority decision. He stated:

The Texas statute undeniably seeks to further the belief of its citizens that certain forms of sexual behavior are "immoral and unacceptable," . . . the same interest furthered by criminal laws against fornication, bigamy, adultery, adult incest, bestiality, and obscenity. Bowers (the case that *Lawrence* overruled) held that this was a legitimate state interest. The Court today reaches the opposite conclusion. . . . This effectively decrees the end of all morals legislation. If, as the Court asserts, the promotion of majoritarian sexual morality is not even a legitimate state interest, none of the above-mentioned laws can survive rational-basis review.

Are Scalia and Santorum correct? Does the Constitution, as interpreted by the *Lawrence* majority, now forbid any morals legislation? The constitutional right of privacy that permits one kind of non-procreative sexual activity, that is contraception, does not necessarily permit all kinds of sexual activity. After all, Justice Goldberg allowed in *Griswold* that laws against adultery and fornication were constitutional. The issue is whether we should leave these questions to the legislature.

Justice Scalia and Senator Santorum conflate a right to make child-bearing decisions, as was recognized in *Griswold* and *Roe*, with a variety of sexual practices. They fail to recognize the clear biological differences between them. Incest, for instance, has vastly different biological consequences than adultery, since, if a child is conceived, the child has a greater risk of birth defects. Adultery may or may not result in the birth of a child, but it may ruin a marriage and harm the children of that marriage. I submit that only when we understand the biological underpinnings of human reproduction can we come to a principled position about when and whether it is legitimate for government to intervene in these profoundly personal and biological matters.

As the founding legal document creating a civil society, a constitution's unstated but primary purpose is to create a civil society that preserves the biologic function and enables reproduction. There are few or no biologic or reproductive dangers with some of the sexual practices that Senator Santorum and Justice Scalia cited—homosexuality, adultery, bigamy, and polygamy. There may be other social and family reasons for prohibiting these practices, but no substantial biological reasons. But a right to privacy based on the ability to make a childbearing decision, which is the ultimate biological decision, does not mandate that every sexual practice must therefore be allowed. Senator Santorum and Justice Scalia are wrong because they failed to understand the differences in who or what the sexual or marriage laws they cite are protecting, if anyone, or if rather they are solely expressions of majority moral sentiment. They failed to differentiate the cases where there are biological interests and those when there are not.

I believe that there is no role for ideological absolutism in defining the scope of the right to privacy. Virtually everyone would support laws forbidding rape, incest, bigamy, and polygamy and would oppose laws forbidding miscegenation, masturbation, fornication, and contraception. The adultery and fornication laws that are still on the books are a dead letter. There is consensus, at least in the United States, that there are some marital, sexual, and reproductive matters that concern society at large and some that do not. The debate centers on the one practice that provides women direct control of human reproduction—abortion.

The pro-choice position reveals a fundamental evolutionary truth that there is a built-in conflict not only between men and women but also between the individual and the society when it comes to reproduction. It is beneficial for society to have a common morality and a legal system. This makes for a society that is conducive to reproduction. Within this cooperative environment, however, men and women are striving for reproductive advantage over their fellow citizens. While it is in everyone's interest to have a common morality and rule of law, it is not in each individual's interest to obey the moral code or law all the time. For instance, a morality that supports marriage may create an environment of stability and social cohesion that is good for everyone collectively, but it may be in an individual's reproductive interest to have children outside of marriage.

I have argued that reproductive freedom is essential for the attainment of human reproductive strategies. Individuals recognize this as it applies to themselves. If a society collectively restricts that freedom in an effort, for instance, to increase its population, a moral conflict ensues for the individual who sees a reproductive advantage in breaking the moral code. The result is that the law is broken surreptitiously, and no effort is made to change the law. Each individual sees the law as hurting the competitive position of his reproductive competitors, but not hurting his own, because he can break the law with impunity when it suits him. The result is that many people feel that abortion should be legal for "rape, incest and me." The problem that reproductive rights advocates face is to get people to believe and to vote for abortion's being legal for "rape, incest, me and you." The answer to this problem can come only from citizens attaining a biological awareness that collective reproductive freedom enhances each individual's reproductive success.

While reproductive freedom enables individuals to make the most of whatever fitness advantages they may have, it is not a right that protects only the elites. Reproductive freedom protected by a right to privacy insures that the weak, the minority, and the powerless are on the same reproductive footing as the powerful. This is not to say that the powerful and those blessed with resources, social position, and good genes (if we knew what they were) won't have greater reproductive success than those without these attributes. But reproductive freedom means that the powerful cannot completely control the reproductive game. If there was no reproductive freedom, the dominant elites could control who reproduced and who didn't. They could enact eugenic laws. They could force or mandate birth control, sterilization, and abortion in cases that suited them. Reproductive freedom levels the reproductive playing field at least as far as the law is concerned. It gives everyone an equal chance under the law to reproduce. It is especially the poor, the unhealthy, and the weak who benefit from reproductive freedom. They more than those with better health and more resources need to control their childbearing. Pregnancy and childbirth are much more fraught with danger for those less healthy and well-to-do.

Without reproductive freedom or a right to privacy the government could enact any law it wished on reproductive matters. Social and biological engineering would be permitted with virtually no restraint, except that the law would have to be rationally related to some valid government goal, an admittedly easy test to meet. Laws preventing a person convicted of non-payment of child support from having a additional child, which are currently enforced more against men than women, would be permitted. Laws prohibiting a teenager from having a child would be permitted on the grounds that teen pregnancy was not universally advantageous for mother or child. Laws that required breastfeeding, or that prohibited drinking and smoking by pregnant women, or that required a pregnant woman to eat a certain diet and take folic acid might be permissible. If the country became overpopulated, then perhaps laws limiting couples to one or two children would be permitted. If a country became under-populated, then laws akin to those in Romania requiring parents to have a certain number of children would be valid. Laws prohibiting births spaced too close together, an admitted danger for mother and child, would also be a permissible public health regulation. If *Roe* and *Casey* were to be overturned, then there would be few if any limits on what the state could do to control childbearing decisions.

Without reproductive freedom all these laws would be constitutional. When the constitution is interpreted to permit laws invading reproductive freedom, there is virtually no limit to what society can control. Childbirth and abortion could be prohibited or required depending on the legislature's goals. Only if the fetus is given the same full constitutional rights as persons born might there be constitutional questions. But even then the legislature under the Rehnquist test is only restricted from enacting laws depriving the fetus of life "without due process of law." Admittedly the constitutional test for depriving a fetus or a person of life would be stricter than that for depriving it of liberty, but there is a strong possibility that as long as the legislature found a compelling reason to deprive the unborn child of life, it could constitutionally do so. Reproductive freedom, backed by stringent restrictions on the power of the legislature to enact laws invading it, is thus a biological and social necessity.

Laws regulating reproduction or proscribing certain sexual conduct are attempts by government not only to change human nature, but also to set new ground rules for the exercise of reproductive strategies. Laws prohibiting birth control are an attempt to require that every sexual act should potentially result in a pregnancy, and laws proscribing abortion are an attempt to require that every pregnancy potentially result in the birth of a child. These laws attempt to dictate biological outcomes, and are profoundly wrong. They say that the government will make better reproductive choices than an individual will. They are an attempt to constrict individual reproductive strategies and choices. This is absurd on its face. Humanity has gotten to where it is by individual reproductive strategies being pursued by individuals free of governmental and societal constraints except in certain biologically harmful cases. Humans have and will make better reproductive decisions than governments will. They make them depending on a multitude of personal and environmental factors. A law saying that these factors are irrelevant is evolutionary idiocy.

The constitutional right of privacy prevents the majority from changing the rules of the reproductive and evolutionary system that humanity has used since its inception. The right of privacy means that humanity can continue to reproduce under the conditions that each individual decides and with the reproductive strategies that each person thinks are most advantageous. Individuals may make decisions that some may think wrong or even immoral. Natural selection will separate the wise decisions from the unwise. This is what nature has provided and is as it should be.

Government attempts to change this by enacting restrictions on reproductive strategies are in my view an illegitimate and unwise exercise of government power. We admittedly don't fully understand the biology of evolution. How can we possibly try to regulate it, manipulate it, or prevent evolution from taking its course? Restrictions on reproductive strategies cannot be left to the whim of the majority. That is why we have a Constitution with limits on the majority and on government power. The right to privacy protects biology and evolution from society. Human experience has shown that humanity will do what it takes to achieve reproductive success, no matter what laws society enacts. As anthropologist E. Adamson Hoebel of the University of Minnesota has said: ". . . biology . . . imposes limitations on what may be culturally achieved. . . ."

We should not be afraid of the sexual and reproductive dynamics that nature has given us. The battle of the sexes is a good thing. Competition between the sexes to control reproduction is a good thing—females to control their childbearing and males to control whom they parent. Social engineering within limits is good in order to create a society in which reproduction is favored. Biological engineering on the other hand is generally unnecessary and counterproductive. Males and females can sort out reproduction on their own without the government tilting the scales.

Though I have presented constitutional, legal, and practical objections to excessive government interference into the private realm, the ultimate solution to the problem is not a political or legal one. As Judge Learned Hand said in *Sources of Tolerance*: "If a community decides that some conduct is prejudicial to itself, and so decides by numbers sufficient to impose its will upon dissenters, I know of no principle which can stay its hand." In Judge Hand's view the broadly worded amendments that are in our Bill of Rights and the Fourteenth Amendment are ultimately of no help since they can be interpreted by judges first one way and then another. Hand called for "a sense of fair play, of give and take, of the uncertainty of the human hypothesis, of how changeable and passing are our surest convictions . . . "

A certain humility and respect for history is called for, as well as a respect for the notion that, when there is a conflict of moral views, we should defer to the liberty and conscience of the individual. This calls for a great deal of forbearance, for often reproductive rights are exercised in a manner and for purposes that many may disagree with on a moral basis. But that is no more a reason to forbid the exercise of these rights than the excesses of tabloid journalism justify the repeal of the First Amendment. I believe that it is immoral to enforce morality that tries to repeal the fundamental laws of human nature and of human reproduction. There is a good reason that there is no consensus on abortion, because individuals see that in many cases the decision to have an abortion is biologically called for and is moral. And they know that banning abortion won't work. The battle over abortion rights is thus better conducted as a moral one, not a legal one. Each side can attempt to win converts to its moral position. Each individual can decide whether or not to make use of abortion in their lives. This is the essence of liberty. This is not for the government to dictate.

# CHAPTER EIGHT

# Beyond Choice

Having the choice whether or not to become a parent and have a child has been and is essential to the survival and well-being of humanity. Even men and women who say they disagree with this proposition have benefited by it. Their ancestors took control of their childbearing and gave a greater chance for their descendants to survive and in turn to reproduce. As Sarah Blaffer Hrdy stated in *Mother Nature*:

> Like it or not, each of us lives with the emotional legacy and decision-making equipment of mothers who acted so as to ensure that at least one offspring survived to reproduce. Prudent allocation of reproductive effort and construction of an advantageous social niche in which her offspring could survive and prosper were linked to ultimate reproductive success.

Modern medical science has not made the risks of childbearing a relic of the past. Even if science eventually does so, safe childbearing is only one part of the process of successful reproduction. Successful reproduction is a lifelong process of nurturing and trade-offs to ensure that children survive in good health and in turn reproduce successfully.

As a result of taking control over its reproduction, humanity has reproduced with remarkable success. There are now over 6 billion of us on the planet. This global reproductive success has coincided with the unprecedented growth in human health, prosperity, and lifespan. Over time human society has become more conducive to childbearing and to survival. Religion and moral codes, the growth of civil society, and scientific, technological, and medical progress have all made this possible. Women and men co-evolved with both sexes fighting for control over their reproduction. Men and women managed to cooperate in order to time and limit their childbearing to the number they could support and raise successfully. Men and women also evolved to live in tribes and societies where their religion, culture, and morality also evolved and demanded robust population growth in order to defend the society, to conquer the environment, and to survive.

In the Judeo-Christian tradition this societal imperative was put in theological terms as a commandment to be fruitful and multiply. However, the moral course for the individual frequently differed from the moral dictates of the society. Being fruitful and multiplying did not mean that women and men did so without forethought, strategies, and limits. While humanity pursued its reproductive strategies in the context of its various civil and religious societies and moral codes, it often did so in spite of them. In America a majority of citizens can honestly say to pollsters that they believe both that abortion is immoral and that it should be kept legal. This is not a contradiction. It is an evolutionary reality. Humanity evolved by making choices but also by having moral codes. Having choice is a moral value. So is preserving life. In a narrow sense the conflict between these two values is irreconcilable. Philosopher Isaiah Berlin said: "The need to choose, to sacrifice some ultimate values to others, turns out to be a permanent characteristic of the human predicament." I have argued that it is the biological realities of the human predicament that create the framework for reconciling the seemingly irreconcilable nature of choice and life.

The central argument for reproductive rights has traditionally been based on the dual concepts of the human dignity and moral autonomy of women. This moral autonomy includes the freedom of women to decide whether and when to become a parent. Both those who sought to limit a woman's freedom to make her own decisions about reproduction and those who sought to expand them based their positions in part on a view of what it meant to be human. Each side also has distinct views on the proper rules for a society to function and for humanity, individually and collectively, to be morally worthy. The pro-life side has argued, somewhat simplistically in my view, that what they called "life" begins at conception and that therefore under all or most circumstances it must be allowed to be born. The increase in biological knowledge of embryonic development since the early nineteenth century and especially in the late twentieth century has been a major impetus behind the growing respect for fetal life and consequential restrictions on abortion.

The pro-choice side has been reluctant to present the biological arguments for reproductive freedom. This may be an outgrowth of the eugenics disaster, which left a dark shadow over the birth control movement. It may also be a reaction against the evolutionary theories of Charles Darwin and his successors, which are thought in some circles to undermine the moral and religious basis for civil society (or at least to provide no moral compass for it). Some believe that Darwin's theories provided support for what was called Social Darwinism, an economic and social theory that discouraged intervention into society to improve the fortunes of the disadvantaged. Under the Social Darwinist banner some politicians found intellectual support for their undemocratic, sexist, and elitist political and social systems. Many believe that the theory of evolution and the discoveries of modern genetics and modern biology support the idea of genetic determinism, undermine the notion of free will and moral autonomy, and somehow make traditional gender roles into something fixed and immutable. Debates have raged in academia about nature and nurture, biology and culture, and genes and the environment. The consensus now is that none of the above are separable one from another and that all of the above influence human behavior. Culture has evolved along with humanity and "genes are the mechanisms of experience," as Matt Ridley has said.

Darwin's theories, modern genetics, and the biological sciences have been used by their opponents as political straw men, easy targets for those who are discomforted by the modern world and by science in general. This intellectual unease has proven by and large unfounded. The Catholic Church says that evolution is not incompatible with Christian beliefs and that it does not undermine religious teachings and morality. There are also those who oppose evolution because they believe it means that society will use it as an excuse to fix male and female gender roles into their traditional patterns. But humans can change and improve. As Sarah Blaffer Hrdy said, humans have free will where nature cuts it some slack. I do not believe that intellectual unease with the implications of evolutionary theory, or with how it has been misused and distorted, should deter the pro-choice movement from using the biological arguments for reproductive choice.

The principles of evolutionary biology do not inevitably lead to a Social Darwinist society where the elites use these principles as a political excuse to ignore the plight of the disadvantaged or to ignore festering social problems like inequality, sexism, poverty, and disease. On the contrary, since the mid–1800s, humanity has come to accept Darwin's theories, and at the same time democracy, liberty, the status of women, health, and prosperity have all increased around the globe. Intellectual belief in human evolution has not led to humanity ignoring the well-being of its fellow humans. Nor does evolutionary biology say that there is no role for law, culture, or religion to try to channel or improve human behavior. Humans have free will despite being a part of a biological system. Social problems and deviant human behaviors are not fated, destined, or immutable. In recent years we have come to appreciate that humanity is not all nature or all nurture. Being biological creatures does not make us biological captives. We are, for the most part, in control of our human destiny, and with some limits humans can change many of their behaviors. What the biological sciences can do is help policymakers understand the evolutionary factors, stated and unstated, conscious and unconscious, that influence how people behave. When we can understand this, we can lessen the risk of failed social programs and the risk of severe unintended consequences of our policy interventions. When it comes to modifying human reproductive strategies, science can give policymakers a needed dose of humility. As science writer Matt Ridley has said, "There are limits to the power of culture to change human behavior."

I have argued that the principles of evolutionary biology, a science that has existed only for the last twenty-five years or so, can assist in providing a moral compass for humanity. The biological sciences can provide the moral and intellectual underpinnings for reproductive freedom for men and women. A study of biology and evolution shows that reproductive freedom is necessary for the creation, nurturing, and survival of human life. Successful reproduction—the birth of a child and the creation of a family—involves many decisions, trade-offs, and obligations, including deciding to reproduce, mating, having sex, giving birth, and extensive parenting and parental investment. Successful reproduction also means controlling when not to reproduce by not mating, by not having sex, not getting pregnant by using contraception, and not giving birth by having an abortion. Abortion can only be understood in its biological context. When humans understand their own biology, they can make better moral choices about the circumstances under which they should bring life into the world.

Those who oppose reproductive freedom argue that society has higher aims than creating good reproductive conditions and that humanity is more than a collection of animals acting out their natural urges. They would argue that divine morality and the commandments require us to respect all human life at whatever stage of development. Abortion, and to some even birth control, take life as well as contribute to a culture of disrespect for all living persons. It is humanity's purpose, they argue, to overcome our animal instincts and whatever evolutionary influences are acting upon us. Finally, they argue that the theoretical forces of natural selection in particular, and science in general, provide no moral compass for humanity.

I would agree with some of these arguments. There are purposes to human society other than reproduction. Life should be respected at all stages of development. We are more than animals. That has been my entire point. Animals by and large do not take conscious control of their reproduction to the extent humans do. Animals do have an amazing variety of strategies of controlling whom they will mate with and who will become a parent of their children. Humanity has evolved to take conscious control of reproduction and has done so in order to survive and to preserve life. Taking control of reproduction is respectful of life. At times it means not conceiving a life, and at times it means not letting unborn life be born. When humanity does this, it often does so in pursuance of a reproductive strategy that will best enable it to preserve and nurture other life. We cannot repeal the laws of natural selection. Nature does not let every life form survive. Humanity uniquely, and to its benefit, can exercise some dominion over this process and maximize the chances for human life to survive and grow. Without this, no other human goals are possible. A world without reproductive freedom is the animal world. It takes us backward, not forward. Opponents of reproductive freedom are trying to take biology, genetics, evolution, and the environment out of human reproduction. They are trying to create a world where whatever nature says will happen will in fact happen. This is bad biology and is bad for humanity. Reproductive freedom is essential for human survival. Being biologically pro-life means that one must be politically pro-choice.

Bans on reproductive options are nothing more or less than eugenics—they target the poor and make them less able to reproduce. The state of the law at the moment is quasi-Social Darwinist. It is the mission of the pro-choice movement to change the law so that everyone has the same chance to reproduce successfully. At the beginning of twenty-first century an adult American is in general free to reproduce, except if he or she is in prison or in some cases if he or she is a convicted child abuser. A poor adult who suffers from infertility has no right to financial assistance in order to seek medical treatment for the infertility, although some states provide it. Although again there is no right, some states provide insurance coverage for genetic screening for some birth defects. A poor adult has no right to financial assistance to terminate a pregnancy, although again a few states provide it. All states provide financial assistance to the poor to pay for childbirth and for some contraception. A poor woman will have great difficulty accessing quality prenatal care. If you are a minor, you have the right to bear a child on your own and to put up a child for adoption but not to terminate a pregnancy without a court order or some amount of parental involvement. Anyone seeking an abortion can be subject to a lecture from the state as to why they should not do it. A woman may terminate a pregnancy on her own without her partner's consent and may on her own anonymously abandon a newborn child to the state. Parents are responsible for the health and welfare of their children and to provide for their education. They are otherwise free to bring up their children as they wish.

This is just a sampling of laws that relate to human reproduction as we have broadly defined it. How this amalgam of laws relates to a particular moral code or theory of government is not easy to discern, nor is there any apparent biological consistency. For the poor, the system is almost pure Social Darwinism. This needs to change. If society is going to encourage childbirth by paying for it for the poor and not paying for abortion, I believe it should pay for fertility services. If society is going to discourage unwanted childbearing, I believe it should pay for contraceptive and abortion services for those who cannot afford them. If society is going to pay for prenatal care to insure the birth of healthy infants, I believe it should pay for genetic screening and make prenatal care more accessible. I believe young people with the requisite judgment should have the right to have an abortion as well as give birth without their parent's consent. And I believe that the consent of the father should be required when a child is put up for adoption but not for childbirth or abortion.

While a rights-based argument can help bring consistency to some of these legislative inconsistencies, I believe a biological argument is a more helpful approach. Once we understand what both an individual's and society's biological goals are and what the biological limits are on what can be achieved through the law, then we can strive to attain these biological goals with the greatest efficiency and effectiveness. Society's biological goal should be to enable successful reproduction by its citizens. It should therefore subsidize abortion, fertility services, and genetic screening for those who cannot afford it, since these services enable successful reproduction. Society should recognize that the decision to have a child is as consequential for a young person as having an abortion, in fact from a health point of view it is more so, and thus should permit those with the requisite maturity to make both choices. Childbirth, abortion, and adoption are reproductive events for the mother and father, but childbirth and abortion have health consequences for the woman alone. There is no health risk for the woman if society requires, as it should, the permission of the baby's father before his child is put up for adoption. However, the health risk when the mother is giving birth or having an abortion overrides his reproductive interest in that event.

The central battle in America today is over whether society should have jurisdiction over the childbearing decisions of its citizens and the circumstances in which abortion should be permitted, if at all. Among the circumstances when abortion is legally permissible include when the woman has been raped or is a victim of incest, when the fetus has a birth defect, or when being pregnant is a serious threat to the woman's life or health. There is a fair amount of consensus that abortion should be permissible under these circumstances. There is less consensus when the woman is unmarried, when she cannot afford the child, when the woman is young and hasn't finished her education, or when she simply does not want to have a child. A woman's social and economic condition, her family situation and her relationship with her partner constitute her biological environment. Only she can judge if this environment is suitable for her to have a child. Only she can judge whether her circumstances are such that it would give her child a better chance of health and survival if she were to have a child at a later date with the same or different partner.

Societies debate time periods—should abortion be allowed in the first trimester, second, or third (the *Roe* framework), or before or after fetal viability (the *Casey* framework)? As a pregnancy progresses, the mother is making an increasing amount of investment in her child, and the fetus is growing and developing daily. As an unborn child gets closer to birth, many people believe that at some point abortion should cease to be an option for the mother. Some set the line at the time when the fetus could survive outside the womb. From the mother's point of view, the age and developmental status of the fetus is irrelevant to her ability to give birth and to parent that child. The health risks of pregnancy and childbirth to the mother and the lifetime of parental investment in front of her are things that are independent of the age of the fetus. Not every woman can evaluate these and make the decision to give birth or not within a short time after she finds out she is pregnant. Life changes during a pregnancy. The woman's health, or the baby's health, may have deteriorated during pregnancy, or her social and economic position might have. The father of the baby may have left her, or even worse, could be physically or mentally abusing her (spousal abuse is at its peak during a pregnancy). She may have lost her job. Whatever the factors might be that militate against having a child, the pregnant woman is the one making the bodily investment in that child. Pregnancy is a biological event with grave consequences to the mother. The fact that the fetus is continuing to grow and has not miscarried indicates that it is in all likelihood developing normally. Because of her already substantial investment in the pregnancy, a woman will be inclined to continue the pregnancy. Modern technology may indicate that not all is well with the pregnancy. But even if all is well with the pregnancy, the law should not require her to give birth when she does not want to. A woman will not want to end a pregnancy for any but the most compelling reasons. I believe that not wanting to be a mother for any reason is a compelling reason. Motherhood is for life. It should not be undertaken lightly. A mother cannot be legislated to love and raise a child properly. Certainly if the law trusts women to give birth, it can trust them not to. *Roe* and *Casey* recognize this in principle but mandate childbirth after fetal viability unless there is a compelling health reason not to.

*Roe* and *Casey* reflect the fact that our society does not trust women. It does not trust women because men don't. Men have used their control of society's law-making institutions to enact laws that give them more control over reproduction than they would have in a state of nature. As a result, many states have debated whether a woman should be allowed to make the abortion decision on her own in consultation with her doctor, or alternatively whether the involvement of others should be required or encouraged. States have considered instituting requirements for married women or young women that a religious counselor, a social worker, a committee of doctors, the woman's husband, the father of the fetus, and in the case of a pregnant minor, her parents, must be consulted and give their approval. I have argued that the woman is the best judge of her reproductive environment; others, however well intentioned, are not. Any advice she seeks should be on her own, not required by law.

Most restrictions on access to abortion do not make biological sense. Waiting periods and other regulations designed to frustrate and delay a woman's access under the guise of patient safety are no more than a ruse. They only serve to delay the abortion or to make the woman give birth when she does not want to, both of which are contrary to her biological interests. The denial of insurance or Medicaid coverage for an indigent woman's abortion is similarly misguided and cruel. It forces some women to give birth when they believe it is not in their biological interest. Poor women weather faster than well-to-do women, and pregnancy and childbirth for them carry extra risks. Women in these circumstances especially need to control pregnancy and childbearing as a matter of their own and their children's survival. The best way for the pro-choice movement to dispel the arguments that evolution means the survival of only the fittest and that evolution does not provide a moral compass is for the movement to make as its first priority the provision of all health services an indigent woman requires to successfully reproduce. This would include Medicaid coverage for and access to prenatal care, abortion, and a full range of contraception, genetic screening, and infertility services.

Along with providing Medicaid coverage for the poor, the other most contentious issue in abortion politics in the United States is parental consent for pregnant teens seeking an abortion. The laws requiring parental consent, or requiring that one or both parents at least be notified of the pending abortion (from the teen's point of view there is often no difference between notification and consent), are designed to force teens who fear their parents or who don't want to disappoint them to give birth. For some teens early childbearing is an option that can provide certain biological benefits. But it is for the teen, with in most cases her kin network, to evaluate the risks and decide this. When parental consent laws intervene, it is the teen's parents who can force her to give birth. Parents cannot force their daughters to have an abortion under current law, although if the law was to be consistent and a minor child was to be treated as the parent's reproductive property, it would allow parents to do this. Parental involvement laws ignore the fact that a minor daughter is not the legal property of her parents. They also gloss over the biological reality that the daughter is the means by which the parent's reproductive strategy is to be carried out. The teen and her parents may or may not have the same reproductive strategy, or they may have divergent views about childbirth in this particular circumstance. If so, whose reproductive strategy should control: the mother of the unborn child or the grandparents of that child?

When the teenage daughter decides on childbirth, in virtually every case she tells her parents because she eventually cannot hide the pregnancy. In a small minority of cases, she doesn't, often with tragic results for her or her child, when, for instance, she tries to give birth on her own. In other cases she does tell her parents and is subject to being disowned or beaten, sometimes to death. When the teen decides on an abortion, in about two-thirds of cases she tells her parents, again with some heightened risk of violence, usually from her father. The laws that require parental involvement do increase the number of cases where daughters tell their mothers about their pregnancies. If one believes that the law should mandate family communication, then this is a good result. Together mother and daughter often work out a solution. The potential reproductive success that the child of a teen mother represents may depend largely on the investment by the teen's parents, the child's grandparents. When the teen and her parents view the environment differently or view her chances of a reproductive success differently, is it society's function to say that the potential child's grandparent's view shall control? I would argue that it is the person with the greater investment in the child and who bears the health risk, the child's mother, the teenage daughter, whose views should control.

The laws that provide for parental involvement also provide for outside judicial supervision of the teen if she cannot tell her parents. This serves to insure that the teen is mentally capable of making the decision. But there are already laws that provide for adult supervision in states without parental involvement laws. No teen can give informed consent to an abortion, or to any medical procedure, unless she has the requisite mental capability. Doctors are required to evaluate this and to bring in the family court on a confidential basis if they have any doubts. Thus, in my view, parental consent laws are redundant, costly, serve only a limited purpose, and don't make biological sense.

The public is in favor of seeking the consent, or at least notifying, the father of the unborn child. The pregnancy represents a potential reproductive success for him too. It also represents, or it should, the beginning of a lifelong commitment to and investment in that child. The father's parental investment, and that of his family, can be essential for the child's survival and success. This is a case where the "should" differs from the "must." The child's father should be involved in the decision to give birth or not, but legal mandates are likely to have negative unintended consequences for the mother. He should be involved because it is his child too, and a male, like a female, has and is entitled to have his own reproductive strategy. On their faces the mother and father's strategies should be given equal weight. The father's strategy may be in alignment with or conflict with the mother's. But the health risk of the pregnancy is born solely by the mother. This risk is not insubstantial. The biological investment in the pregnancy is solely the mother's, and as a result the likelihood is that the child care responsibility will be mostly hers. For this reason, the childbearing and abortion decisions must be hers alone, even if the mother is in good health and the father says he will bring up the child. A pregnant woman faced with a law mandating the unborn child's father's involvement, when they do not agree on having the child or not, will simply go outside the system either to give birth or to have an abortion. Putting the woman at this risk does not justify the limited benefits that might accrue from forcing some communication between the parents and increasing the father's rights. A man must take control of his own reproductive destiny, not try to control his wife's. He can use condoms and DNA testing to parent only the children he wants.

We have explored throughout this book the contours of the right to procreate—the right to reproduce. Reproduction and procreation involve much more than passing on genes to the next generation. Reproduction is a biological process with male and female reproductive strategies that have evolved to best ensure the survival of children. The process is one of meeting, mating, sexual activity, protection, birth, nurturing, parenting, maturing, surviving, and in turn successfully reproducing. This is the reason why adoption is not a realistic alternative for many women faced with an unwanted pregnancy. If successful human reproduction were only a matter of passing on genes, then it would make perfect sense to let someone else bring up one's children. But biology and reproduction involve far more than passing on genes. Genes are expressed in an environment, which for a child the parent largely controls. It is the rare parent who will let another person create an environment for their genetic child. This is why the pro-life argument that a pregnant woman should "tough it out," have the child, and give it up for adoption makes little biological sense. Humanity is altruistic because it permits childrearing to be done by strangers. Hrdy noted that women especially have evolved to nurture small babies. But adoption is the exception. A woman in general will not want to run the risks of pregnancy and childbearing in order to deliver her child to strangers. The shortage of babies for adoption is not the fault of abortion, although legal abortion did decrease the number of children available. A more important reason for the shortage is the societal acceptance of single motherhood. Single women are no longer subject to censure for having a child and raising it on their own.

Humanity has benefited by attempting to control all the moving parts of the reproductive process. In general, the only random part of the process is which part of each parent's genetic code gets transferred to his or her child. But even though the reproductive process is not a random one, this does not mean that it is entirely under human control. The process is partly conscious and sub-conscious, and partly instinct and partly choice. It is a process with false starts, mistakes, and sadness, and a process with the greatest possible joy and rewards. It is a process where it is not always possible to determine whether any of us acted wisely or unwisely. How each person gets to their reproductive goals is not always by a straight-line journey with no pitfalls, detours, or wrong turns.

This human journey with all its mistakes has gotten us to where we are and for that reason alone is deserving of our collective respect and forbearance. It is a process that we should not permit our governments to interfere with for no substantial reason. The presumption must be to keep governmental hands off this intensely personal process. If individual humans are likely to make mistakes in their reproductive strategies, collective humanity is much more likely to make even worse mistakes. We have seen this most recently in Romania and China. We have seen that even more putatively benign interventions in the reproductive process, such as with teen pregnancy prevention programs or incentives to childbearing in some countries, may have minimal effects and unintended consequences. Governmental restrictions on certain human behavior, sexual or reproductive, raise serious questions about the legitimacy of the government's action from a moral point of view. It is not that human behavior can't be influenced or changed by law. Humans are not genetic and reproductive robots. But there are biological limits to what law and culture can achieve in changing the biological process, just as Marxists found out there are limits to what changes politics can bring about in the social and economic spheres. More importantly, we should not want to change these biological and evolutionary processes, even if we had the power to do so. What makes us think that we can develop rules to cover every human circumstance? Any attempt to enact rules to control human reproduction within the context of each person's particular environment would have all the simplicity, clarity, and compassion of the internal revenue code.

In the ranking of moral values, life must rank at the top or near the top. As I have argued, life is more than biological existence. It involves biological creation, survival and re-creation by going through a biological reproductive process. In most cases a woman's pregnancy ends in the birth of a child, and not abortion, because that is in alignment with her reproductive strategy. In some cases it is not, and the pregnancy is terminated early. I have argued that society should respect this and not interfere with it. While reproduction is an intensely private endeavor, there are public, species-wide consequences to some of humanity's private reproductive choices. I suggest that individual reproduction involves, indeed commands, obligations to one's progeny and to the community. The law should set out some of these obligations but not all.

A justification of unfettered reproductive choice based solely on a human rights or women's rights basis, while important and vital, leaves out too many other interests and considerations. For a woman especially, being able to determine her reproductive destiny is a vital component of her freedom. Her reproductive choices, like those of men, have consequences, as do other exercises of individual liberty. Choices are made in contexts. At the beginning of this book I related how my wife said she would not have an abortion if her baby had hip displaysia. But there might be other circumstances where my wife might. Each of us has to imagine circumstances where having an abortion would be the right decision. The possible parameters are enormous. Just as the environment alters reproductive strategies, so too does the environment validate, or not, reproductive choices. The future of reproductive rights will be determined by the extent that we come to respect this reality. Humanity's existence on earth shouldn't be a suicide pact. We must give individual humans the benefit of the doubt and the maximum liberty possible to carry out their reproductive strategies, but we need not permit humanity to do so in a way that endangers society. That is why the standard of judicial review that courts use to see if a law restricting reproductive freedom passes constitutional muster is so vital. Our courts must use the strictest scrutiny possible when they examine these laws.

I believe we can best advance reproductive freedom, not just by extolling it as a fundamental element of human freedom and dignity, but by supporting it an indispensable part of our biological destiny. When the pro-choice movement gets on the side of human betterment and survival, it will win. The pro-life side has pretended to do this by defending "life." Their position, by eliminating individual control over one's own reproduction, is, as I have argued, inimical to the long-term biological interests of humanity. The only thing more important than life is the propagation of life. The pro-choice movement can be on the side of humanity's long-term reproductive interests by supporting the reproductive strategies that humans make. Reproductive freedom is just as important to a woman who wants to have a child as it is to a woman who doesn't want to. There is no "us" and "them" in reproductive freedom. Everyone benefits from it. Being on the side of women and men as they try to carry out their reproductive strategies can only help the pro-choice movement.

As those who oppose reproductive choice try to impose stricter limits on abortion access and even criminalize it entirely, we who support reproductive freedom must reconcile biology with the religious and moral codes that evolved as we did. Biologist E. O. Wilson of Harvard University once said: "The human mind evolved to believe in Gods. It did not evolve to believe in biology." The challenge for humanity is to believe in biology and evolution as positive forces for humanity. We are here because of them, no matter what our religious beliefs. We must become proud that we have taken control of our reproduction. This has been a major factor in advancing human evolution and survival. While the right to privacy is important in insuring that the majority cannot try to change the biological rules of life, the word "privacy" should not be our banner. It connotes secrecy and shame. We must eliminate shame from the debate over reproductive freedom. Our argument must not be for the legality of abortion, but for abortion itself.

In 1915 my grandmother was given a banquet on the eve of her trial for publishing *The Woman Rebel*. Each member of the audience of over 100 women was asked to sign a public statement that they used birth control. Only three women volunteered to sign. My grandmother knew that birth control would not become and remain legal until women publicly and proudly acknowledged its use.

Few women today publicly and proudly acknowledge having had an abortion. We can no longer be ashamed of abortion. Abortion won't become safely legal until we recognize and admit how reproductive freedom, including the right to an abortion, furthers human destiny. We got over our shame with birth control. It is time we did so with abortion.

# Epilogue

After the Republican victory in the 2004 presidential election, it became all the rage in both the pro-choice movement and the Democratic Party to talk about "reframing" the abortion debate. The precipitating cause was that exit polls revealed 22 percent of the electorate selected "moral values" as their most important issue, and that 80 percent of them voted for President Bush. Anti-abortion groups hailed this as proof that they had carried the day for the President and deserved payback in the form of new Justices on the Supreme Court who would vote to overturn *Roe v. Wade*. The Democratic candidate himself, John Kerry, reportedly told one Democratic audience after the election that Democrats needed to make the American people understand that the party didn't like abortion, and encouraged the party to work on getting more pro-life candidates onto Democratic tickets. Several leading members of the Democratic Party indicated that moral values had cost the party the election, and that the solution was not just to reframe how Democrats talked about abortion but actually to soften their stance, particularly on the issues of parental consent and "partial-birth abortion".

A closer look at the exit polls and comparisons with prior years told a less than clear-cut story. First, the term "moral values" was left to the voter to interpret. It was by no means clear whether same sex marriage, rather than abortion, or indeed just moral values generally, were the "moral values" voters had in mind. The validity of the polling technique used was questioned because the pollsters actually listed "moral values"—along with the economy/jobs, terrorism, Iraq, health care, taxes, and education—as a possible response to the question about what voters considered most important. In other open-ended polls taken around election time that did not suggest particular answers, "moral values" received far fewer votes as the most important issue. Finally, polling done in the 1996 and 2000 elections by the *Los Angeles Times* revealed that 40 percent and 35 percent of voters respectively had named "moral values" as the most important issue in those elections. Thus, it would seem that the percentage of the electorate who claimed "moral values" as their most important issue actually declined significantly in 2004, and was replaced by concern over terrorism and Iraq, which together received 34 percent of the electorate's vote as the most important issues.

Further examination of the exit polls revealed that, consistent with the last thirty years of polling, the American public's opinion about abortion had not changed one iota. The exit polls reported that 21 percent of the electorate believed abortion should be "always legal" while 16 percent believed it should be "always illegal", with 60 percent somewhere in the middle (34 percent saying it should be "mostly legal" and 26 percent "mostly illegal"). Compare this to the original Gallup poll on abortion from 1975 which I cited earlier, where 21 percent said abortion should be "always legal" and 22 percent "always illegal" with 54 percent in the middle. The results are virtually identical within the margins of error for the polls. The Democratic Party leaders who were so quick to fault abortion failed to note that the public opinion on abortion in 2004 had not changed a bit from previous years. Abortion was not the deciding factor in an election governed by issues of war, judgment, leadership, and character.

These issues, as well as economic and tax issues, led some solidly pro-choice voters to vote for the anti-choice candidate and vice versa. Of those in the 21 percent camp who said abortion should always be legal, fully 25 percent of them voted for President Bush—the candidate opposed to abortion rights. At the other end of the spectrum, of the 16 percent camp who said abortion should always be illegal, 22 percent of them voted for Senator Kerry, who supports the legality of abortion. When the math is done, this was a swing of about 3.5 percent in President Bush's favor, which was almost exactly his margin of victory in the popular vote. But the swing was not because of abortion.

Nevertheless, many Democratic leaders leapt to be first to jettison their support for abortion always being legal, available, and accessible. Hillary Clinton, in January 2005, repeated her husband's formulation that abortion should be "safe, legal and rare". She framed the abortion issue as Naomi Wolf did, that abortion "represents a sad, even tragic choice to many, many women". She urged that both sides come together to prevent unsafe and unintended pregnancies, and she indicated qualified support for parental consent laws for abortion.

The Rockridge Institute, a progressive think tank, similarly proposed an abortion framework based on a negative view of abortion with prevention being the theme and said:

">. . . abortion (is) the result of an awful situation—a woman with an unintended pregnancy. Treating the woman as someone in need of empathy and taking responsibility to avoid this situation in the future leads Progressives to take a prevention approach and support policies such as: increasing funding and access to family planning clinics, improving access to contraception and emergency contraception, supporting the use of sex-education and other programs that have been proven effective in lowering teen pregnancy, [and] keeping abortion safe and legal.

Furthermore, Progressives also support social safety nets and community assets like prenatal care, health care, family leave, improved public schools, and aftercare programs which make it easier for women to raise their children in a healthy, supportive environment."

The Rockridge Institute report continued:

"These prevention policies are consistent with Progressives' stated goals of decreasing unintended pregnancies, decreasing abortions, decreasing the risk of sexually transmitted diseases, protecting the health of women, and promoting environments in which women can choose to raise their children."

It is most definitely time to reframe the debate over abortion. That is why I spent 2000-2003 writing this book and all of 2004 traveling the country talking about the ideas in it. The reader will have already noticed that I part company with the approach of both the Democratic Party and those Progressives aligned with the Rockridge Institute. First, these groups are talking in the negative: abortion is bad, tragic, wrong; we need prevention, prevention, and more prevention. Second, they are selling a progressive, liberal viewpoint. That is what the Democratic party does, and should do.

But the reproductive freedom movement is different from the Democratic Party, or it should be. The people we need to reach do not share the liberal, progressive viewpoint of the Democratic Party. They are moderate to conservative, Republicans and independents. Many or most have a different worldview and values than progressives do. The best way to advance reproductive freedom is not by trying to convince moderates and conservatives of the rightness of the liberal, progressive, Democratic world view. Conservatives and moderates can support reproductive freedom without buying the liberal worldview. They can keep their own worldview and incorporate reproductive freedom within it. How do we do this?

First, we need to start talking in the positive. We need to tell the American people what we are for, not what we are against. We need to encompass our beliefs and goals within one big idea, and that idea is family. Human reproduction is all about family and family formation. We don't marry, mate, and have children haphazardly, randomly, or by chance—even though we are subject to unconscious forces, desires, needs, and passions. The path we take may be messy, uneven, and not a straight line. But it gets most of us to where we want to be: in a family of our choosing with the children and grandchildren we want to have. Every child being a wanted child is a powerful message. This is what reproductive freedom gives us. Moderates and conservatives want to form families just like progressives do. This desire cuts across all worldviews and value sets. Each value set can incorporate this and not be in conflict with its basic tenets.

Abortion rights cannot stand on their own. They must be incorporated into the larger framework of family formation, healthy children, parental responsibility, and a community where each potential child (from conception onwards) has the best possible environment for reaching adulthood healthy, educated, and ready to assume the responsibility of forming a family for themselves. That is what humanity has formed communities and societies and government to do. It is nothing to be ashamed of.

# Acknowledgments

I would first like to thank all of my colleagues at Planned Parenthood all over the world who over the years have given me so much support and inspiration. This book is equally dedicated to them, as well as to my wife and children. I want to especially acknowledge Sylvia Clark, my colleague at Planned Parenthood of the Rocky Mountains, who was so supportive of the ideas in this book.

I am indebted to my agent, Jillian Manus, who took on this project with the enthusiasm that only a beleaguered pro-choice Republican could.

My editor, Lisa Kaufman, was a model of clarity, tact, and vision. She made this a better book. I would also like to thank Peter Osnos, publisher of PublicAffairs, for venturing out on this limb with me.

My research assistant, Jim Rossi, was a marvel at finding obscure articles and studies on the intricacies of modern biology. He had a unique ability to translate their technicalities into everyday English and to clarify all the academic disputes in modern Darwinism and evolutionary biology. I am indebted to Jim for all his moral as well as intellectual support.

During the course of my research and writing I consulted with many experts, including Steven M. L. Aronson, Professor Anne Fausto-Sterling, Austin Gager, Stanley Henshaw, Fran Kissling, Professor Bobbi S. Low, the Rev. Louis Pojman, Professor Mike Wallace, and Kristina Wertz. I am grateful as well to the doctors at Fertility Clinic in New York.

Many colleagues went above and beyond the call and read all or portions of the manuscript and offered helpful and critical suggestions. They include: May Del Rio, Professor Norman Dorsen, Beth Frederick, Nicki Nichols Gamble, Douglas Gould, William Hamilton, Richard Hauskenecht, M.D., Judith Helzner, Jane Johnson, Professor Esther Katz, Margaret Lampe, Jim Le Fevre, Joyce Moss, Hugh Nissensen, Peter Wilderotter, and William Zangwill. I am deeply indebted to my good friend Sean Connor who waded through multiple drafts and who by his persistent questioning made this, I hope, a more persuasive book.

I am especially grateful to Professor Lionel Tiger, the Charles Darwin Professor of Anthropology at Rutgers University, for all his wisdom and patience over the years.

The staff of Planned Parenthood of New York City, especially Norma Liebowitz, the manager of the Margaret Sanger Clinic, and Leslie Rottenberg, the clinic's social work director, were extremely helpful in my research. I am indebted to every staff member at PPNYC for all their support over the years. In my book, they are all heroes.

I also would like to thank the staff at International Planned Parenthood Federation/Western Hemisphere Region at whose offices I wrote this book. I am honored to serve as the chair of the International Planned Parenthood Council. I am especially indebted to Hernan Sanhueza and Carmen Barroso, the directors of the Western Hemisphere Region, for allowing me the use their offices. My thanks also to Nicole Mitzel, who made sense of my bibliography. And special thanks to Noel Negron, Sharon Harrison, and Bernice Davis for all their help to me over the years.

Finally, my wife, Jeannette Watson, publisher and bookseller, has been and remains my biggest source of inspiration and support. I thank her for letting me share her story which opens the book and for being so supportive throughout.

# Bibliography

The literature on human sexuality, reproduction, evolution, and the law is vast. I cite below many of the sources, both books and scientific articles, that I relied on in the writing of this book. In addition to those cited, I relied extensively on the materials produced by The Alan Guttmacher Institute and the Population Council. Interested readers should visit their websites where all their publications are available: http://www.agi-usa.org/ and http://www.popcouncil.org/ respectively. In addition, I relied on publications from the World Health Organization at http://www.who.int/en/, from the United Nations Population Division at http://www.un.org/popin/, and from the Centers for Disease Control and Prevention at http://www.cdc.gov/.

Abma, Joyce, and Freya L. Sonenstein. "Teenage Sexual Behavior and Contraceptive Use: An Update." Washington: National Center for Health Statistics and the Urban Institute, 1998.

Ahmed, Saifuddin, et al. "HIV incidence and sexually transmitted disease prevalence associated with condom use: a population study in Rakai, Uganda." *AIDS* 15.16 (2001): 2171–2179.

Akerlof, George A., Janet L. Yellen, and Michael L. Katz. "An Analysis of Out-of Wedlock Childbearing in the United States." *The Quarterly Journal of Economics* 111.2 (1996): 277–317.

Alexander, Michele G., and Terri D. Fisher. "Truth and Consequences: Using the Bogus Pipeline to Examine Sex Differences in Self-Reported Sexuality." *The Journal of Sex Research* 40.1 (2003): 27–35.

Anderson, Kermyt G., and Bobbi S. Low. "Nonmarital first births and women's life histories." Prepared for *The Biodemography of Fertility*. Eds. J. Rodgers and H. P. Kohler. New York: Kluwer, 2002.

Andrews, Lori B. *Future Perfect: Confronting Decisions About Genetics*. New York: Columbia UP, 2001.

Angier, Natalie. *Woman: An Intimate Geography*. London: Virago, 1999.

Archer, Gregory S., et al. "Behavioral variation among cloned pigs." *Applied Animal Behaviour Science* 82.2 (2003): 151–161.

———. "Hierarchical Phenotype and Epigenetic Variation in Cloned Swine." *Biology of Reproduction* 69 (2003): 430–436.

Arkes, Hadley. *Natural Rights and the Right to Choose*. New York: Cambridge UP, 2002.

Asbell, Bernard. *The Pill: A Biography of the Drug That changed the World*. New York: Random House, 1995.

Asch, Adrienne. "Prenatal Diagnosis and Selective Abortion: A Challenge to Practice and Policy." *American Journal of Public Health* 89.11 (1999): 1649–1657.

Averett, Susan L., Daniel I. Rees, and Laura M. Argys. "The Impact of Government Policies and Neighborhood Characteristics on Teenage Sexual Activity and Contraceptive Use." *American Journal of Public Health* 92 (2002): 1773–1778.

Baird, Donna Day, and Beverly I. Strassmann. "Women's Fecundability and Factors Affecting It." *Woman and Health* (2000): 126–137.

Bandarage, Asoka. *Women, Population and Global Crisis: A Political-Economic Analysis*. Atlantic Highlands, N.J.: Zed Books, 1997.

Bankole, Akinrinola, and Susheela Singh. "Couples' Fertility and Contraceptive Decision-Making In Developing Countries: Hearing the Man's Voice." *International Family Planning Perspectives* 24.1 (1998): 15–24.

Barash, David P., Ph.D., and Judith Eve Lipton, M.D. *The Myth of Monogamy: Fidelity and Infidelity in Animals and People*. New York: W. H. Freeman and Company, 2001.

Barber, N. "On the relationship between marital opportunity and teen pregnancy—The sex ratio question." *Journal of Cross-Cultural Psychology* 32.3 (2001): 259–267.

Basu, Alaka Malwade, ed. *The Sociocultural and Political Aspects of Abortion: Global Perspectives*. Westport, Conn.: Praeger, 2003.

Bateson, Patrick, ed. *Mate Choice*. New York: Cambridge UP, 1983.

Becker, Stan, and Elizabeth Costenbader. "Husbands' and Wives' Reports of Contraceptive Use." *Studies in Family Planning* 32.2 (2001): 111–129.

Beekman, Madeleine, Jan Komdeur, and Francis L. W. Ratnieks. "Reproductive conflicts in social animals: who has power?" *Trends in Ecology & Evolution* 18.6 (2003): 277–282.

Belsky, Jay, and Patricia Draper. "Reproductive Strategies and Radical Solutions." *Society* March/April 1987: 20–24.

Belsky, Jay, Laurence Steinberg, and Patricia Draper. "Childhood Experience, Interpersonal Development, and Reproductive Strategy: An Evolutionary Theory of Socialization." *Child Development* 62 (1991): 647–670.

Belsky, Jay. "Modern Evolutionary Theory and Patterns of Attachment." Pp. 141–161. *Handbook of Attachment Theory and Research*. Eds. J. Cassidy and P. Shaver. New York: Guilford, 1999.

———. "Variation in Susceptibility to Environmental Influence: An Evolutionary Argument." *Psychological Inquiry* 8 (1997): 182–186.

Berg, Cynthia J., et al. "Pregnancy-Related Mortality in the United States 1987–1990." *Obstetrics & Gynecology* 88.2 (1996): 161–166.

Berlin, Isaiah. *Liberty*. Ed. Henry Hardy. New York: Oxford UP, 2002.

Betzig, Laura. "Where are the bastards' daddies?" *Behavioral & Brain Sciences* 16 (1993): 285–286.

Bhathena, R. K. "The long-acting progestogen-only contraceptive injections: an update." *British Journal of Obstetrics and Gynaecology* 108 (2001): 3–8.

Biddlecom, Ann E., and Bolaji M. Fapohunda. "Covert Contraceptive Use: Prevalence, Motivations, and Consequences." *Studies in Family Planning* 29.4 (1998): 360–372.

Birdsall, Nancy, Allen C. Kelley, and Steven W. Sinding, eds. *Population Matters: Demographic Change, Economic Growth, and Poverty in the Developing World*. New York: Oxford UP, 2001.

Bitler, Marianne, and Madeline Zavodny. "Did Abortion Legalization Reduce the Number of Unwanted Children? Evidence from Adoptions." *Perspectives on Sexual and Reproductive Health* 34.1 (2002): 25–33.

Blanc, Ann K. "The Effect of Power in Sexual Relationships on Reproductive and Sexual Health: An Examination of the Evidence." Population Council, Power in Sexual Relationships Meeting, 2001.

Bock, Gisela, and Pat Thane, eds. *Maternity and Gender Policies: Women and the Rise of the European Welfare States 1880s–1950s*. New York: Routledge, 1994.

Boonin, David. *A Defense of Abortion*. Cambridge Studies in Philosophy and Public Policy Ser. New York: Cambridge UP, 2003.

Brener, N., et al. "Trends in Sexual Risk Behaviors Among High School Students—United States, 1991–2001." *Morbidity and Mortality Weekly Report* 51.38 (2002): 856–859.

Brodie, Janet Farrell. *Contraception and Abortion in Nineteenth-Century America*. Ithaca, N.Y.: Cornell UP, 1994.

Brown, Lester R., Gary Gardner, and Brian Halweil. *Beyond Malthus: Nineteen Dimensions of the Population Challenge*. The Worldwatch Environmental Alert Ser. New York: Norton, 1999.

Brown, Sarah S., and Leon Eisenberg, eds. *The Best Intentions: Unintended Pregnancy and the Well-Being of Children and Families*. Institute of Medicine. Washington: National Academy Press, 1995.

Browne, Kingsley R. *Biology at Work: Rethinking Sexual Equality*. New Brunswick, N.J.: Rutgers UP, 2002.

Browning, Don S., et al. *From Culture Wars to Common Ground: Religion and the American Family Debate*. The Family, Religion, and Culture Ser. Louisville, Ky.: Westminster John Knox Press, 1997.

Buchanan, Allen, et al. *From Chance to Choice: Genetics and Justice*. New York: Cambridge UP, 2000.

Buechler, Steven M. *Social Movements in Advanced Capitalism: The Political Economy and Cultural Construction of Social Activism*. New York: Oxford UP, 2000.

———. *Women's Movements in the United States: Woman Suffrage, Equal Rights, and Beyond*. New Brunswick, N.J.: Rutgers UP, 1990.

Burnham, Terry, and Jay Phelan. *Mean Genes: From Sex to Money to Food: Taming Our Primal Instincts*. Cambridge, Mass.: Perseus, 2000.

Burtchaell, James Tunstead, ed. *Abortion Parley*. National Conference on Abortion, University of Notre Dame, 1979. New York: Andrews and McMeel, 1980.

———. *Rachel Weeping and Other Essays on Abortion*. Toronto: Life Cycle Books, 1990.

Buss, David M. "Paternity Uncertainty and the Complex Repertoire of Human Mating Strategies." *American Psychologist* Feb. 1996: 161–162.

———. *The Evolution of Desire: Strategies of Human Mating*. New York: Basic Books, 1994.

Buss, David M., Todd K. Shackelford, and Gregory J. LeBlanc. "Number of children desired and preferred spousal age difference: context-specific mate preference patterns across 37 cultures." *Evolution and Human Behavior* 21 (2000): 323–331.

Caldwell, John C. "Rethinking the African AIDS Epidemic." *Population and Development Review* 26.1 (2000): 117–135.

Callahan, Daniel. *Abortion: Law, Choice and Morality*. Toronto: Macmillan, 1970.

Callahan, Sidney, and Daniel Callahan, eds. *Abortion: Understanding Differences*. The Hasting Center Series in Ethics. New York: Plenum Press, 1984.

Cannold, Leslie. *The Abortion Myth: Feminism, Morality, and the Hard Choices Women Make*. Hanover, N.H.: Wesleyan UP, 2000.

Carlson, Elof Axel. *The Unfit: A History of a Bad Idea*. Cold Spring Harbor, New York: Cold Spring Harbor Laboratory Press, 2001.

Cates, Willard Jr., David A. Grimes, and Kenneth F. Schulz. "The Public Health Impact of Legal Abortion: 30 Years Later." *Perspectives on Sexual and Reproductive Health* 35.1 (2003): 25–28.

Chapman, Tracey, et al. "Sexual Conflict." *Trends in Ecology & Evolution* 18.1 (2003): 41–47.

Chesler, Ellen. *Woman of Valor: Margaret Sanger and the Birth Control Movement in America*. New York: Anchor Books, 1992.

Christensen, Clayton M. *The Innovator's Dilemma: When New Technologies Cause Great Firms to Fail*. New York: HarperBusiness, 2000.

Clarke, Alice L., and Bobbi S. Low. "Testing Evolutionary Hypothesis with Demographic Data." *Population and Development Review* 27.4 (2001): 633–660.

Cochran, Gregory, and Paul W. Ewald. "High-Risk Defenses: The body's self-destructive tactics against infection." *Natural History* Feb. 1999:40–43.

Cohen, Marshall, ed. *The Philosophy of John Stuart Mill: Ethical, Political and Religious*. New York: Modern Library, 1961.

Colborn, Theo, Dianne Dumanoski, and John Peterson Myers. *Our Stolen Future: Are We Threatening Our Fertility, Intelligence, and Survival?—A Scientific Detective Story*. New York: Plume, 1997.

Colker, Ruth. *Abortion & Dialogue: Pro-Choice, Pro-Life, & American Law*. Indianapolis: Indiana UP, 1992.

———. *Pregnant Men: Practice, Theory, and the Law*. Indianapolis: Indiana UP, 1994.

Cook, Kimberly J. *Divided Passions: Public Opinions on Abortion and the Death Penalty*. The Northeastern Series on Gender, Crime, and Law. Boston: Northeastern UP, 1998.

Coughlan, Michael J. *The Vatican, the Law and the Human Embryo*. Iowa City: University of Iowa Press, 1990.

Critchlow, Donald T. *Intended Consequences: Birth Control, Abortion, and the Federal Government in Modern America*. New York: Oxford UP, 1999.

———, ed. *The Politics of Abortion and Birth Control in Historical Perspective*. University Park: Pennsylvania State UP, 1996.

Crowder, K. D., and S. E. Tolnay. "A new marriage squeeze for black women: The role of racial intermarriage by black men." *Journal of Marriage and the Family* 62.3 (2000): 792–807.

D'Emilio, John, and Estelle B. Freedman. *Intimate Matters: A History of Sexuality in America*. New York: Harper & Row, 1988.

D'Emilio, John, William B. Turner, and Urvashi Vaid, eds. *Creating Change: Sexuality, Public Policy, and Civil Rights*. New York: St. Martin's Press, 2000.

Dennett, Daniel C. *Freedom Evolves*. New York: Viking, 2003.

Diamond, Jared. *Why Is Sex Fun?: The Evolution of Human Sexuality*. Science Masters Ser. New York: BasicBooks, 1997.

DiCenso, Alba, et al. "Interventions to reduce unintended pregnancies among adolescents: systematic review of randomized controlled trials." *BMJ* 324 (2002): 1–9.

DiClemente, R. J., et al. "Association of adolescents' history of sexually trans-mitted disease (STD) and their current high-risk behavior and STD status." *Sexually Transmitted Diseases* 29.9 (2002): 503–509.

Donohue, John J., and Steven D. Levitt. "The Impact of Legalized Abortion on Crime." *The Quarterly Journal of Economics* 116.2 (2001): 379–420.

———. "Further Evidence That Legalized Abortion Lowered Crime: A Reply to Joyce." NBER Working Paper Ser. 9532. Cambridge: National Bureau of Economic Research, 2003 http://www.nber.org/papers/w9532.

Donzelot, Jacques. *The Policing of Families*. Trans. Gilles Deleuze. Johns Hop-kins Paperbacks ed. Baltimore: Johns Hopkins UP, 1997.

Duncan, Greg J., et al. "How Much Does Childhood Poverty Affect the Life Chances of Children?" *American Sociological Review* 63 (1998): 406–423.

Durrant, Russil and Bruce J. Ellis. *Evolutionary Psychology: Core Assumptions and Methodology*. In M. Gallagher & R.J. Nelson (Eds.), *Comprehensive Handbook of Psychology, Volume Three: Biological Psychology* (pp. 1–33). New York: Wiley & Sons.

Dworkin, Ronald. *Life's Dominion: An Argument About Abortion, Euthanasia, and Individual Freedom*. New York: Knopf, 1993.

Eberstadt, Nicholas. *Prosperous Paupers and Other Population Problems*. New Brunswick, N.J.: Transaction, 2000.

Ellertson, Charlotte, et al. "Emergency Contraception: Randomized Comparison of Advance Provision and Information Only." *Obstetrics & Gynecology* 98.4 (2001): 570–575.

Ellison, Peter T. *On Fertile Ground: A Natural History of Human Reproduction*. Cambridge, Mass.: Harvard UP, 2001.

Ennenga, George R. vB. "Artificial Evolution." *Artificial Life* 3.1 (1997): 51–61.

Essock-Vitale, Susan M., and Michael T. McGuire. "Women's Lives Viewed from an Evolutionary Perspective. I. Sexual Histories, Reproductive Success, and Demographic Characteristics of a Random Sample of American Women." *Ethology and Sociobiology* 6 (1985): 137–154.

Ethics Committee of the American Society for Reproductive Medicine. "Human somatic cell nuclear transfer (cloning)." *Fertility and Sterility* 74.5 (2000): 873–876.

———. "Sex selection and preimplantation genetic diagnosis." *Fertility and Sterility* 72.4 (1999): 595–598.

————. "Preconception gender selection for nonmedical reasons." *Fertility and Sterility* 75.5 (2001): 861–864.

Ewald, Paul W. "Guarding Against the Most Dangerous Emerging Pathogens: Insights from Evolutionary Biology." *Emerging Infectious Diseases* 2.4 (1996): 245–257.

————. "The Evolution of Virulence: A Unifying Link Between Parasitology and Ecology." *The Journal of Parasitology* 81.5 (1995): 659–669.

Ewald, Paul W., and Gregory M. Cochran. "*Chlamydia pneumoniae* and Cardiovascular Disease: An Evolutionary Perspective on Infectious Causation and Antibiotic Treatment." *The Journal of Infectious Diseases* 181.Suppl 3 (2000):s394–401.

Feng, Yi, Jacek Kugler, and Paul J. Zak. "The Politics of Fertility and Economic Development." *International Studies Quarterly* 44 (2000): 667–693.

Finkle, Jason L., and C. Alison McIntosh, eds. *The New Politics of Population: Conflict and Consensus in Family Planning*. Population and Development Review, Supplement to Vol. 20. New York: The Population Council, 1994.

Fisher, Helen. *Anatomy of Love: A Natural History of Mating, Marriage, and Why We Stray*. New York: Fawcett Columbine, 1992.

————. *The First Sex: The Natural Talents of Women and How They Are Changing the World*. New York: Random House, 1999.

Foner, Eric. *The Story of American Freedom*. New York: Norton, 1998.

Foster, E. Michael, Damon Jones, and Saul D. Hoffman. "The economic impact of nonmarital childbearing: How are older, single mothers faring?" *Journal of Marriage and the Family* 60.1 (1998): 163–174.

Fu, Haishan, et al. "Contraceptive Failure Rates: New Estimates From the 1995 National Survey of Family Growth." *Family Planning Perspectives* 31.2 (1999): 56–63.

Fukuyama, Francis. *Our Posthuman Future: Consequences of the Biotechnology Revolution*. New York: Farrar Straus and Giroux, 2002.

————. *The Great Disruption: Human Nature and the Reconstitution of Social Order*. New York: Touchstone, 2000.

Furstenberg, Frank F. Jr. "The Effect of Welfare Reform on the Family: The Good, the Bad and the Ugly." Presented at the Joint Center for Poverty Research Preconference "Family Management and Child Development in Low Income Families," 1998, Chicago. Philadelphia: U of Pennsylvania, 1998.

————. "Why Pregnancy Prevention Programs Don't Work and What To Do About It." Presented at the Joint Center for Poverty Research Conference "Synthesizing the Results of Demonstration Programs for Teen Mothers," 1997, Northwestern. Philadelphia: U of Pennsylvania, 1998.

Gangestad, Steven W., and Randy Thornhill. "Menstrual cycle variation in women and preferences for the scent of symmetry." *Proc. R. Soc. Lond.* 265 (1998): 927–933.

Garrow, David J. *Liberty and Sexuality: The Right to Privacy and the Making of Roe v. Wade.* New York: Macmillan, 1994.

Geronimus, Arline T. "Black/White Differences in the Relationship of Maternal Age to Birthweight: A Population-Based Test of the Weathering Hypothesis." *Social Science and Medicine* 42.4 (1996): 589–597.

———. "Teenage Childbearing and Personal Responsibility." *Political Science Quarterly* 112.3 (1997): 405–430.

———. "Understanding and Eliminating Racial Inequalities in Women's Health in the United States: The Role of the Weathering Conceptual Framework." *Journal of American Medical Women's Association* 56 (2001): 133–136.

———. "What Teen Mothers Know." *Human Nature* 7.4 (1996): 323–352.

———. "Why Teenage Childbearing Might Be Sensible: Research and Policy Implications." Prepared for Symposium, "Teenage Pregnancy: Invention or Epidemic?" New Orleans: American Assoc. for the Advancement of Science, 1990.

Geronimus, Arline T., et al. "Excess Mortality Among Blacks and Whites in the United States." *The New England Journal of Medicine* 335 (1996): 1552–1558.

Geronimus, Arline T., John Bound, and Timothy A. Waidmann. "Health inequality and population variation in fertility-timing." *Social Science & Medicine* 49 (1999): 1623–1636.

Geronimus, Arline T., Sanders Korenman, and Marianne M. Hillemeier. "Does Young Maternal Age Adversely Affect Child Development? Evidence from Cousin Comparisons in the United States." *Population and Development Review* 20.3 (1994): 585–609.

Ginsburg, Faye D., and Rayna Rapp, eds. *Conceiving the New World Order: The Global Politics of Reproduction.* Berkeley: U of California P, 1995.

Glasier, A. F., and D. Baird. "The effects of self-administering emergency contraception." *New England Journal of Medicine* 339.1 (1998): 1–4.

Glasier, A. F., et al. "Would women trust their partners to use a male pill?" *Human Reproduction* 15.3 (2000): 646–649.

Goodkind, Daniel. "Should prenatal sex selection be restricted? Ethical questions and their implications for research and policy." *Population Studies* 53 (1999): 49–61.

Gordon, Linda. *The Moral Property of Women: A History of Birth Control Politics in America* (third edition). Chicago: University of Illinois Press, 2002.

———. *Woman's Body, Woman's Right: Birth Control in America* (second edition). New York: Penguin, 1990.

Gorney, Cynthia. *Articles of Faith: A Frontline History of the Abortion Wars.* New York: Simon & Schuster, 1998.

Gottlieb, Stephen E. *Morality Imposed: The Rehnquist Court and Liberty in America.* New York: New York UP, 2000.

Gowaty, Patricia Adair, ed. *Feminism and Evolutionary Biology: Boundaries, Intersections, and Frontiers.* New York: Chapman & Hall, 1997.

———. "Multiple mating by females selects for males that stay: another hypothesis for social monogamy in passerine birds." *Animal Behaviour* 51 (1996): 482–484.

Graham, Cynthia A., et al. "The Effects of Steroidal Contraceptives on the Well-being and Sexuality of Women: A Double-blind, Placebo-controlled, Two-centre Study of Combined and Progestogen-only Methods." *Contraception* 52 (1995): 363–369.

Green, Shirley. *The Curious History of Contraception.* London: Ebury Press, 1971.

Greene, Margaret E., and Ann E. Biddlecom. "Absent and Problematic Men: Demographic Accounts of Male Reproductive Roles." *Population and Development Review* 26.1 (2000): 81–115.

Grogger, Jeff, and Stephen Bronars. "The Socioeconomic Consequences of Teenage Childbearing: Findings from a Natural Experiment." *Family Planning Perspectives* 25 (1993): 156–161 & 174.

Gruter, Margaret, and Paul Bohannan, eds. *Law, Biology and Culture: The Evolution of Law.* Santa Barbara: Ross-Erikson, 1983.

Hamburger, Philip. *Separation of Church and State.* Cambridge, Mass.: Harvard UP, 2002.

Hamilton, Alexander, John Jay, and James Madison. *The Federalist: A Commentary on The Constitution of The United States.* Introduction Edward Mead Earle. New York: Modern Library, 1937.

Hamilton, William D., and Marlene Zuk. "Heritable True Fitness and Bright Birds: A Role for Parasites?" *Science* 218 (1982): 384–387.

Hamilton, William J., and Robert Poulin. "The Hamilton and Zuk Hypothesis Revisited: A Meta-Analytical Approach." *Behaviour* 134 (1997): 299–320.

Hand, Learned. *The Spirit of Liberty: Papers and Addresses of Learned Hand.* Ed. Irving Dilliard. New York: Knopf, 1952.

Hansen, Michéle, et al. "The Risk of Major Birth Defects after Intracytoplasmic Sperm Injection and in Vitro Fertilization." *The New England Journal of Medicine* 346.10 (2002): 725–730.

Hardy, Ian C. W., ed. *Sex Ratios: Concepts and Research Methods.* New York: Cambridge UP, 2002.

Hart, H. L. A. *Law, Liberty, and Morality*. New York: Vintage, 1963.

———. *The Concept of Law* (second edition). Oxford: Oxford UP, 1965.

Hatcher, Robert A., et al. *Contraceptive Technology* (seventeenth edition). New York: Ardent Media, 1998.

Hewlett, Sylvia Ann. *Creating a Life: Professional Women and the Quest for Children*. New York: Talk Miramax Books, 2002.

Hill, Elizabeth M., and Bobbi S. Low. "Contemporary Abortion Patterns: A Life History Approach." *Ethology and Sociobiology* 13 (1992): 35–48.

Himes, Norman E. *Medical History of Contraception*. New York: Schocken, 1970.

Ho, H. N., et al. "Sharing of human leukocyte antigens in couples with unexplained infertility affects the success of in vitro fertilization and tubal embryo transfer." *American Journal of Obstetrics and Gynecology* 170.1 (1994): 63–71.

Hofferth, Sandra L., and Lori Reid. "Early Childbearing and Children's Achievement and Behavior over Time." *Perspectives on Sexual and Reproductive Health* 34.1 (2002): 41–49.

Hoffman, Saul D. "Teenage Childbearing Is Not So Bad After All . . . Or Is It? A Review of the New Literature." *Family Planning Perspectives* 30.5 (1998):236–239 & 243.

Hoffman, Saul D., and E. Michael Foster. "Could It Be True After All? AFDC Benefits and Non-Marital Births to Young Women." Prepared for 1997 meeting of the Population Association of America. Chicago: Joint Center for Poverty Research, 1997.

Holmes, King K., et al, eds. *Sexually Transmitted Diseases* (third edition). New York: McGraw-Hill, 1999.

Hord, Charlotte, et al. "Reproductive Health in Romania: Reversing the Ceausescu Legacy." *Studies in Family Planning* 22.4 (1991): 231–239.

Hotz, V. Joseph, Susan Williams McElroy, and Seth G. Sanders. "Teenage Childbearing and Its Life Cycle Consequences: Exploiting a Natural Experiment." NICHD, 1999.

Hrdy, Sarah Blaffer. *Mother Nature: Maternal Instincts and How They Shape the Human Species*. New York: Ballantine, 1999.

Huezo, Carlos M., M.D., and Charles S. Carignan, M.D.. *Medical and Service Delivery Guidelines for Family Planning* (second edition). London: International Planned Parenthood Federation, 1997.

Hull, N. E. H., and Peter Charles Hoffer. *Roe v. Wade: The Abortion Rights Controversy in American History*. Lawrence: Kansas UP, 2001.

Hurst, Jane. *The History of Abortion in the Catholic Church: The Untold Story*.

Abortion in Good Faith Ser. Washington: Catholics for a Free Choice, 1981.

Immerman, Ronald S., and Wade C. Mackey. "Establishing a Link Between Cultural Evolution and Sexually Transmitted Diseases." *Genetic, Social, and General Psychology Monographs* 123.4 (1997): 441–459.

Jacob, Suma, et al. "Paternally inherited HLA alleles are associated with women's choice of male odor." *Nature Genetics* 30.2 (2002): 175–179.

Jaffee, Sara, et al. "Why are children born to teen mothers at risk for adverse outcomes in young adulthood? Results from a 20-year longitudinal study." *Development and Psychopathology* 13 (2001): 377–397.

Jain, Anrudh, ed. *Do Population Policies Matter?: Fertility and Politics in Egypt, India, Kenya, and Mexico.* New York: Population Council, 1998.

Jennions, M. D., and M. Petrie. "Why do females mate multiply? A review of the genetic benefits." *Biological Reviews of the Cambridge Philosophical Society* 75.1 (2000): 21–64.

Jones, Rachel K., Jacqueline E. Darroch, and Stanley K. Henshaw. "Patterns in the Socioeconomic Characteristics of Women Obtaining Abortions in 2000–2001." *Perspectives on Sexual and Reproductive Health* 34.5 (2002): 226–235.

Jordan, W. C., and M. W. Bruford. "New perspectives on mate choice and the MHC." *Heredity* 81.3 (1998): 239–245.

Joyce, Theodore. "Did Legalized Abortion Lower Crime?" *Journal of Human Resources* 38.1 (2003): 1–37.

Judson, Olivia. *Dr. Tatiana's Sex Advice to All Creation.* New York: Metropolitan Books, 2002.

Kaestner, Robert, and June O'Neill. "Has Welfare Reform Changed Teenage Behaviors?" NBER Working Paper Ser. Cambridge: National Bureau of Economic Research, 2002.

Kalmuss, Debra, et al. "Preventing Sexual Risk Behaviors and Pregnancy Among Teenagers: Linking Research and Programs." *Perspectives on Sexual and Reproductive Health* 35.2 (2003):87–93.

Kamen, Paula. *Her Way: Young Women Remake the Sexual Revolution.* New York: New York UP, 2000.

Katz, Katheryn D. "The Clonal Child: Procreative Liberty and Asexual Reproduction." *Albany Law Journal of Science and Technology* 8.1 (1997): 1–63.

Keller, Matthew C., Randolph M. Nesse, and Sandra Hofferth. "The Trivers-Willard hypothesis of parental investment No effect in the contemporary United States." *Evolution and Human Behavior* 22 (2001): 343–360.

Kemper, Theodore D. *Social Structure and Testosterone: Explorations of the Socio-Bio-Social Chain.* New Brunswick, N.J.: Rutgers UP, 1990.

Kennedy, David M. *Birth Control in America: The Career of Margaret Sanger.* New Haven: Yale UP, 1970.

Kiddugavu, Mohammed, et al. "Hormonal contraceptive use and HIV–1 infection in a population-based cohort in Rakai, Uganda." *AIDS* 17.2 (2003): 233–240.

Kimmey, Jimmye. *Legal Abortion: A Speaker's Notebook.* New York: Association for the Study of Abortion, 1975.

Kirby, Douglas, et al. "The Impact of Condom Distribution in Seattle Schools on Sexual Behavior and Condom Use." *American Journal of Public Health* 89 (1999): 182–187.

Kogan, Barry S. *A Time to be Born and a Time to Die: The Ethics of Choice.* New York: Aldine de Gruyter, 1991.

Kohl, James Vaughn "Re: effects of fathers on puberty onset in girls." E-mail to Teresa Binstock, forwarded to the author. 13 Aug. 2002.

Kohl, James Vaughn, and Robert T. Francoeur. *The Scent of Eros: Mysteries of Odor In Human Sexuality.* Lincoln: Authors Choice, 2002.

Kuczewski, Mark G., and Ronald Polansky, eds. *Bioethics: Ancient Themes in Contemporary Issues.* Cambridge, Mass.: MIT Press, 2000.

Lancaster, Jane B. "The Evolutionary History of Human Parental Investment in Relation to Population Growth and Social Stratification." Pp. 466–489. *Feminism and Evolutionary Biology.* Ed. P.A. Gowaty. New York: Chapman & Hall, 1997.

Lancaster, Jane B., and Beatrix A. Hamburg, eds. *School-Age Pregnancy and Parenthood: Biosocial Dimensions.* New York: Aldine de Gruyter, 1986.

Lassonde, Louise. *Coping with Population Challenges.* Trans. Graham Grayston. London: Earthscan, 1997.

Laumann, Edward O., and Robert T. Michael, eds. *Sex, Love, and Health in America: Private Choices and Public Policies.* Chicago: University of Chicago Press, 2001.

Laumann, Edward O., and Robert T. Michael, et al. *The Social Organization of Sexuality: Sexual Practices in the United States.* Chicago: University of Chicago Press, 1994.

Lavreys, L., et al. "Hormonal contraception and risk of HIV–1 acquisition: results of a 10 year prospective study." *Antiretroviral Therapy* 8 suppl. 1 (2003): 206.

Lawson, Annette, and Deborah L. Rhode, eds. *The Politics of Pregnancy: Adolescent Sexuality and Public Policy.* New Haven: Yale UP, 1993.

Leigh, Andrew, and Justin Wolfers. "Abortion and Crime." *AQ: Journal of Contemporary Analysis* 72.4 (2000): 28–30.

Levine, Judith. *Harmful to Minors: The Perils of Protecting Children from Sex.* Minneapolis: University of Minnesota Press, 2002.

Levine, Phillip B. "The Impact of Social Policy and Economic Activity Throughout the Fertility Decision Tree." *Joint Center for Poverty Research: Working Paper Series.* 16 July 2002. http://www.jcpr.org/wp/WPprofile.cfm?ID=348

Levine, Phillip B., and Douglas Staiger. "Abortion as Insurance." Cambridge: National Bureau of Economic Research, 2002.

Lewinsohn, Richard. *A History of Sexual Customs.* Trans. Alexander Mayce. New York: Harper & Brothers, 1958.

Linn, Gary S., and Horst D. Steklis. "The Effects of Depo-Medroxyprogesterone Acetate (DMPA) on Copulation-Related and Agonistic Behaviors in an Island Colony of Stumptail Macaques (Macaca arctoides)." *Physiology & Behavior* 47 (1990): 403–408.

Lott, John R. Jr., and John Whitley. "Abortion and Crime: Unwanted Children and Out-of-Wedlock Births." Yale Law School Program for Studies in Law, Economics, and Public Policy Working Paper Ser. 254. New Haven, Conn.: Yale Social Science Research Network Paper Collection, 2001. http://papers.ssrn.com/paper.taf?abstract_id=270126

Low, Bobbi S. "Ecological Demography: A Synthetic Focus in Evo-lutionary Anthropology." *Evolutionary Anthropology* 1 (1993):106–112.

———. *Why Sex Matters: A Darwinian Look at Human Behavior.* Princeton: Princeton UP, 2000.

Low, Bobbi S., Alice L. Clarke, and Kenneth A. Lockridge. "Toward and Ecological Demography." *Population and Development Review* 18.1 (1992): 1–31.

Low, Bobbi S., Carl P. Simon, and Kermyt G. Anderson. "An Evolutionary Ecological Perspective on Demographic Transitions: Modeling Multiple Currencies." *American Journal of Human Biology* 14 (2002): 149–167.

———. "The Biodemography of Modern Women: Tradeoffs When Resources Become Limiting." Prepared for *The Biodemography of Fertility.* Ed. J. Rogers and H-P. Kohler. New York: Kluwer, 2002.

Ludtke, Melissa. *On Our Own: Unmarried Motherhood in America.* New York: Random, 1997.

Luker, Kristin. *Abortion and the Politics of Motherhood.* Berkeley: University of California Press, 1985.

———. *Dubious Conceptions: The Politics of Teenage Pregnancy.* Cambridge, Mass.: Harvard UP, 1996.

———. *Taking Chances: Abortion and the Decision Not to Contracept.* Berkeley: University of California Press, 1975.

Lundberg, Shelly, and Elaina Rose. "Child Gender and the Transition to Marriage." Seattle: University of Washington Dept. of Economics, 2003.

Macunovich, Diane J. "Fertility and the Easterlin hypothesis: An assessment of the literature." *Journal of Population Economics* 11 (1998): 53–111.

Maguire, Daniel C., ed. *Sacred Rights: The Case for Contraception and Abortion in World Religions.* New York: Oxford UP, 2003.

———. *Sacred Choices: The Right to Contraception and Abortion in Ten World Religions.* Sacred Energies Ser. Minneapolis: Fortress Press, 2001.

Majerus, Michael E. N. *Sex Wars: Genes, Bacteria, and Biased Sex Ratios.* Princeton: Princeton UP, 2003.

Mann, Joshua R., Curtis C. Stine, and John Vessey. "The Role of Disease-Specific Infectivity and Number of Disease Exposures on Long-Term Effectiveness of the Latex Condom." *Sexually Transmitted Diseases* 29.6 (2002): 344–349.

Marks, Lara V. *Sexual Chemistry: A History of the Contraceptive Pill.* New Haven, Conn.: Yale UP, 2001.

Martin, C. W., et al. "Potential impact of hormonal male contraception: cross-cultural implications for development of novel preparations." *Human Reproduction* 15.3 (2000): 637–645.

Martin, Harold L., et al. "Hormonal Contraception, Sexually Transmitted Diseases, and Risk of Heterosexual Transmission of Human Immunodeficiency Virus Type 1." *Journal of Infectious Diseases* 178.4 (1998): 1053–1059.

Maxwell, Mary. *The Sociobiological Imagination.* Albany: State University of New York Press, 1991.

Mayr, Ernst. *What Evolution Is.* New York: BasicBooks, 2001.

McCann, Carole R. *Birth Control Politics in the United States 1916–1945.* Ithaca, N.Y.: Cornell UP, 1994.

McCoy, Norma L., and Joseph R. Matyas. "Oral Contraceptives and Sexuality in University Women." *Archives of Sexual Behavior* 25.1 (1996): 73–90.

McDonagh, Eileen L. *Breaking the Abortion Deadlock: From Choice to Consent.* New York: Oxford UP, 1996.

McFarlane, Deborah R., and Kenneth J. Meier. *The Politics of Fertility Control: Family Planning and Abortion Policies in the American States.* New York: Chatham, 2001.

McLaren, Angus. *A History of Contraception: From Antiquity to the Present Day.* Cambridge: Basil Blackwell, 1990.

McMichael, Anthony J. "Population, environment, disease, and survival: past patterns, uncertain futures." *The Lancet* 359.9312 30 Mar. 2002. 13 May 2002 http://www.thelancet.com/journal/vol359/iss9318/full/llan.359.9312.editorial_and_review

Means, Cyril C. Jr. "The Law of New York Concerning Abortion and the Status of the Foetus, 1664–1968: A Case of Cessation of Constitutionality." *New York Law Forum* Fall Issue preprint (1968).

Merrick, Thomas W. "Population and Poverty: New Views on an Old Controversy." *International Family Planning Perspectives* 28.1 (2002): 41–46.

Merz, J. F., C. A. Jackson, and J. A. Klerman. "A Review of Abortion Policy: Legality, Medicaid Funding, and Parental Involvement, 1967–1994." *Women's Rights Law Reporter* 17 (1995): 1–61.

Meyer, D., and G. Thomson. "How selection shapes variation of the human major histocompatibility complex: a review." *Annals of Human Genetics* 65.1 (2001): 1–26.

Milinski, Manfred, and Claus Wedekind. "Evidence for MHC-correlated perfume preferences in humans." *Behavioral Ecology* 12.2 (2001): 140–149.

Miller, Brent C., et al, eds. *Preventing Adolescent Pregnancy: Model Programs and Evaluations*. Newbury Park, CA: Sage Publications, 1992.

Miller, Maureen, et al. "Sexual behavior changes and protease inhibitor therapy." *AIDS*. 2000 Man 10; 14(4): F33-9.

Mindell, David P., Jeffrey W. Shultz, and Paul W. Ewald. "The AIDS Pandemic Is New, But Is HIV New?" *Systematic Biology* 44.1 (1995): 77–92.

Mohr, James C. *Abortion in America: The Origins and Evolution of National Policy*. New York: Oxford UP, 1978.

Mokyr, Joel. *The Lever of Riches: Technological Creativity and Economic Progress*. New York: Oxford UP, 1990.

Moore, A. J., et al. "Sexual conflict and the evolution of female mate choice and male social dominance." *Proceedings of the Royal Society of London, Series B—Biological Sciences* 268.1466 (2001): 517–523.

Morris, Aldon D, and Carol McClurg Mueller, eds. *Frontiers in Social Movement Theory*. New Haven: Yale UP, 1992.

Murray, John Courtney, S.J. *We Hold These Truths: Catholic Reflections on the American Proposition*. New York: Sheed and Ward, 1960.

New York State. Task Force on Life and the Law. *Assisted Reproductive Technologies: Analysis and Recommendations for Public Policy*. New York:1998.

Nicholson, Susan Teft. *Abortion and The Roman Catholic Church*. Studies in Religious Ethics Ser. 2. Knoxville: Religious Ethics, Inc., 1978.

Noonan, John T. Jr. *A Private Choice: Abortion in America in the Seventies*. New York: The Free Press, 1979.

———. *Contraception: A History of Its Treatment by the Catholic Theologians and Canonists*. Cambridge, Mass.: Harvard UP, 1965.

————, ed. *The Morality of Abortion: Legal and Historical Perspectives.* Cambridge, Mass.: Harvard UP, 1970.

Novak, Michael. *On Two Wings: Humble Faith and Common Sense at the American Founding.* San Francisco: Encounter Books, 2002.

Ochoa, Gabriela, and Klaus Jaffé. "On Sex, Mate Selection and the Red Queen." *Journal of Theoretical Biology* 199 (1999): 1–9.

Ojeda, Auriana, ed. *Should Abortion Rights Be Restricted?.* At Issue Ser. San Diego: Greenhaven Press, 2003.

Omran, Abdel R., ed. *Liberalization of Abortion Laws: Implications.* Chapel Hill: Carolina Population Center at UNC Chapel Hill, 1976.

Ott, Mary A. et al. "The Trade-Off Between Hormonal Contraceptives and Condoms Among Adolescents." *Perspectives on Sexual and Reproductive Health* 34.1 (2002): 6–14.

Padian, N., S. Shiboski, and N. Jewell. "The relative efficiency of female-to-male HIV sexual transmission." *International Conference on AIDS* 6.1 (1990): 159.

Pagel, Mark, and Walter Bodmer. "A naked ape would have fewer parasites." *Proc. R. Soc. Lond. B: Biology Letters* Suppl. 1 (2003): 117–119.

Parsons, Jack. *Population versus Liberty.* London: Pemberton, 1971.

Penn, D.J., and W. K. Potts. "The evolution of mating preferences and major histocompatibility complex genes." *American Naturalist* 153.2 (1999): 145–164.

Pernick, Martin S. "Public Health Then and Now: Eugenics and Public Health in American History." *American Journal of Public Health* 87.11 (1997): 1767–1771.

Petchesky, Rosalind Pollack. *Abortion and Woman's Choice: The State, Sexuality, and Reproductive Freedom.* Longman Series in Feminist Theory. New York: Longman, 1984.

Phipps, Maureen Glennon, Jeffrey D. Blume, and Sonya M. DeMonner. "Young maternal age associated with increased risk of neonatal death." *Obstetrics & Gynecology* 100.3 (2002): 481–486.

Piccinino, Linda J., and William D. Mosher. "Trends in Contraceptive Use in the United States: 1982–1995." *Family Planning Perspectives* 30.1 (1998): 4–10 & 46.

Pinker, Steven. *The Blank State: The Modern Denial of Human Nature.* New York: Viking, 2002.

Pojman, Louis P. *Life and Death: A Reader in Moral Problems.* Boston: Jones and Bartlett, 1993.

————. *Life and Death: Grappling with the Moral Dilemmas of Our Time.* Boston: Jones and Bartlett, 1992.

Pojman, Louis P., and Francis J. Beckwith, eds. *The Abortion Controversy: A Reader.* The Jones and Bartlett Series in Philosophy. Boston: Jones and Bartlett, 1994.

Posner, Richard A. *Frontiers of Legal Theory.* Cambridge: Harvard UP, 2001.

———. *Sex and Reason.* Cambridge, Mass.: Harvard UP, 1992.

———. *The Problematics of Moral and Legal Theory.* Cambridge, Mass.: Harvard UP, 1999.

———. *The Problems of Jurisprudence.* Cambridge, Mass.: Harvard UP, 1990.

Potts, Malcolm. "Sex and the Birth Rate: Human Biology, Demographic Change, and Access to Fertility-Regulation Methods." *Population and Development Review* 23.1 (1997): 1–39.

———. "The myth of a male pill." *Nature Medicine* 2.4 (1996): 398–399.

President's Council on Bioethics. *Beyond Therapy: Biotechnology and the Pursuit of Happiness.* Washington D.C., 2003

Raine, Tina, et al. "Emergency Contraception: Advance Provision in a Young, High-Risk Clinic Population." *Obstetrics & Gynecology* 96.1 (2000): 1–7.

Ramjee, Gita, et al. "The Acceptability of a Vaginal Microbicide Among South African Men." *International Family Planning Perspectives* 27.4 (2001).

Ranjit, Nalini, et al. "Contraceptive Failure in the First Two Years of Use: Differences Across Socioeconomic Subgroups." *Family Planning Perspectives* 33.1 (2001): 19–27.

Rank, Mark R. "Fertility Among Women on Welfare: Incidence and Determinants." *American Sociological Review* 54 (1989): 296–304.

Reagan, Leslie J. *When Abortion Was a Crime: Women, Medicine, and Law in the United States, 1867–1973.* Berkeley: University of California Press, 1997.

Reed, James. *From Private Vice to Public Virtue: The Birth Control Movement and American Society Since 1830.* New York: BasicBooks, 1978.

Richens, John, John Imrie, and Andrew Copas. "Condoms and seat belts: the parallels and the lessons." *Lancet* 355 (2000): 400–403.

Riddle, John M. *Eve's Herbs: A History of Contraception and Abortion in the West.* Cambridge: Harvard UP, 1997.

Riddle, John M., and J. Worth Estes. "Oral Contraceptives in Ancient and Medieval Times." *American Scientist* 80 (1992): 226–233.

Ridley, Mark. *The Cooperative Gene: How Mendel's Demon Explains the Evolution of Complex Beings.* New York: The Free Press, 2001.

Ridley, Matt. *Genome: The Autobiography of a Species in 23 Chapters.* New York: HarperCollins, 2000.

———. *Nature Via Nurture: Genes, Experience, and What Makes Us Human.* New York: HarperCollins, 2003.

Ringheim, Karin. "Factors that Determine Prevalence of Use of Contraceptive Methods for Men." *Studies in Family Planning* 24.2 (1993): 87–99.

Roberts, Dorothy. *Killing the Black Body: Race, Reproduction, and the Meaning of Liberty*. New York: Vintage, 1999.

Rosenzweig, Mark R. "Welfare, Marital Prospects and Nonmarital Childbearing." Philadelphia: University of Pennsylvania, 1995.

Rothman, Barbara Katz. *The Tentative Pregnancy: Prenatal Diagnosis and the Future of Motherhood*. New York: Viking, 1986.

Roughgarden, Joan. "Social Selection Theory." Prepared for American Association for the Advancement of Science Conference. Denver: AAAS, 2003.

———. *Evolution's Rainbow: Diversity, Gender and Sexuality in Nature and People*. Reader for Biology 19N, Winter 2003. Berkeley: Stanford University Bookstore, 2002.

Rowe, David C. *Biology and Crime*. Los Angeles: Roxbury, 2002.

Russell, Andrew, Elisa J. Sobo, and Mary S. Thompson, eds. *Contraception Across Cultures: Technologies, Choices, Constraints*. Cross-Cultural Perspectives on Women Ser. New York: Berg, 2000.

Sailer, Steven. "Does Abortion Prevent Crime?" *Slate Magazine* 23 Aug. 1999.

Saletan, William. *Bearing Right: How Conservatives Won the Abortion War*. Berkeley: University of California Press, 2003.

Samuels, Sarah E,. and Mark D. Smith, eds. *The Pill: From Prescription to Over the Counter*. Menlo Park, Calif.: The Kaiser Forums, 1994.

Sanders, Stephanie A., et al. "A prospective study of the effects of oral contraceptives on sexuality and well-being and their relationship to discontinuation." *Contraception* 64 (2001): 51–58.

Sanger, Margaret. *Margaret Sanger: An Autobiography*. Introduction Kathryn Cullen-DuPont. New York: Cooper Square Press, 1999.

———. *The Pivot of Civilization*. Classics in Women's Studies Ser. Introduction H. G. Wells. Foreword Peter Engelman. New York: Humanity Books, 2003.

———. *Women and the New Race*. New York: Blue Ribbon Books, 1920.

Savin-Williams, Ritch C., and Lisa M. Diamond. "Sex." Prepared for *The Handbook of Adolescent Psychology* (2002). Eds. R.M. Lerner and L. Steinberg.

Schettler, Ted, et al, eds. *Generations at Risk: Reproductive Health and the Environment*. Cambridge, Mass.: MIT Press, 1999.

Schieve, Laura A., et al. "Low and Very Low Birth Weight in Infants Conceived with Use of Assisted Reproductive Technology." *The New England Journal of Medicine* 346.10 (2002): 731–737.

Schmitt, David P., et al. "Universal Sex Differences in the Desire for Sexual Variety: Tests From 52 Nations, 6 Continents, and 13 Islands." *Journal of Personality and Social Psychology* 85.1 (2003): 85–104.

Schoen, Robert, et al. "Why Do Americans Want Children?" *Population and Development Review* 23.2 (1997): 333–358.

Schroedel, Jean Reith. *Is the Fetus a Person?: A Comparison of Policies Across the Fifty States*. Ithaca, N.Y.: Cornell UP, 2000.

*Scientific Evidence on Condom Effectiveness for Sexually Transmitted Disease (STD) Prevention.* Workshop Summary, 2000, Herndon. Washington: National Inst. of Allergy and Infectious Diseases, 2001.

Seaman, Barbara. *The Doctors' Case Against the Pill* (twenty-fifth anniversary edition). Alameda, Calif.: Hunter House, 1995.

Serbanescu, Florina, et al. "The Impact of Recent Policy Changes on Fertility, Abortion, and Contraceptive Use in Romania." *Studies in Family Planning* 26.2 (1995): 76–87.

Setty-Venugopal, Vidya, and Ushma D. Upadhyay. "Birth Spacing: Three to Five Saves Lives." *Population Reports* Ser. L, No. 13 (2002).

Shrage, Laurie. *Abortion and Social Responsibility: Depolarizing the Debate.* Studies in Feminist Philosophy Ser. New York: Cambridge UP, 2003.

Silver, Lee M. *Remaking Eden: How Genetic Engineering and Cloning Will Transform the American Family.* New York: Avon, 1998.

Singer, Peter. *A Darwinian Left: Politics, Evolution and Cooperation.* New Haven, Conn.: Yale UP, 1999.

———. *Writings on an Ethical Life.* New York: HarperCollins, 2000.

Sjögen, Berit, and Claes Gottlieb. "Testosterone for male contraception during one year: attitudes, well-being and quality of sex life." *Contraception* 64 (2001) 59–65.

Smith, Gordon C. S., Jill P. Pell, and Richard Dobbie. "Interpregnancy interval and risk of preterm birth and neonatal death: retrospective cohort study." *BMJ* 327 (2003): 313–320.

Smith, Jennifer S., et al. "Cervical cancer and use of hormonal contraceptives: a systematic review." *The Lancet* 361 (2003): 1159–1167.

Smith-Rosenberg, Carroll. *Disorderly Conduct: Visions of Gender in Victorian America.* New York: Oxford UP, 1985.

Solinger, Rickie, ed. *Abortion Wars: A Half Century of Struggle, 1950–2000.* Berkeley: University of California Press, 1998.

———. *Beggars and Choosers: How the Politics of Choice Shapes Adoption, Abortion, and Welfare in the United States.* New York: Hill and Wang, 2001.

———. *Wake Up Little Susie: Single Pregnancy and Race Before Roe v. Wade.* New York: Routledge, 1992.

Sonenstein, Freya, et al. "Fertility Motivation, Decision Making, and Intention to Engage in Sex, Contraception, Pregnancy, Abortion and Birth." Prepared for NICHD Workshop, "Improving Data on Male Fertility and Family Formation." Washington: Urban Institute, 1997.

———. "Changes in Sexual Behavior and Condom Use among Teenaged Males: 1988 to 1995." *American Journal of Public Health* 88 (1998): 956–959.

Sorenson, Susan, Douglas Wiebe, and Richard Berk. "Legalized Abortion and the Homicide of Young Children: An Empirical Investigation." *Analyses of Social Issues and Public Policy* 2.1 (2002): 239–256.

South, Scott J., and Kim M. Lloyd. "Marriage Markets and Nonmarital Fertility in the United States." *Demography* 29 (1992): 247–261.

Stark, M., et al. "Contraceptive Method and Condom Use Among Women at Risk for HIV Infection and Other Sexually Transmitted Diseases—Selected U.S. Sites, 1993–1994." *MMWR* 45.38 (1996): 820–823.

State of New York. *Report of the Governor's Commission Appointed to Review New York State's Abortion Law.* New York: Chairman Charles W. Froessel, 1968.

Steinbock, Bonnie. "Rethinking the Right to Reproduce." *Harvard School of Public Health.* 23 Feb. 2001. http://www.hsph.harvard.edu/Organizations/healthnet/HUpapers/ reproright.html.

Steklis, Horst D., et al. "Effects of Medroxyprogesterone Acetate on Socio-Sexual Behavior of Stumptail Macaques." *Physiology & Behavior* 28 (1982): 535–544.

Stern, Kathleen, and Martha K. McClintock. "Regulation of ovulation by human pheromones." *Nature* 392 (1998): 177–179.

Stock, Gregory. *Redesigning Humans: Our Inevitable Genetic Future.* New York: Houghton Mifflin, 2002.

Strassman, B. I., and J. H. Warner. "Predictors of fecundability and conception waits among the Dogon of Mali." *American Journal of Physical Anthropology* 105.2 (1998) 167–184.

Sunstein, Cass R. *Designing Democracy: What Constitutions Do.* New York: Oxford UP, 2001.

Taylor, Timothy. *The Prehistory of Sex: Four Million Years of Sexual Culture.* New York: Bantam, 1996.

Tenner, Edward. *Why Things Bite Back: Technology and the Revenge of Unintended Consequences.* New York: Vintage, 1997.

Thomasma, David C., et al, eds. *Cambridge Quarterly of Healthcare Ethics: The International Journal for Healthcare Ethics and Ethics Committees.* 8.4 (1999).

Thornhill, Randy, and Steven W. Gangestad. "The Scent of Symmetry: A Human Sex Pheromone that Signals Fitness?" *Evolution and Human Behavior* 20 (1999): 175–201.

Tiger, Lionel. "On Human Nature: Living with Abortion" *The Sciences* Sept./Oct. 1992: 12–15.

———. *The Decline of Males.* New York: Golden Books, 1999.

———. *The Pursuit of Pleasure* (second edition). New Brunswick, N.J.: Transaction, 2000.

Tiger, Lionel, and Robin Fox. *The Imperial Animal* (second edition). New Brunswick, N.J.: Transaction, 1998.

Tone, Andrea. *Controlling Reproduction: An American History.* Worlds of Women Ser. 2. Wilmington: Scholarly Resources, 1997.

———. *Devices and Desires: A History of Contraceptives in America.* New York: Hill and Wang, 2001.

Tribe, Laurence H. *Abortion: The Clash of Absolutes.* New York: Norton, 1990.

Trivers, Robert L. "Parental Investment and Sexual Selection." Pp. 136–179. *Sexual Selection and the Descent of Man 1871–1971.* Ed. Bernard Campbell. Chicago: Aldine, 1972.

Trivers, Robert L., and Dan E. Willard. "Natural Selection of Parental Ability to Vary the Sex Ratio of Offspring." *Science* 179 (1973): 90–92.

Trussell, James, Barbara Vaughan, and Joseph Stanford. "Are All Contraceptive Failures Unintended Pregnancies? Evidence from the 1995 National Survey of Family Growth." *Family Planning Perspectives* 31.5 (1999): 246–247 & 260.

United States. Commission on Civil Rights. *Constitutional Aspects of the Right to Limit Childbearing.* Washington: GPO, 1975.

———. Committee on the Judiciary, United States Senate, Ninety-Seventh Congress, First Session. *Constitutional Amendments Relating to Abortion: Hearings Before the Subcommittee on The Constitution.* 2 vols. Washington: GPO, 1981.

———. Committee on the Judiciary, United States Senate, Ninety-Fourth Congress, First Session. *Abortion—Part IV: Hearings Before the Subcommittee on Constitutional Amendments.* Washington: GPO, 1976.

———. Committee on the Judiciary, United States Senate, Ninety-Third Congress, Second Session. *Abortion—Part 1: Hearings Before the Subcommittee on Constitutional Amendments.* Washington: GPO, 1974.

Van Devanter, Nancy, et al. "Effect of an STD/HIV Behavioral Intervention on Women's Use of the Female Condom." *American Journal of Public Health* 92.1 (2002): 109–115.

Velasco-Hernandez, J. X., H. B. Gershengorn, and S. M. Blower. "Could widespread use of combination antiretroviral therapy eradicate HIV epidemics?" *The Lancet* 2.8 (2002): 487–501.

Watkins, Elizabeth Siegel. *On the Pill: A Social History of Oral Contraceptives 1950–1970*. Baltimore: Johns Hopkins UP, 1998.

Wedekind, Claus, et al. "MHC-dependent mate preferences in humans." *Proc. R. Soc. Lond.—Ser. B* 260 (1995): 245–249.

Weisfeld, Glenn E., and Carol C. Weisfeld. "Marriage: An Evolutionary Perspective." *Human Ethology & Evolutionary Psychology* 23.suppl. 4 (2002): 47–54.

Weller, Aron. "Communication through body odour." *Nature* 392 (1998): 126–127.

Whitten, Wes. "Pheromones and regulation of ovulation." *Nature* 401 (1999): 232.

Wiederman, Michael W. *Understanding Sexuality Research*. Toronto: Wadsworth, 2001.

Wiker, Benjamin. *Moral Darwinism: How We Became Hedonists*. Downers Grove: InterVarsity Press, 2002.

Williams, Constance Willard. *Black Teenage Mothers: Pregnancy and Child Rearing from Their Perspective*. Lexington, Ky.: Lexington Books, 1991.

Wilson, Edward O. *The Future of Life*. New York: Knopf, 2002.

Wilson, James Q. *The Marriage Problem: How Our Culture Has Weakened Families*. New York: HarperCollins, 2002.

Wilson, Margo, and Martin Daly. "Life expectancy, economic inequality, homicide, and reproductive timing in Chicago neighbourhoods." *BMJ* 314.1271 (1997).

Wolf, Naomi. "Our Bodies, Our Souls." *New Republic* 16 Oct. 1995: 26+.

Wolfe, Alan. *Moral Freedom: The Impossible Idea That Defines the Way We Live Now*. New York: Norton, 2001.

Wright, Robert. *The Moral Animal: Why We Are the Way We Are: The New Science of Evolutionary Psychology*. New York: Vintage, 1995.

Zhang, Junsen, Jason Quan, and Peter Van Meerbergen. "The Effect of Tax-Transfer Policies on Fertility in Canada, 1921–88." *The Journal of Human Resources* 29.1 (1993): 181–201.

Zimmer, Carl. *Evolution: The Triumph of an Idea*. New York: HarperCollins, 2001.

———. "Taming Pathogens: An Elegant Idea, But Does It Work?" *Science* 300 (2003): 1362–1364.

# Index

PublicAffairs is a publishing house founded in 1997. It is a tribute to the standards, values, and flair of three persons who have served as mentors to countless reporters, writers, editors, and book people of all kinds, including me.

I.F. STONE, proprietor of *I. F. Stone's Weekly*, combined a commitment to the First Amendment with entrepreneurial zeal and reporting skill and became one of the great independent journalists in American history. At the age of eighty, Izzy published *The Trial of Socrates*, which was a national bestseller. He wrote the book after he taught himself ancient Greek.

BENJAMIN C. BRADLEE was for nearly thirty years the charismatic editorial leader of *The Washington Post*. It was Ben who gave the *Post* the range and courage to pursue such historic issues as Watergate. He supported his reporters with a tenacity that made them fearless and it is no accident that so many became authors of influential, best-selling books.

ROBERT L. BERNSTEIN, the chief executive of Random House for more than a quarter century, guided one of the nation's premier publishing houses. Bob was personally responsible for many books of political dissent and argument that challenged tyranny around the globe. He is also the founder and longtime chair of Human Rights Watch, one of the most respected human rights organizations in the world.

For fifty years, the banner of Public Affairs Press was carried by its owner Morris B. Schnapper, who published Gandhi, Nasser, Toynbee, Truman, and about 1,500 other authors. In 1983, Schnapper was described by *The Washington Post* as "a redoubtable gadfly." His legacy will endure in the books to come.

Peter Osnos, *Founder and Editor-at-Large*

LaVergne, TN USA
01 September 2009
156659LV00004B/67/A